Coordination and Growth
Essays in Honour of Simon K. Kuipers

Coordination and Growth

Essays in Honour of Simon K. Kuipers

Edited by

Gerard H. Kuper
Elmer Sterken
Els Wester

Department of Economics
University of Groningen, The Netherlands

Springer Science+Business Media, LLC

Library of Congress Cataloging-in-Publication Data
Coordination and growth: essays in honour of Simon K. Kuipers / edited by Gerard H. Kuper, Elmer Sterken, Els Wester.
p.cm.
Includes bibliographical references.
ISBN 978-1-4613-5609-7 ISBN 978-1-4615-1549-4 (eBook)
DOI 10.1007/978-1-4615-1549-4
1. Kuipers, S.K. (Simon Klaas) 2. Economists--Netherlands. 3. Macroeconomics. I. Kuipers, S.K. (Simon Klaas) II. Kuper, G.H. (Gerard H.) III. Sterken, E. (Elmer) IV. Wester, E.

HB111.K85 C66 2001
338.9--dc21

2001038473

Printed on acid-free paper.

Preface: Personal Recollections by Jan Pen[1]

The editors excused me from the obligation to write a scientific article; instead I'm allowed to write a personal note. Indeed, I know Simon for a very long time. Longer than the other authors do. Our first encounter took place when he was a student, which must have been in the beginning of the 1960s. On behalf of the students he was member of a committee in charge of organising an excursion abroad. On the very last moment the number of participants turned out to be too large: an extra professor had applied. The question was whether one of the students should be excluded. No, Simon said, and he got his way. He persisted in a very polite way, and that was a characteristic that I would again witness many times later.

In the forty years that I know him I saw him develop from student to assistant professor (with Frits J. de Jong), PhD candidate (with De Jong as *promotor* (supervisor) and Pen as *co-referent* (consulting supervisor)), colleague in the same faculty (he for general economics, I for public finance), dean of the university and chairman of the board of the university. So, every now and then he was my boss. Together we were members of the editorial board of *De Economist*, founded in 1852, of which Simon is now Honorary Editor. In that capacity we had a meeting every three months at the house of one of the editors, followed by a dinner together with our wives. One can write a book about that circle of friends.

I have very good memories of the recent period, during which Simon was my host on the *fifth floor* of the WSN-building where the Faculty of Economics is housed. That was from 1986 through 1992. After my retirement from the Faculty of Law, Simon invited me to move into a room

[1] Translated by Els Wester and Richard Gigengack.

on the same floor as he. It was a room with a nice view, surrounded with nice people. I could sit there at times that suited me, mostly in the morning. There I read, wrote, looked out of the window and held conversations with who ever felt the desire to walk in. For me, after having spent years with jurists, a new fertile period set in. I was impressed by the skill of the new generation and spoke more with Simon than ever before. He reported about these meetings himself[2] – I can restrict myself to my side of the story.

My account starts in the 1960s. Simon was not one of my students, but attended classes in public finance every now and then. That was not unusual – Duisenberg, who graduated in 1961, also dropped in sometimes. The fact is that there was a rumour about me telling another story about macroeconomics than the man who was paid for that, *viz*. Frits de Jong. That rumour was correct. Of course it was all about Keynes. De Jong's lectures were strongly oriented towards monetary phenomena. He was interested in the creation and contraction of money, in hoarding and dishoarding and in the velocity of money. Moreover, he interpreted the difference between S and I as a matter of time, in the spirit of the Swedish school. In fact it was a variant of Dennis Robertson's ideas, whose elegant book *Money* I had read for my Master's exam in 1946. If you believed this story there was nothing new in Keynes. In my lectures Keynes was pictured as the man of autonomous investment that influences national income through its impact. Money follows expenditures, banks accommodate. The two approaches can be concisely summarised as *MV versus C+I* (the title of an article that I wrote at that time in the journal of the central bank of Belgium.) Students like that: a dispute between two people they can see and hear.

With hindsight there is a case for both points of view and in any case Frits de Jong was right in his contention that formally the two theories can be converted into each other. But at the time I opposed that although Keynesian and monetary models may be formally equivalent, the stories differ. One narrator places different accents than the other; the language differs. Frits de Jong did not embrace the proposition that stories are part of our profession. In that respect Simon Kuipers resembles his master: in his opinion storytelling easily degenerates into journalism. Upon that we disagree – in my opinion economic research, no matter how theoretical or empirical, should be crowned with a story, preferably excitingly told. The listener or reader should think: "And that's the way it is!"

I had a rather intensive contact with Simon when he was working on his PhD thesis: *The Significance of Demand and Supply Factors in One-Sector Models of Economic Growth* (1970). It dealt with growth, more specifically

2 Brakman, S., H. Garretsen and S.K. Kuipers (eds.) (1993), *Met Jan Pen in debat*, Amsterdam: Amsterdam University Press.

with disequilibrium growth. Frits de Jong, supervisor, stayed for a year in the United States and I was consulting supervisor, a not very clearly defined role. The drafts that were submitted to me were in a pretty advanced stage. It seemed very original to me but not always easy to understand. I learned a lot about disequilibria, whether or not simultaneously occurring, – excess demand, excess supply, capital shortage, labour abundance *etc. etc.* – classified in full-page charts. It was pure macroeconomics, a field in which I had occasionally been active myself, but I couldn't always find the relations between the new and the existing literature. The prose, *staccato* with lots of enumerations, didn't sound like music to me. It was more like a lecture note than a thesis. However, the prevailing impression was: here is a creative expert speaking. Nowadays we would call it pioneering. Several rumours circulate about the conversations between the PhD candidate and me, but for sure Simon never changed anything to please me. Again I learned to appreciate his determination. On a few points I maintained my criticism – I don't believe for instance that a negative marginal product of capital is a real phenomenon; the thesis asserts the contrary. The doctorate was bestowed *cum laude*, which I totally agreed with. The thesis itself is only as a mimeograph available. It belongs in the category scarce tracts in economics, copies of which are worth much money.

The way in which Simon developed as a monetarist, a Keynesian or whatever, in the course of time, can easily be discovered by consulting his publications. That's not a job, however, to tackle at any odd moment. He is extremely diligent and his work continuously evolves. The dissertation alone demands a few days of study. Before 1970 he rewrote, in collaboration with others, the standard textbook of Korteweg and Keesing *Het moderne geldwezen.* This book originates in the 1930s, but the first edition, delayed by World War II, was published in 1946. Even at that time it wasn't really modern. Various teams set about to modernise it. In the end only the team from Groningen remained. The result was a miraculous multiplication. More and more volumes and parts came along and they became more and more voluminous. I have in my library the 14th edition (1986) of Part III. The subject is monetary theory. It's loaded with models. One of the chapters analyses the influence of money creation on the price level with eighty-eight equations. And that is only one part of the book that consists of 407 pages.

Anyone who is aware of the relatively limited mathematical knowledge of the original authors acknowledges the enormous advance in professional and technical skill. On the other hand, it also becomes clear how these models can obscure the mind. After working through Part III you are not only longing for a holiday, but also get the impression that in the world of models everything is possible. Depending on the assumptions the model produces results. The more modern the theory the richer the possibilities.

One of the great multipliers was the theory of expectations – if those are rational *à la* Lucas every policy is suppressed. In my opinion it is a foolish story, but you will never hear that qualification from Simon. At least not explicitly and not in writing. In private conversations he has firm opinions but in the scientific business he is tolerant.

Anyone who wants to get an impression of Simon's tolerance in science should compare the pure theoretical dissertations that are completed under his supervision. There is a world of difference between the works. They are predominantly Keynesian, in the sense that they describe disequilibrium situations, but the nature of disequilibrium diverges.

Jan Snippe constructed a world described by a quarterly model with one macro-firm in which national income stops now and again. Nothing happens then. The sole firm then gets going again, don't ask how. Halfway through his (funda)mental research the PhD student realised that this wasn't the way things work. His mind also threatened to stop, but Simon appreciated the effort – Snippe obtained his doctorate with everyone's approval and later became a respected banker. Lex Hoogduin was a Keynesian of the fundamental-uncertainty type: the essentials of money were supposed to be located in that uncertainty. I thought this rather strange and I got the impression that Simon also struggled with the idea, but that doesn't matter – it was a solid thesis and the new-born PhD nowadays manages the econometric research department of *De Nederlandsche Bank* (the Dutch central bank).

Hans van Ees en Harry Garretsen recreated Keynes, following the Walrasian idea that there exists a fundamental equilibrium that would emerge were it not that prices show rigidities. I thought that this was too much of a concession to the neoclassicals, but Simon went along with it. Subsequently, Fieke van der Lecq started to explain those nominal rigidities – a splendid thesis, but about a problem that is hardly a problem. Those rigid prices in fact are not rigid at all and if they adjust slowly there are obvious reasons for it. The shopkeeper has to change his price tags and that is an annoying job even with a computer. This thesis was much more theoretical and profound than the others were. The nice thing about Simon is that he gives everyone the opportunity to tell his or her own story. If it is told in a reasoned way, he will always help and support.

With such an approach, however, his own story remains hidden. This becomes clear when we examine the best book that emerged from the Groningen School in recent years: *Evenwicht, conjunctuur en groei* (1994) (Equilibrium, the Trade Cycle and Growth), by S.K. Kuipers, H. van Ees, H. Garretsen, G.H. Kuper, E. Sterken and E. Wester. It is a textbook and the product of many authors. Its is based on lectures given in the 1980s and the beginning of the 1990s. It gives a complete picture of macroeconomics and the book is modern in the sense that the latest developments are covered. It is crystal clear and shows that it is possible to have two theories at the same moment that have completely different conclusions. Neoclassical theory, the Keynesian theory for the short run, the Keynesian monetary theory, the New Keynesian theory, Keynesian and neoclassical growth theory, *etc*. It is a well-stocked shop window and the economist may choose his wares.

Such an abundant supply of choices of course has a drawback. If we accept the authors, no theory is better than another. Almost no recommendations are given, not even on empirical grounds. Nor is anything discouraged. Some readers will appreciate this tolerance; others will see it as a drawback. I personally would have been rather more "directive" – that is to say I would have told a story that I found to be more convincing at the time I wrote it. If only in a concluding chapter.

Moreover, my favourite story is not found in the book. It is a Post Keynesian story and at its centre lies the vertical demand curve. A few elements: if expenditure is high enough production depends on the production function and the available labour, capital and nature. In that case neoclassical growth theory applies, in which technical progress explains about eighty percent (the labour share) of growth. However if expenditure is deficient, a Keynesian model determines production. We have a different regime then. Prices don't matter (with the interest rate as an exception), because we are talking about the general price level and this doesn't influence aggregate demand. Nor, for that matter, does the nominal wage rate influence the demand for labour (this is Chapter XIX of the *General Theory*). Aggregate demand is vertical because every price rise of domestic origin also creates income. Not the money supply but last year's price level and inflation determine the price level today. Inflation depends predominantly on the increase of the nominal wage rate minus the increase of the productivity of labour (if desired one can incorporate the influence of government, for instance through taxes).

The increase in nominal wages arises from the negotiations between employers and workers. The money supply accommodates, that is what banks are for. The central bank has hardly any control of the money supply. The crucial element in this story is the increase of the nominal wage rate, which should be explained by economists – that part of the theory is missing in *Evenwicht, conjunctuur en groei*. It's about power, bargaining theory, the "polder model". Neither can one find the vertical demand curve in the book. Unfortunately, I think, because the idea can be the basis of macroeconomic thinking in terms of growth rates. It is not the ultimate truth, but a starting point.

My comments above on the development of ideas in Groningen show that I had frequent conversations with Simon, but that I didn't do the best I could to convince him of the Post Keynesian story. Admittedly it is an apocryphal story. An inelastic aggregate demand curve conflicts with the traditional economic way of thinking. Economists usually attach a decisive role to prices – and they are right, in microeconomics. But the macroeconomic world is constructed differently. There, incomes dominate the picture, prices have only indirect and – in my view – weak effects. The fundamental difference between micro- and macroeconomics is at the root of all economic wisdom. In my days this was standard material for introductory courses, at least for law students. They were warned of the fallacy of composition. These warnings I miss in modern teaching. It may be that, 25 meters above the ground, a work of art portrays the "micro-macro-leap" on the front of the WSN-building, but on the lower floors it doesn't show very much.

About such things Simon and I used to converse when I walked into his room in Paddepoel, about ten years ago. There is an ongoing trend in our meetings, which started during my lectures at the Boteringestraat in the 1960s and that now ends with the presentation of this volume. The contact which Simon and I had all the time is difficult to characterise. Even in the beginning it was not the standard relationship between a teacher and a student. From the very start I saw him as a person in his own right, a man who could perhaps be convinced, but only with very good arguments. In that it helped that we didn't belong to different schools; we are both eclectic and aimed at a kind of synthesis between neoclassical and Keynesian ideas. It is not very helpful for our communication that we are both rather busy. I prefer writing and Simon nowadays leans more towards managing. Moreover, I am impatient and not inclined to listen very long. Simon is better at that than I am. For me he is the personification of Groningen. He was born in Sauwerd, ten kilometres from the city. He went to university at 44 Boteringestraat, the same building where he now holds office as the highest-level boss of the university. He lives within walking distance of the WSN-building. As ever, he goes to work by bike. During the last half century I met many *Groningers* and tried to understand the workings of their mind. I came to the well-considered conclusion that they all differ. It is therefore convenient that there is one man I know whom I can consider to be symbolic for all of them – something like Marshall's Representative Firm: Simon is the Representative Agent from Groningen.

Haren, February 2001

Jan Pen

Contributors

Bas Bakker, International Monetary Fund, Washington DC

Steven Brakman, Department of Economics, University of Groningen

Nanne Brunia, Department of Economics, University of Groningen

Sijbren Cnossen, Erasmus University Rotterdam and Maastricht University

Jouke van Dijk, Department of Spatial Sciences, University of Groningen

Ruud Dorenbos, NEI, Rotterdam, Division of Labour and Education, and World Bank Institute, Human Development Division

Hans van Ees, Department of Economics, University of Groningen

Casper van Ewijk, CPB Netherlands Bureau for Economic Policy Analysis, Tinbergen Institute and University of Amsterdam

Martin Fase, Econometric Research and Special Studies Department, De Nederlandsche Bank N.V. and University of Amsterdam

Harry Garretsen, Department of Applied Economics, University of Nijmegen

Reyer Gerlagh, IVM, Institute for Environmental Studies, Vrije Universiteit, Amsterdam

Arnold Heertje, Department of Economics, University of Amsterdam

Lex Hoogduin, Deputy Executive Director of the Netherlands Bank

Jan Jacobs, CCSO and Department of Economics, University of Groningen

Jan Kakes, Monetary and Economic Policy Department, De Nederlandsche Bank

Piet Keizer, Department of Economics, Maastricht University

Michiel Keyzer, SOW-VU, Centre for World Food Studies, Vrije Universiteit, Amsterdam

Theo van de Klundert, Faculty of Economics, Tilburg University and Groningen University

Gerard Kuper, Department of Economics, University of Groningen

Fieke van der Lecq, Economisch Statistische Berichten, Rotterdam

Ruud de Mooij, CPB Netherlands Bureau for Economic Policy Analysis and OCFEB

Joan Muysken, Department of Economics and Maastricht Economic Research Institute on Innovation and Technology, Maastricht University

Jan Pen, Haren

Elmer Sterken, Department of Economics, University of Groningen

Els Wester, Department of Economics, University of Groningen

Arjen van Witteloostuijn, Department of Economics, University of Groningen

Adriaan van Zon, Department of Economics and Maastricht Economic Research Institute on Innovation and Technology, Maastricht University

Contents

Chapter 1

Introduction

Gerard H. Kuper, Elmer Sterken and Els Wester[1]
Department of Economics, University of Groningen

1. INTRODUCTION

In 1954, Arrow and Debreu published their seminal paper "Existence of an equilibrium for a competitive economy" (see Arrow and Debreu, 1954). The principal contribution of their study is the axiomatic validation of the Walrasian benchmark model of price taking, individual rationality, and market clearing. As is known, one can show that equilibria exist in competitive frictionless markets, albeit under strong conditions. The frictionless world, although intellectually appealing and allowing for strong policy conclusions, does not provide a framework to address many of the problems macroeconomists like to solve. Describing empirical regularities, analysing economic policy, and forecasting economic developments is typically hard using the pure Walrasian system. Take for instance the issue of the existence of money as a medium of exchange in the Walrasian system. Up to now economic theory has not been able to show the *raison d'être* of money or financial intermediaries in equilibrium. Modern macroeconomics therefore acknowledges the Arrow-Debreu results, but proceeds on formalising departures from the frictionless world such that the goals of fitting the macroeconomic stylised facts, analysing economic policy, and forecasting future economic developments can be achieved.

One of the serious flaws of the Arrow-Debreu theory itself though is its lack of clarity how equilibrium is achieved. What is the mechanism that

[1] We owe thanks to Heleen Kruger-Groen and Lies Baars-Drent for editorial assistance.

ensures that all "Hicksian" excess demands for all goods and services equal zero at all times? Who or what is responsible for informing all agents regarding notional supply and demand? How are prices adjusted towards their instantaneous equilibrium values? Although it is not necessary to formally describe the *tâtonnement* process to be able to proof that equilibria exist, several metaphors of the clearing process have been proposed, of which the most interesting one is that of the Walrasian auctioneer. The auctioneer investigates all needs of agents who demand or supply goods, processes this information, and computes equilibrium prices. But who wants to be a Walrasian auctioneer in a frictionless world? What are the incentives to coordinate supply and demand? So, even in a frictionless economy the problem of coordinating economic activity is unsolved.

It is certain that coordination issues cannot be solved within the Arrow-Debreu framework. We need frictions or imperfections to be able to describe processes of intermediation, price adjustment, auctioning, and coordination of economic activity in general. On the one hand, the introduction of imperfections helps to address the issue of coordination, but on the other hand it makes it more difficult to understand fully the issues at hand. In models that include imperfections, one cannot use the Arrow-Debreu results and one needs to address the important issues of the nature (or absence) of equilibria all over again. In other words, the macroeconomic theory of imperfections is rich but difficult. Nevertheless, most modern macroeconomists like the challenge to think in terms of frictions. Departing from the Arrow-Debreu framework indeed leads to a better understanding of regularities in macroeconomic data, a more realistic formulation of policy advice, and a further development of macroeconomic theory. One can explain *e.g.* the existence of money as a medium of exchange in a general equilibrium model if one assumes that it is costly to search for a trading partner (see Kiyotaki and Wright, 1993). And if there are information asymmetries we are able to explain the existence of banks (see Diamond and Dybvig, 1983).

Macroeconomists use various instruments and/or metaphors to model frictions and imperfections. These instruments vary from transaction costs to information problems, from missing markets to sticky prices and wages, from irrationality to monopolistic competition. Some macroeconomists prefer to stick closely to the Arrow-Debreu frictionless world. The most prominent school of thought is the "New Classical" school. New Classical economists in fact only allow for some minor frictions like transaction costs, installation costs, and information asymmetries in the sense that one group of agents is earlier informed than the other group of agents. Some macroeconomists reject almost all classical axioms. Following Keynes (1936), stickiness of wages is a prominent type of imperfection. Sometimes the axioms are even stronger: some schools of thought simply do not assume that equilibrium can be achieved due to serious lacks of rationality and information. The divergence of thoughts leads to interesting debates on core macroeconomic issues and solutions to policy debates.

Departing from the Walrasian world leads most likely to a better insight in the coordination issue. The opportunities to come closer to a better understanding of the functioning of markets and the price mechanism increase once we allow for various types of frictions. The downside of introducing multiple frictions is that a true understanding of the working of market economies becomes increasingly complex. The price we have to pay for understanding macroeconomic behaviour is high in terms of theoretical insight and intellectual ability of the prototype macroeconomist. There are thousands of types of frictions, out of which the theorist has to pick the appropriate ones to tackle the important issues he/she faces. It is likely that *e.g.* for short-run problems other types of frictions are appropriate than for issues in economic growth. Price stickiness is likely to exist in the short run, but is highly unlikely in the long run.

This book addresses the core of macroeconomic theory, namely coordination of macroeconomic activity. The *Festschrift* presented is a tribute to the professional career of Simon K. Kuipers. Simon Kuipers's work as a macroeconomist can best be described as the permanent quest for the appropriate frictions to understand major macroeconomic issues. This quest passed various, mostly Keynesian, 'pools of frictions'. Simon Kuipers showed a major interest in the theory of capital (following *e.g.* Harrod), growth theory (following Solow), monetary theory (following Tobin), and disequilibrium theory (following Malinvaud and Benassy). The nature of the frictions varies from pure quantity rationing, like in the Malinvaud analysis, to imperfect substitution of various capital goods (like in the vintage models) or assets (in the general monetary equilibrium models proposed by Tobin). The art of choosing the appropriate type of frictions can only be mastered by someone who has a wide knowledge of macroeconomic theory. It is without any doubt that Simon Kuipers fits the profile of Master of Macroeconomics.

The book contains chapters in various fields. In the remainder of this introduction we provide a framework to position the chapters in the main fields of interest of Simon Kuipers. We do not describe the professional life and work of Simon Kuipers in this introduction. Fase and Van de Klundert (1998) present an excellent overview of his academic work (reprinted in Chapter 2). The authors stress Kuipers's interest in economic theory and policy and complement him with his analytical rigour. We could not do better here, but do present a complete bibliography of all the written work of Simon Kuipers at the end of this volume. In subsequent chapters, we address the main issues, ranging from theoretical issues in coordination, to coordination of economic policy, monetary economics, and growth theory.

2. THEORETICAL ISSUES IN COORDINATION

At the microeconomic level coordination problems are likely to occur. If an agent is unaware of the most likely behaviour of a likely trading partner and uses expectations concerning the behaviour of his trading partner, even bilateral exchange is likely to end up in multiple equilibria. The major problem for each agent is how to pick an equilibrium outcome (Cooper and John, 1988). One can imagine that if coordination problems of this type are likely to occur at the micro level, aggregation to the macro level does not create full clarity on how to attain the preferred full equilibrium outcome. It is highly unlikely that the price mechanism alone will be able to coordinate macroeconomic activity of an economy to the extent that that the final outcomes are Pareto-efficient.

What kind of mechanisms or institutions might be complementary to the price mechanism (or even be full substitutes) to be able to at least move in the direction of full equilibium? Van de Klundert and Van der Lecq focus on the role of norms or rules of behaviour (Chapter 3). Norms can help to form adequate expectations of others' behaviour. Norms can be such that confirming with them is procedurally rational. Such norms evolve into self-enforcing conventions. Other norms might be linked more to ethical aspects. Van de Klundert and Van der Lecq typically address the role of ethics in the relation between citizens and the government. They assume heterogeneity of the population. A fraction of citizenry likes to claim its rights as opposed to a group that is more focused on cooperation. Van de Klundert and Van der Lecq present a game theoretic model that includes a cultural evolutionary mechanism. They argue that a civil society can last, provided that people are willing to cooperate.

A second complementary mechanism to the price mechanism in coordinating economic activity might be communication. As Keizer argues in Chapter 4 the coordination and communication mechanism might be interrelated processes. The lack of attention by economists for communication issues is caused by the historical separation of economics and sociology. Due to specialisation economists focused their attention on the coordination issue, while sociologists tried to explain the processes of communication between the principal groups that constitute society, including the economy. Keizer shows that a proper understanding of the economic coordination problem requires the integration of the ideas on efficiency of both the coordination and communication mechanisms.

3. ECONOMIC POLICY

Issues in coordination of macroeconomic activity require tedious economic reasoning. It is by far not easy to derive clear-cut answers to most theoretical problems in modern macroeconomics. The central issue is whether we can use the price mechanism to obtain full equilibrium in a macroeconomic system. Is it just the price mechanism, or do we need other mechanisms, like for instance norms and institutions? One important institution is the government. Is the government able to complement the price mechanism? Is the government able to stabilize a market economy at the full employment level? Is the government able to ensure an efficient allocation of endowments to all agents? It is clear that the role of the government in coordinating economic activity is an important one. Therefore it is interesting to study issues in economic policy that are focused on the coordination of the allocation of endowments.

At the core of the macroeconomic debate is the discussion on the flexibility of wages. Since labour market inefficiencies immediately translate into imbalances that prevent full equilibrium, coordinating labour market allocation is central to all types of economic policy. Bakker discusses this issue for a small open economy, the Netherlands (Chapter 5). The central idea is that wage formation obtained by bilateral negotiations by employers and employees might not lead to a socially desirable outcome. Since both types of agents cannot oversee the joint interest of wage moderation, the role of the government in the negotiation process is essential. The government prevents myopic outcomes by striving for wage moderation, and through that an increase in international competitiveness, output growth and growth of employment. The tripartite negotiations in the Netherlands in the second half of the 1980s and the 1990s therefore helped to increase employment growth, leading to a better fiscal position of the government as well.

Coordinating economic activity via the market price mechanism is most common to all western economies. The most extreme form of economic policy is the one that completely rules out the price mechanism and plans quantity variables. In that case we have a central planner that coordinates activity. The central planner collects all relevant information and distributes endowments, organises new production, and factor input demands. Strangely enough this extreme way of coordinating economic activity is closely related to the classical Ramsey (1928) model that tries to explain the optimal rate of saving in a dynamic economy. As Blanchard and Fischer (1989) show the outcome that a central planner prescribes in an Arrow-Debreu dynamic economy is identical to the outcome that individual optimizing agents will obtain without the interference of the central planner. This theoretical equivalence seems to be far from reality for the issue of transition from centrally-planned economies to market economies. Van Dijk and Dorenbos study the labour market in two transition economies shortly after the start of the transition (Chapter 6). The labour market changed from a job-rights allocation to a job-search market. This is a typical, almost laboratory, experiment that allows for a precise analysis of the emergence of new coordinating mechanisms. Van Dijk and Dorenbos analyse the case of Hungary and Poland and use a microeconometric analysis of wage determination. They conclude that indicators of (potential) productivity tend to show up as determinants of wage formation even shortly after the transition. This would lead to the conclusion that the price mechanism is powerful and quickly to implement as a coordination device after all.

One of the main contributions of Keynes (1936) is the notion that coordination problems at the microeconomic level, *i.e.* between individual agents, might have serious effects at the macroeconomic level. It is basically this issue that New Keynesian economists tend to stress in more modern work. If the government is involved and we analyse economic policy – even within governmental bodies, but certainly between them – coordination problems might arise. Between sovereign states competing governments might pursue noncooperating policies that end up in suboptimal outcomes (think of beggar-thy-neighbour policies). Cnossen, Van Ewijk and De Mooij analyse decision making by the government and the resulting coordination problems (Chapter 7). They argue that it is important to be aware of the level of decision making. According to the subsidiarity principle economic decisions should always be made at the lowest possible level. But there might be cases that control at a higher level avoids the problem of ending up in suboptimal noncooperative outcomes. Control at a higher level comes at a cost though. It requires more information and tends to neglect the diversity of preferences at the lower level. Cnossen *et al.* give a survey of such a coordination problem applied to the tax coordination within Europe. Now that the Economic and Monetary Union is established, it is time to think about the desirability of tax harmonisation. The authors conclude that greater diversity is wanted in the VAT, but more harmonisation of all other taxes is desirable, without losing the autonomy of individual governments.

Thinking about coordination requires knowledge about the process of intermediation. The Walrasian auctioneer is an omnipotent intermediary, able to allocate all resources efficiently and instantaneously to the highest bidding agents. If intermediation fails, the role for the government in coordinating wants and resources increases. In this respect it is interesting to analyse the consequences of the so-called "new economy". The development of information and communication technology allows for better intermediation, new organisational forms, the creation of virtual market places, and a reform of traditional economic activity. True believers of the new economy are convinced of the possibilities to obtain permanent higher growth rates, lower inflation, and a dampening of business fluctuations. If this all is true the traditional role for economic policy will change. This is the issue that Van Witteloostuijn raises (Chapter 8). He describes the differences between the new and the old economy at the micro, meso, and macro level. It is not completely clear what the consequences of a strong upraise of the new economy for economic policy might be. On the one hand the improvement of intermediation helps to improve coordination without government interference. On the other hand there are ample developments that hint at an increase of, most likely unwanted, fluctuations. In the latter category one can think of the increases in possibilities for herd behaviour, which might lead to large, speculative bubbles in prices, or a reduction of inventories, that traditionally dampen fluctuations.

4. MONETARY ECONOMICS AND POLICY

There is no natural role for money as a medium of exchange in a full general equilibrium model. One of the goods will take the role of *numeraire*, but intrinsic worthless money will have no price. General equilibrium theory therefore faces the problem of explaining the existence of a monetary economy as opposed to a barter economy. One can rephrase this finding into the notion that the theory of value, which is focused on explaining real relative prices, is separated from theories that explain the general price level, which is the focus of monetary theory. There are numerous attempts by classical theorists to integrate money in full equilibrium systems. These approaches all introduce some kind of friction that either introduces money by definition or uses optimizing agents that try to avoid the costs of not using money. These approaches vary from Samuelson's money in the utility function (Samuelson, 1947), to Clower's cash-in-advance (Clower, 1967), to Samuelson's intergenerational coordination problems (Samuelson, 1958), to legal restrictions (Wallace, 1983), to search and bargaining models (see Trejos and Wright, 1995). It goes without saying that all these approaches seem to be artificial and ignore the true nature of a monetary economy. It seems to be more appropriate to start from the notion that an economy in principle lacks stability, that agents behave under uncertainty (some economists even believe in fundamental uncertainty), and the idea that money fulfils an important role as hedge against uncertainty and mechanism to create stability. Especially if information problems arise, money and uncertainty seem to be happily married (Goodhart, 1989). In this more Keynesian view, money itself is an important institution that facilitates coordination of activity. Through its special properties of low production elasticity, its large substitution elasticities with other assets, and its liquidity, money is something special in the minds of economic agents.

How does money act as a coordinating device? Suppose we are in a world that is characterized by a large degree of uncertainty for all agents. Agents might want to write contracts for all bilateral exchange deals. If writing contracts would be without any costs, agents could use all the time they need to write the rules of the game for all possible outcomes. In reality this type of contract is simply too costly. As a result people write incomplete contracts. The unforeseen outcomes can be governed by legal enforcement or by conventional agreements or even by societal trust. As Van der Lecq (1998) argues, low bilateral trust that coincides with a large societal trust might be a stimulating environment to use money as a hedge against uncertainty. Van Ees and Sterken use this notion in an empirical analysis of the relation between the use of money and societal trust (Chapter 9). Using data for 40 countries they illustrate that the income velocity of money and trust are related. Countries that complement societal trust with a sound legal system typically allow monetary exchange.

The Keynesian heritage stresses the role of monetary theory in explaining the coordination of macroeconomic activity. Monetary policy, in various forms, is therefore seen as a powerful instrument in achieving stability at full employment. Despite this notion, there seems to be a fashion in the type of monetary theory macroeconomist like to use or to develop. Even more important, there is a fashion in using types of monetary policy to achieve the final goals of either stabilizing output and/or prices. Acknowledging the important role of the monetary system, should a central bank try to use a monetary aggregate, should it try to target nominal income, or try to control the interest rate? And what is the theoretical notion that supports a certain implementation of policy? Is it the quantity theory of money, Sidrauski's dynamic monetary model (Sidrauski, 1967), or a more short-run Keynesian type of sticky price model (Clarida *et al.*, 1999)? Brakman, Garretsen and Hoogduin review the confidence in monetary policy by central bankers and the confidence economic agents apparently have in central bankers themselves (Chapter 10). Are central bankers like Greenspan the wizards of coordination? Apparently we expect nowadays from central bankers that they can use some sort of optimal control models to steer inflation. Given the favourable recent economic period economic agents might have become overoptimistic in this respect. It is likely that Greenspan is not our Walrasian coordinator and we should not expect him to play that role.

One of the important aspects of recent insights into economic policy is the notion that precise ideas on expectations formation are important to implement policies successfully. If the private sector is highly uncertain about the true nature of *e.g.* monetary policy, it is likely to ask for higher risk premiums in setting wage and price contracts. To that extent, the use of policy rules is quite popular both in fiscal and monetary policy. In general, monetary policy rules can be either active or passive. A most extreme rule for instance is the Chicago rule, which prescribes the nominal interest rate to be equal to zero to prevent welfare loss due to anticipated inflation. More activist rules are proposed by McCallum (adjusting the monetary growth to obtain the desired growth rate of nominal GDP) and by Taylor (adjusting the nominal interest rate to obtain desired levels of inflation and output). So what is the value added of using policy rules? Fase addresses this issue in an analysis of monetary policy rules for Economic and Monetary Union (Chapter 11). He illustrates the use of both the McCallum and the Taylor rule in a small empirical New Keynesian model for EMU. He concludes that using policy rules of either sort is successful in terms of minimizing the rate of inflation at a low reduction of output. Moreover, interest rate targeting – which is rather popular nowadays – seems to outperform monetary targeting.

Apart from the recent interest in monetary policy rules, monetary theory developed into the field of information economics. Assuming that information is most likely to be distributed unevenly, one can show that for instance in the credit market equilibrium rationing can occur. So the simple coordination of a single market is hampered in the sense that even though market participants are willing to fulfil all price and non-price demands, still some of them are rationed. This microeconomic result, that can be founded either by adverse selection, or moral hazard, or costly state verification, is powerful, and most likely to be transmitted to the macroeconomic level. Especially if one considers revaluation of collateral due to shocks in asset prices to be important, a financial accelerator or credit cycles are likely (see Bernanke *et al.*, 1996 and Kiyotaki and Moore, 1997). This notion has created attention for the so-called credit channel of monetary policy. At the core of the credit channel is the Tobin-like assumption that credit is special and not a full substitute of other assets. If credit is special, and if the central bank is able to control the supply of credit, and if prices are not fully flexible, then the span of monetary policy is extended from the traditional money channel to the credit market. As in the hey-days of the money channel when the demand for money was at the core of attention of monetary researchers, there seems to be a shift of focus from the demand for money to the demand for credit. Kakes and Jacobs present an econometric analysis of the demand for credit in the Netherlands in the years 1983-1997 (Chapter 12). They show special interest in asymmetry, both in monetary policy itself and in the business cycle. The authors show that monetary expansions have more impact on the quantity of credit than monetary contractions. This result is opposite to what is usually found in empirical studies on the credit view. Secondly, this study does not give support for asymmetries in credit along the business cycle.

5. ECONOMIC GROWTH

Most economists agree on the notion that in the short run more types of frictions are relevant than in the long run. Take for instance the stickiness of wages and prices. Short-run nominal rigidities seem to be highly likely, but it is rather unusual to assume that nominal rigidities will last over decades. One of the finest counterexamples is the price of a bottle of Coca Cola. The price for a bottle of Coca Cola has been 5 dollar cents for almost 75 years (see Levy and Young, 2001).

Also other types of frictions, like switching costs, absence of new market entrants, *etc.* seem to be less valid in growth theory. Nevertheless, there is a debate for more than a century now on the role of long run real rigidities. This debate varies from Keynesian views on lasting disequilibria to almost frictionless growth in the classical tradition. Central to this discussion are key assumptions, like the (dis)functioning of the price mechanism, substitution of production factors, and formation of expectations.

Since the times of David Ricardo, economists emphasised the importance of physical capital formation, and hence increasing investment, for economic growth. During the first decades after the Second World War economic policies, in particular in developing countries, were characterised by an emphasis on large-scale industrialisation, which had to be brought about by government interventions. Underlying these theories a Harrod-Domar production function was assumed in which GDP is proportional to the capital stock. Hence GDP growth directly relates to the investment share through savings. Stability is a matter of coincidence. Hence, a typical Harrod-Domar economy alternates between long and prolonged periods of capital shortage with increasing unemployment, and labour shortage. This outcome, obviously, results from the fixed prices and wages and lack of substitution between the various inputs in the production process. In other words, there is no mechanism that coordinates economic activity in its way to full equilibrium.

The neoclassical economists challenged the importance of physical capital accumulation for economic growth by showing that investment does not affect the long-run equilibrium growth rate. The impact of physical capital accumulation on economic growth is restricted to the adjustment period to the long-run equilibrium of the economy. More in general, the idea that government interventions by means of large-scale industrialisation would stimulate economic growth is rejected by the neoclassical economists by referring to the advantages of free markets. Following the seminal papers of Solow (1956) and Swan (1956) various authors tried to remedy the shortcomings of the neoclassical model. These studies focus on, for instance, the aggregate nature of the production function; the homogeneity assumption of output and inputs in single sector framework; the exogeneity of savings rate. Moreover, in the 1970s, the report of the Club of Rome raised serious doubts about the usefulness of mainstream growth theory. In Chapter 13, Gerlagh and Keyzer review the literature on growth theory. They focus on maintaining growth in rich countries, initiating growth in poor countries and avoiding decline due to exhaustible natural resources.

The long-run exogeneity of economic growth, as well as the convergence implications of the traditional neoclassical growth models stem from the important assumption of decreasing returns to capital. However, if an extra amount of capital would always increase production by the same amount (*constant returns to capital*), the conclusions regarding the exogeneity of long-run growth and the convergence hypotheses drastically change. Since the mid-1980s (Baumol, 1986; Romer, 1986; Lucas, 1988), the study of economic growth and its policy implications re-entered the research agenda. The "new growth" theory emphasises issues which played only a marginal role in the traditional growth theory, such as the accumulation of knowledge, human capital, increasing returns to scale, externalities, learning-by-doing, and research and development. Romer (1990) argues that technological knowledge is not a totally excludable good. In Chapter 14, Van Zon and Muysken focus on public goods aspects of technological change. This public good character invokes market failures leading to underinvestment. They discuss policy simulations for the Netherlands.

An important implication of new growth models is that they exhibit scale effects, meaning that variations in the levels of key variables such as the investment rate, research effort, and policy variables (tax rates) exert permanent influences on national growth rates. However, the empirical evidence does not support the presence of scale effects. The contribution of Heertje (Chapter 15) critically discusses recent work on imperfect competition and growth in non-scale models.

Brunia and Kuper turn back to Harrod. In Chapter 16, they introduce an adjustment mechanism in a typical Post Keynesian model to come up with an expected, or *ex ante*, classification of regimes using a new data set for the Netherlands in the 19th century. It is argued that entrepreneurs invest in a situation of capital shortage based on the assumption that the existence of monopoly profits induces new firms to enter the market. The share of labour in income is found to be the crucial variable that captures information on future profitability of investment.

6. THE COORDINATION RESEARCH AGENDA

Although it is not even fully clear where we stand today, it is tempting to shed light on the future of research in coordination issues in macroeconomics. Given the completion of pure neoclassical thinking in the 1954 Arrow-Debreu paper, we don't take any risk by arguing that the route of tackling frictions is more appropriate if one really wants to understand coordinating mechanisms. How far should we go in assuming frictions? What kind of models should we use? Is there any hope to come up with definite answers?

Since the debate in macroeconomics is rather old, it would be odd to forecast a quick solution to all the issues. There seem to be a couple of modern developments that can stimulate this field of research, though. First, the use of suitable microeconomic theory, like game theory, contract theory, information economics, imperfect competition, *etc.* seems to be more accessible in the field of macroeconomics. This allows macroeconomists to model more precisely the microeconomic nature of posssible imperfections. Secondly, the methodology to analyse full-fledged dynamic equilibrium models that allow for imperfections is readily available. A few decades ago, it seemed that New Classical economists were the sole proprietors of stochastic dynamic equilibrium models. Today, these techniques seem to be common knowledge. Thirdly, microeconomic data are better available and allow for empirical analyses of distribution effects of macroeconomic (policy) actions. Up to now, only macroeconometric models were used to estimate the core parameters, while nowadays microeconometrics helps in finding more suitable results.

Modern macroeconomics centres around the coordination issue. In this book modest attempts are made to increase our knowledge in this field. It will take further effort to reach more definite answers in this interesting, but rather difficult field of research.

REFERENCES

Arrow, K. and G. Debreu (1954), "Existence of an Equilibrium for a Competitive Economy," *Econometrica* 22, pp. 265-290.

Baumol, W.J. (1986), "Productivity Growth, Convergence and Welfare: What the Long-run Data Show," *The American Economic Review* 76, pp. 1072-1085.

Bernanke, B., M. Gertler and S. Gilchrist (1996), "The Financial Accelerator and the Flight to Quality," *Review of Economics and Statistics* 78, pp. 1-15.

Blanchard, O. and S. Fischer (1989), *Lectures on Macroeconomics*, Cambridge: MIT Press.

Clarida, R., J. Gali and M. Gertler (1999), "The Science of Monetary Policy: A New Keynesian Perspective," *Journal of Economic Literature* 37, pp. 1661-1707.

Clower, R.W. (1967), "A Reconsideration of the Microfoundations of Monetary Theory," *Western Economic Journal* 6, pp. 1-9.
Cooper, R. and A. John (1988), "Coordinating Coordination Failures in Keynesian Models," *Quarterly Journal of Economics* 103, pp. 441-463.
Diamond, D. and P. Dybvig (1983), "Bank Runs, Deposit Insurance and Liquidity," *Journal of Political Economy* 91, pp. 401-419.
Fase, M.M.G. and Th. van de Klundert (1998), "Simon Kuipers: An Economist in Search of Rigour and Relevance," *De Economist* 146(1), pp. 1-21.
Goodhart, C.A.E., 1989, *Money, Information and Uncertainty*, London: MacMillan.
Keynes, J.M. (1936), *The General Theory of Money, Interest and Employment*, London: MacMillan.
Kiyotaki, N. and J. Moore (1997), "Credit Cycles," *Journal of Political Economy* 105, pp. 211-248.
Kiyotaki, N. and R. Wright (1993), "A Search-Theoretic Approach to Monetary Economics," *The American Economic Review* 83, pp. 63-77.
Lecq, S.G. van der, 1998, *Money, Coordination and Prices*, PhD Thesis, University of Groningen.
Levy, D. and A. Young (2001), "The Real Thing: Price Rigidity of the Nickel Coke: 1886-1959," Working Paper, Emory University, Atlanta.
Lucas, R.E. (1988), "On the Mechanics of Development Planning," *Journal of Monetary Economics* 22, pp. 3-42.
Ramsey, F. P. (1928), "A Mathematical Theory of Saving," *The Economic Journal* 38, pp. 543-559.
Romer, P.M. (1986), "Increasing Returns and Long-Run Growth," *Journal of Political Economy*, 94, pp. 1002-1037.
Romer, P.M. (1990), "Endogenous Technological Change," *Journal of Political Economy* 98(5), pp. S71-S102.
Samuelson, P. (1947), *Foundations of Economic Analysis*, Cambridge: Harvard University Press.
Samuelson, P. (1958), "An Exact Consumption-Loan Model of Interest With or Without the Social Contrivance of Money," *Journal of Political Economy* 66, pp. 467-482.
Sidrauski, M. (1967), "Rational Choice and Patterns of Growth in a Monetary Economy," *The American Economic Review* 57, pp. 534-544.
Solow, R.M. (1956), "A Contribution to the Theory of Economic Growth," *Quarterly Journal of Economics* 70, pp. 65-94.
Swan, T. (1956), "Economic Growth and Capital Accumulation," *Economic Record* 32, pp. 334-361.
Trejos, A. and R. Wright (1995), "Search, Bargaining, Money and Prices: Recent Results and Policy Implications," *Journal of Money, Credit, and Banking* 25, pp. 558-576.
Wallace, N. (1983), "A Legal Restrictions Theory of the Demand for Money and the Role of Monetary Policy," *Federal Reserve Bank of Minneapolis Quarterly Review,* Winter, pp. 1-7.

Chapter 2

Simon Kuipers: An Economist in Search of Rigour and Relevance[1]

Martin M.G. Fase and Theo van de Klundert
Econometric Research and Special Studies Department, De Nederlandsche Bank N.V. and University of Amsterdam; Faculty of Economics, Tilburg University and Groningen University

Key words: History of economic thought, Neo-Keynesian growth theory, Monetary economics

Abstract At the end of 1997 and after twenty-five years of duty, Professor Simon Kuipers retired as managing editor of *De Economist*. As a token of indebtedness and gratitude, this article reviews Kuipers's written work. The article focuses on two topics that dominate Kuipers's endeavours. First, his contributions to macroeconomic theory, with particular emphasis on his (neo-) Keynesian approach are examined. Second, Kuipers's contributions to actual monetary and economic policy are discussed, emphasis being placed on his empirical work.

1. INTRODUCTION

The retirement of Simon Kuipers as managing editor of *De Economist* is a welcome opportunity to look back and review his professional work over the last thirty years. A substantial number of his publications appeared in this journal, which underlines his long-lasting commitment to one of the oldest periodicals in our discipline.

Kuipers can be characterised as a macroeconomist interested in pure theoretical contributions as well as in applications. His applied work relates

[1] Reprinted from *De Economist* 146(1), pp. 1-21, with permission of Kluwer Academic Publishers and the authors. The editors of this volume are grateful to Mrs. M. Brouwer of De Nederlandsche Bank N.V. for providing them with an electronic version of this article.

to policy analysis and policy prescriptions in many fields, ranging from monetary economics to distortions in the labour market. Kuipers supported econometric work and made his own contributions in line with the Dutch tradition initiated by Tinbergen. Kuipers has an open eye for the different schools of thought in macroeconomics, but it seems fair to classify him as a true Keynesian. He admires neoclassical theory for its rigour and compactness, but doubts its relevance as markets in reality lack an auctioneer.

Keynesianism nowadays is different from what it used to be thirty years ago. The present survey of Kuipers's work is therefore also an exercise in the history of economic thought. In the neo-Keynesian world prices are considered to be rigid. Economic subjects have to make quantity adjustments inducing complicated interactions between variables in the real sphere. Post Keynesian authors emphasise adjustment through changes in the distribution of income, which in turn feed back on demand and supply along different channels. New Keynesians, who are of a more recent vintage, respond to the challenge by New Classical economists and explain why and to what extent prices are rigid or why market coordination is far from perfect.[2] This is all in the work of Kuipers, which made rereading his work such a fascinating enterprise.

To get a clear picture of Kuipers as an economist we organise this survey along two broad sections. In Section 2 we review the pure theoretical contributions, starting with the theories of economic growth along Keynesian lines in Subsection 2.2. The empirical estimation of vintage models supports some of the results of these models, as will be shown in Subsection 2.2. Business cycles belong to the core of Keynesian thinking. Kuipers's contributions in the field are discussed in Subsection 2.3. The section on theoretical developments closes with an original attempt to reconcile neoclassical and Keynesian growth theory in a Mashallian framework. Section 3 is devoted to applied work. In Subsection 3.1 we review Kuipers's contributions to monetary policy analysis. His vision on monetary integration, fiscal stabilisation policy and labour market issues are discussed in Subsection 3.2. The survey is concluded by presenting a profile of Professor S.K. Kuipers as an inspiring economist.

[2] See for an elementary introduction Kuipers *et al.* (1994), Chapter 6.

2. TWENTY YEARS OF MACROECONOMIC THEORY (1969-1989)

Simon Kuipers contributed to economic theory in many ways. There is however a clear and consistent *leitmotiv* in his theoretical work. From 1969 to 1989 a lot of effort is spent on constructing large theoretical models of economic growth. His aim was to develop a New Keynesian growth theory as an addendum or perhaps even as an alternative to neoclassical growth theory. With the introduction of Keynesian elements, disequilibrium situations become prominent and one has to deal also with the business cycles. Kuipers went even further by disentangling medium-run disequilibria in empirical studies of the Dutch economy. After 1990 his macroeconomic interest shifted somewhat more towards applications, but on many occasions he kept reminding us of the severe limitations of Walras's auctioneer. In this section we discuss the theoretical contributions of the period 1969-1989 without following a strict chronological path, considering four topics in particular. Emphasis is put on consistency and topicality.

2.1 Theories of Economic Growth

The phenomenon of economic growth has always fascinated Kuipers. Inspired by Harrod and other Keynesian authors there is a constant search for a neo-Keynesian growth theory opposed to or complementary with neoclassical growth theory. The discussion starts in 1969 with the publication in this journal of a triptych written in cooperation with H. de Haan entitled "An Investigation into the Influence of Monetary Factors on the Real Process of Growth in some Traditional Theories of Economic Growth" (De Haan and Kuipers, 1969a, 1969b, 1969c).

If all markets function perfectly, as assumed in the neoclassical theory, money does not matter for the real sector of the economy. However, if the real rate of interest is fixed exogenously neo-Keynesian features prevail. The capital coefficient is constant and where all savings are invested the stock of capital grows according to the well-known Harrod-Domar formula. This gives rise to a distinction between situations of capital abundance (the warranted rate of growth being higher than the growth of labour supply) and capital shortage (the opposite being true of both growth rates). In case of capital abundance, firms envisage excess capacity, which leads to a fall in investment and a corresponding decline in effective demand. The economy is unstable and unemployment rises. This is earmarked as "the typical Keynesian situation". If there is capital shortage, unemployment also rises permanently, but in this case because of an increasing gap between the demand for work and the supply of jobs.

In the neo-Keynesian growth model with a constant price level and a monetary sector there is a way out of this dilemma. The rate of growth of the money supply determines the real rate of interest. As observed above, when the rate of interest is fixed, the stock of capital grows at a constant rate. If this rate of growth differs from the rate of growth of the labour supply monetary authorities could change the growth rate of money supply to attain a neoclassical steady state. A necessary condition for this to happen is that the growth rate of the money supply equals the exogenously determined growth rate of the labour force.

If the capital-output ratio is fixed for one reason or another, the neoclassical growth theory does not apply, however. In Kuipers (1976) it is the substitution process itself which was under attack. Prices are flexible but capital is not fully malleable. It is assumed that during the transition from one technique to another with a higher capital-labour ratio a certain proportion of the existing capital stock has to be scrapped. This idea is modelled by the introduction of a malleability coefficient. In the extreme case of absence of malleability the capital coefficient cannot be changed, so that depending on initial conditions the Keynesian situation of capital abundance may arise. In the words of the author: "The Keynesians are right when the degree of malleability is so low that in the eyes of entrepreneurs too high an amount of capital scrapping is necessary to change the production technique" (Kuipers, 1976, p. 541). As a consequence, the system will be rather unstable, just as in the case of a fixed real interest rate.

It goes without saying that a full swing neo-Keynesian growth theory requires the integration of a well-specified demand block and a sensible supply block. This difficult task is accomplished in Kuipers (1973), which draws heavily on his PhD thesis: "The significance of demand and supply factors in one sector models of economic growth" (1970). This model of Kuipers became very complicated but was handled with great skill. Here it is only possible to hint at the most important mechanisms in the model in order to prepare the ground for an understanding of the main conclusions.

In his model savings depend on the gross profit margin (capital share of national income). Investment is also determined by the profit margin (q), because the firms desired capital increases with q. In addition, investment depends on actual output as a proxy for expected output. The resulting investment equation is non-linear in its arguments. Entrepreneurs adjust output (X) to total demand, so that investment and savings must be equated by adjusting quantities. This gives rise to an inverted U-curve relating output (X) to the profit margin (q). The intuition is that for low values of q a rise in the profit margin raises investment more than savings, so that output increases. The reverse may be true of relatively high values of q. However, for low values of q there is a complication coming from the supply side of the model. Entrepreneurs will not adjust output to demand if the real wage is higher than the marginal product of labour. So if the satisfaction of demand would bring the level of the marginal product of labour below that of the real wage, entrepreneurs will restrict output. Excess demand in the market for goods will be accompanied by excess supply in the labour market. This is a situation which Malinvaud (1977) labelled "classical unemployment". In his paper of 1973, Kuipers rejected this constraint as being unrealistic. Instead he assumed that the entrepreneur will reorganise the production process when q has fallen below a critical level (q_c). Therefore, below q_c output is restricted by a supply-side relation relating the capital-output ratio to the profit margin. Accordingly, output is then determined by effective supply.

There is a second inverted U-curve in Kuipers's model originating from the dynamic wage and price equations which are of the Post Keynesian type. Wage increases are negatively related to unemployment and prices rise in accordance with excess demand. Both unemployment and excess demand are functions of output and the profit margin, which explains the similarity between the output and the wage curve in the X-q space.

The functions of the model are specified so that the output-capital ratio (x) appears as one of the variables in the two reduced forms discussed above. In the short run the stock of capital is constant, whereas in a long-run steady state growth equilibrium the capital-output ratio is constant (meaning that in Kuipers's analysis with fixed capital x and X are equivalent). Therefore, in case of steady growth the output curve and the wage curve can be presented in the x-q space, as illustrated in Figure 1.

On the segment AB of the output curve production is supply-constrained. The segment BCD consists of points where production is demand-constrained. There is a maximum level for the output-capital level or capital productivity x_{max}, because it is assumed that substitution between capital and labour is only possible in a bounded region. As a consequence, there is an upper limit for x. Capital productivity at full employment is denoted by $\bar{x}$ On the segment AB of the output curve. It is assumed that the full-employment level $\bar{x}$ is always less than the technical maximum x_{max}. "Thus, unemployment due to capital shortage will not arise. This is likely to be true in Western countries; in the underdeveloped countries this is not so" (Kuipers, 1973, p. 584).

Steady state growth will obtain at points of intersection of the output curve and the wage curve. Such equilibria should be stable in the short run as well as in the long run in order to be of interest. Stability analysis takes a lot of effort and Kuipers displays great ingenuity in mastering this difficult topic. In Figure 1 two stable equilibria are shown. In point S_1 output is restricted by effective demand, while in point S_2 output is restricted by the size of the labour force. There is a third possibility not shown in the figure, which relates to the case that output is restricted by effective demand. Such an equilibrium would lie on the segment BC of the output curve. In the latter case the market for goods is in equilibrium, but the labour market is not. Hence, steady state growth is accompanied by a constant rate of unemployment. Distributive shares are determined by demand as well as by supply factors. If output is determined by effective supply the market for goods is in excess demand and the labour market is in excess supply. Then in a situation of steady state growth the rate of unemployment and the degree of excess of goods are both constant. The income distribution is primarily determined by supply factors. If output is determined by labour, the market of goods is in excess demand. The income distribution is again primarily determined by supply factors. The main conclusion of the analysis is that long-run disequilibria may exist, which calls for deliberate policy measures to restore equilibrium.

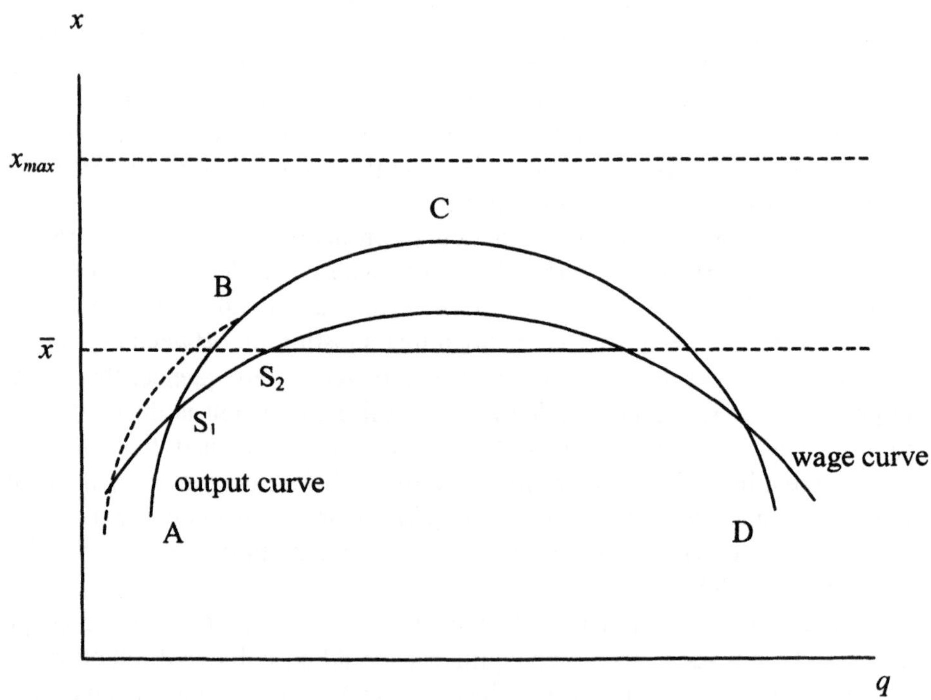

Figure 1.

Vintage models of capital accumulation used to be popular in the 1970s, at least in the Netherlands. In Kuipers (1975) a clay-clay vintage structure characterises the supply side of the model. Demand is modelled along conventional lines. In comparison with his 1973 model, Kuipers now takes a short-cut by using changes in the rate of capacity utilisation to equate demand and supply in the goods market. Wage and price equations are not very different from the earlier macroeconomic model. Emphasis lies on the comparative dynamics of steady state growth paths. For instance, a rise in the propensity to save leads to a fall in the life span of machines and a decline in the profit rate. This sounds familiar from neoclassical theory. But there is more. The utilisation rate of capital increases with the result that the unemployment rate declines. The negative relation between the rate of unemployment and the rate of capacity utilisation follows from the specification of the wage and price equations. The increase in the rate of capital utilisation comes as a surprise, because effective demand declines on impact of shocks. However, the fall in profits reduces gross investment leading to a higher degree of capacity utilisation. Output in the newest vintage decreases, whereas it increases in the older more labour intensive vintages. As a consequence, the demand for labour rises.

The example shows that full-fledged neo-Keynesian growth models are rather complex. Comparative dynamic results can be derived by careful mathematical analysis, but the economic intuition behind these outcomes is not always easy to grasp. It therefore seems appropriate to use the models for classificatory purposes as is illustrated in many of Kuipers's contributions to the field.

2.2 Empirical Estimation of Vintage Models

The vintage model has no special merit in this connection, but it has played an important role in empirical studies for the Dutch economy and the delineation of regimes of labour and capital shortage in the past. In Kuipers, Muysken and Van Sinderen (1970) the clay-clay vintage model is calibrated applying data for output, gross investment, employment, labour supply (adjusted for frictional unemployment), working hours, and real wages for the Netherlands over the period 1921-1976. The authors propose six minor amendments to the procedure introduced by Den Hartog, Van de Klundert and Tjan (1975), Den Hartog and Tjan (1976), but the method of estimation is basically the same. The main contribution of Kuipers *et al.* is that they apply the model to the pre-war period 1921-1939 as well as to the post-war period 1959-1976. An important assumption is that the actual development has to be characterised as a regime of labour shortage or capital shortage. In the first regime, labour falls short of capacity demand for labour with actual demand for labour to a large extent being determined by labour supply. In the other regime, labour supply exceeds capacity demand and actual demand for labour is determined by capacity demand and the degree of capacity utilisation.

Before discussing the results of Kuipers *et al.* it may be useful to take a closer look at the concepts of labour shortage and capital shortage. First, the term capital abundance, which is equivalent to labour shortage, no longer appears in Kuipers's later publications. Perhaps the reason was that this term caused confusion, because it is associated overly strongly with a low propensity to invest and Harrodian instability. Second, output capacity and the corresponding capacity demand for labour can be the outcome of three different situations defined as follows: (a) If there is no factor substitution, output capacity depends on the existing stock of capital and a constant capital coefficient (capital-output ratio). This fairly extreme assumption is made in Kuipers (1988) and discussed below; (b) If there is substitution one may assume that it is limited for technical reasons. This view is taken in Kuipers (1973) and as a special case in Kuipers (1976), where output capacity is determined by the stock of capital and the capital coefficient on the border of the substitution interval; (c) If there is full substitution but factor prices are rigid, the capital coefficient chosen by entrepreneurs is fixed. Output capacity is again determined by the available stock of capital and the fixed capital coefficient. This view is taken in De Haan and Kuipers (1969), Kuipers (1973 and 1975) and Kuipers *et al.* (1979).

The article of 1973 is special because of the distinction made between the possibility of capital shortage following definition (b) (which is subsequently ruled out in the paper as an uninteresting case) and the possibility of supply-constrained output. In the latter case firms restrict output, because real wages are too high compared with labour productivity if the demand for goods is fully satisfied. Real wages are fixed and profit-maximising entrepreneurs stick to the technique with the lowest cost. Output capacity then follows from definition (c). It is somewhat confusing to have different definitions for the same thing. For expositionary purposes it might perhaps be advisable to stick to definitions (a) or (c) in theoretical work.

In the clay-clay vintage model factor substitution is associated with changes in the life-span of equipment (capital). So long as older equipment has a positive yield (defined as the difference between revenue and labour cost) it will remain in use. Output capacity is determined by the total amount of equipment in use. Capital shortage arises if labour demand at capacity falls short of labour supply. Kuipers has elaborated this empirically for the sample periods 1921-1939 and 1959-1975.

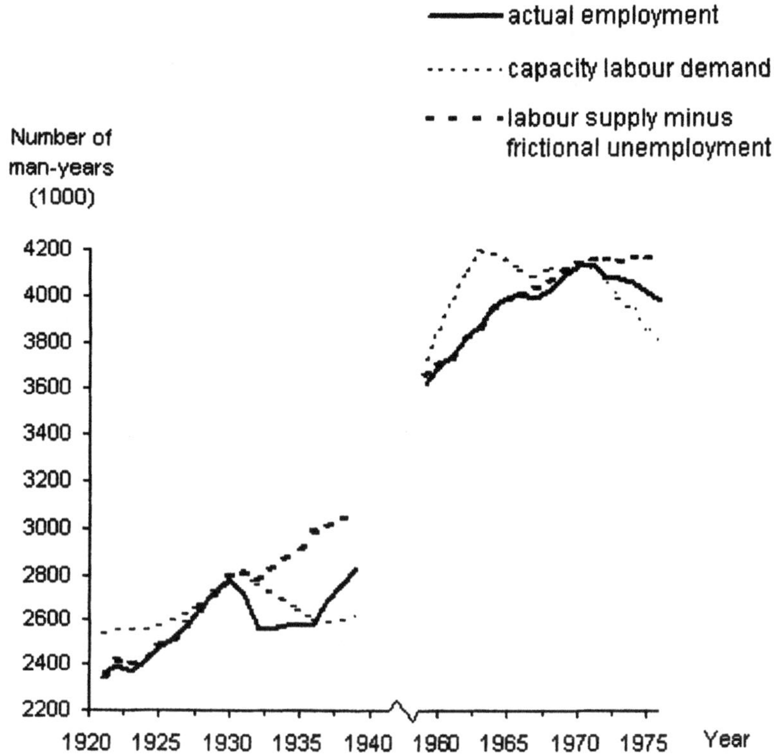

Figure 2. Source: Kuipers, Muysken and Van Sinderen (1979), *op. cit.*, p. 501

The results of estimating capacity labour demand are shown in Figure 2 along with effective labour demand and exogenous labour supply. In both epochs there have been alternating periods of labour shortage and capital shortage. With respect to the inter-war period, the Dutch economy changed regimes in 1930 from a situation of having labour shortage to one of having capital shortage. With regard to the post-war period there is a similar switch around 1969. The situation of labour shortage in the 1960s turned into capital shortage in the 1970s. The change of regime in the epochs examined was the result of different factors. In the pre-war period, capital shortage was caused by very low levels of investment. The life-span of equipment was constant and determined purely by wear and tear. In the post-war period, capital shortage arose because substantial increases in the real wage rate induced economic obsolescence of existing equipment. Capacity utilisation was low in years of labour scarcity, but may also be affected by effective demand especially in case of capital scarcity. In the 1930s the degree of capacity utilisation was extremely low due to a shortage of effective demand. Building on Kuipers and Van Zon (1982), Kuipers and Kuper

(1985) showed that the results obtained with clay-clay vintage models can be reproduced in a more general setting by applying a putty-clay vintage model and that capital shortage continued until the mid-1980s. The main conclusion that macroeconomic disequilibria are not necessarily short-lived therefore rests on firm grounds (see also Kuipers, 1990).

2.3 The Trade Cycle under Different Regimes

Kuipers's penetrating analysis of the trade cycle culminates in his contribution to the Festschrift for the well-known Dutch economist Witteveen. In his treatise *Structuur en Conjunctuur,* Witteveen (1956) explains how the characteristics of the trade cycle in a situation of capital shortage differ fundamentally from those in a situation of labour shortage. In Kuipers (1988) this issue is taken up again, applying disequilibrium theory developed by Barro and Grossman (1976) and Malinvaud (1977, 1980). The non-market clearing framework used for the analysis of the trade cycle has several elements in common with the dynamic model in Malinvaud (1980). The main differences introduced by Kuipers relate to the monetary sector (which exhibits traditional Keynesian features) and to the nominal wage and price dynamics (which are modelled with static expectations). As a result of these assumptions the model of Kuipers is essentially different from that of Malinvaud.

The production structure is characterised by fixed input coefficients. Output capacity and the corresponding demand for labour therefore correspond to definition (a), presented in Section 2.2. Capital shortage prevails if output capacity (X^*) falls short of output at full employment $\overline{X}$. Labour shortage implies the opposite: capacity output is higher than full employment output. In each situation there are several possibilities with respect to short-run equilibria as shown in Table 1, using a terminology borrowed from Malinvaud (1977, 1980). Under capital shortage the economy exhibits Keynesian unemployment if effective demand (Y) falls short of capacity output.

Table 1. Disequilibrium regimes

Capital shortage: $X^* < \overline{X}$	Labour shortage: $\overline{X} < X^*$
Keynesian unemployment	Keynesian unemployment
$Y < X^* < \overline{X}$	$Y < \overline{X} < X^*$
Classical unemployment	Underconsumption
$X^* < Y < \overline{X}$	$\overline{X} < Y < X^*$
$X^* < \overline{X} < Y$	Repressed inflation
	$\overline{X} < X^* < Y$

Classical unemployment prevails if effective demand is higher than capacity output. Under labour shortage there are three short-run equilibria. If effective demand is lower than full employment output, there is a situation of Keynesian unemployment. If effective demand exceeds both full employment output and capacity output, we have repressed inflation or simply inflation. Firms are rationed in the output market and in the labour market. There is a third possibility, which is termed underconsumption. This implies that firms are rationed in the labour market but face excess supply in the market for goods. In contrast to Malinvaud, who does not find this possibility interesting, Kuipers considered this interesting and examined the situation of underconsumption carefully. According to this analysis Kuipers's dynamical system can be reduced to two differential equations. Under capital shortage the state variables are output capacity, which is governed by investment, and the real wage rate, depending on nominal wages and prices. In case of labour shortage things are more complex. The reduction to a system of two differential equations now requires some simplifying assumptions with respect to the behaviour of consumers and investors. In all cases considered, the process of adjustment, however, is cyclical and the economy may eventually attain a Walrasian equilibrium.

From this analysis of Kuipers it appeared that the traditional overinvestment theory explains the upper turning point of the trade cycle in case of capital shortage. In the opposite case of labour shortage, the traditional underinvestment theory applies at the upper turning point of the cycle. However, the upper turning point does not occur at a low but at a high level of economic activity with rising prices. This result is not in agreement with the Keynesian underinvestment theory. In Kuipers's model, investment is low in the expansionary phase because consumptive demand is high. The other characterisations of cycle, the downswing, the lower turning point and the upswing do not correspond so well with Witteveen's view nor with the views expressed by the proponents of the underinvestment theory and the overinvestment theory.

The results on the business cycle obtained by Kuipers are interesting in their own right. However, to what extent these results are robust with respect to the manner of linking different dynamic sub-systems remains to be seen. Numerical simulations as in Malinvaud (1980) are required to clarify this issue. Although Kuipers acknowledges in some of his publications the usefulness of simulation experiments, he actually refrains from applying this method in his work.

2.4 A Marshallian Synthesis

In most of Kuipers's publications, the neo-Keynesian growth theory is treated as a special case of the neoclassical growth theory or the other way around. In the latter case the neo-Keynesian growth theory seems to be the norm and neoclassical growth theory is put in the background as in for instance Kuipers (1973). The view expressed in Kuipers (1981 and 1982) is different in that it is based on a very special hierarchy of models. A distinction is made à la Marshall between the short run, the medium run and the long run. In the short run, output capacity and prices are given and quantity rationing applies along the lines set out above. Short-run equilibria may be stable under reasonable assumptions as shown in Kuipers (1982).

In the medium run output capacity and prices are endogenous, but the expected prices that are relevant with respect to technology choice are constant. This implies that the medium run is a period within which the entrepreneurs try to get rid of the existing underutilisation or overutilisation. The dynamics of the medium run are studied for a special case: the Harrodian model under capital shortage. The special regimes considered in this connection are Keynesian unemployment ($Y < X^* < \overline{X}$) and classical unemployment ($X^* < Y < \overline{X}$). Kuipers has shown that Harrod's warranted process of growth is stable under both regimes. (Regime switches are ruled out in advance). The model of the medium run therefore tends towards a situation characterised by full utilisation of productive capacity. This contrasts with the usual view that Harrod's model of economic growth is unstable (see in this connection Van Ewijk, 1982). Stability in the model of Kuipers is assured by assuming that entrepreneurs base their investment decisions on past and present experiences with respect to capacity utilisation. Investment decisions are considered as medium-term decisions because capital goods have a life time of more than one period.

In the analysis of the long run all variables are determined endogenously. Price expectations are now revised and the production technique is adjusted accordingly from medium-term period to medium-term period. It is assumed here that equilibrium in the medium run is stable and that the adjustment in the direction of full capacity utilisation proceeds so quickly that it is safe to base the long-run analysis on full utilisation in every (medium-term) period. If all expectations are fulfilled, it can be shown that there is a tendency to balanced growth in the real sphere of the model. Real wages adjust in case of unemployment. Capital accumulation and wage formation interact in a stable manner. In case of unemployment, real wages decline and accumulation increases so that more workers are employed. The process of adjustment may be cyclical but is always damped. The monetary system requires the rate of growth of the money stock less than the growth of output. This conclusion differs from the one with respect to money growth in De Haan and Kuipers (1969), as discussed above. The reason for this difference is that in Kuipers (1981), a change in the price level induces a change in production technology, because the net rate of profit depends on the rate of inflation.

The question of how the New Keynesian and the neoclassical growth theory fit into a common framework can now be answered. In Kuipers's view, the Keynesian growth theory is a theory of the medium run and the neoclassical growth theory is one of the long term. The question that still remains is where to put the business cycle. The length of the medium run is set by Kuipers at a period of two to five years. The business cycle may last for at least as many years. Therefore, the Marshallian synthesis does not lead to an integration of cycles and growth. This challenge is taken up more recently by supporters of the real business cycle theory. However, one may doubt whether a full-fledged integration can do without the Keynesian elements that flourish so prominently in Kuipers's writings.

3. TWENTY-FIVE YEARS OF MONETARY ANALYSIS AND ECONOMIC POLICY WATCHING

Simon Kuipers has left a prominent mark as a critical watcher and analyst of macro-economic policy over the past thirty years.[3] Besides his devotion to economic theory as outlined in the previous section, his interests and capabilities are also in the field of every day macro-economic policy issues. A common approach, also followed by Kuipers himself, is to distinguish three macro-economic instruments for economic policy, namely monetary, fiscal and labour market policy. Below we discuss Simon Kuipers's main contributions in the fields of monetary policy, with fiscal and labour market policy as well as his view on EMU to be discussed in Subsection 3.2. Our approach is to focus on the topicality of the subject studied by him, his theoretical framework and the main policy implications which very often Kuipers also based on applied econometric research.

[3] With others, Kuipers was also involved in revising and rewriting the well-known and at the time widespread monetary textbook in Dutch by Korteweg and Keesing from the 1970s onwards.

3.1 Monetary Matters

3.1.1 Holtrop's monetary analysis

The first paper of Simon Kuipers in the field of Dutch monetary policy was on Holtrop's monetary approach (Kuipers and Wilpstra, 1973). This paper is mainly a response to a paper by Engering, in which Holtrop's econometric verification of his own monetary analysis was criticised. Kuipers and Wilpstra show that Engering's critique is in most cases invalid. The main purpose of Holtrop's method of monetary analysis was to create a framework to locate inflationary and deflationary disturbances. In those days the importance of the method of Holtrop (and the Nederlandsche Bank) as a practical tool for monetary analysis was its diagnostic meaning, enabling Holtrop to recognise the origin and character of monetary disturbances in the Dutch economy and to delineate approximately the Bank's responsibilities. The basic source of any monetary disturbances is to be found in inflationary or deflationary processes. A necessary and sufficient condition for the occurrence of any monetary equilibrium, the absence of either inflation or deflation, is that the algebraic sum of spontaneous inflationary and deflationary disturbances should be zero. Holtrop's main analytical problem was to translate this abstract notion into an operational framework. Therefore, much attention was given to the distinction between domestic and external monetary impulses. Holtrop's model for an open economy is given in a nutshell by the following equation:

$$\Delta Y = 1/(k+m)(D+E) \qquad (1)$$

It endogenises nominal national income (Y) in terms of the marginal liquidity ratio (k), the marginal import coefficient (m), and domestic (D) and foreign (E) monetary shocks. In a closed economy, as stated by Holtrop, the marginal import coefficient vanishes and therefore national income increases by $1/k$ times the sum of domestic and foreign monetary shocks. Kuipers and Wilpstra, however, showed that by taking dynamics into account, the result remains the same for a closed economy but changes for an open economy. For an open economy the income multiplier of domestic monetary shocks is absent, while the income multiplier of a foreign shock is equal to the inverted marginal import coefficient. Therefore, according to Kuipers and Wilpstra, the empirical verification by Holtrop would be improved by introducing dynamics in Holtrop's model. In addition, Kuipers and Wilpstra focus, as typical (in the terminology of Fase, 1994) for the third round of discussion on Dutch monetarism, on Holtrop's statistical verification. The basic equation of Holtrop's monetary analysis is hard to test, because as a matter of fact it is an identity, rather than an estimable reduced-form equation. Therefore, Kuipers and Wilpstra postulate equation (1) as a reduced-form equation. Their analysis confirms Holtrop's hypothesis that an increase in nominal national income is mainly explained by monetary impulses. Therefore, they conclude is that money has a significant influence on the increase on national income and that money matters. Kuipers and Wilpstra also show that changes in nominal income are not dominated by foreign monetary impulses, as Holtrop's regression results indicate, but that the impact of domestic and foreign monetary impulses is more or less the same.

3.1.2 Demand for money

In 1978 Kuipers and Wilpstra (1978) published an empirical study about the demand for money in the Netherlands, with a focus on the stability of the demand for money. This issue is the cornerstone of the monetarist belief in the effectiveness of monetary policy. Keynesians are generally much less optimistic in this respect. The theoretical specification used by Kuipers and Wilpstra is based on an earlier study by Fase and Kuné (1974), which they criticized on several points. This criticism concerned the stability tests performed, the small size of the interest-rate elasticity and the fact that Fase and Kuné used only a broad definition of money. However, Kuipers and Wilpstra found in their preferred money demand equation an interest elasticity of -0.32, which is slightly higher than the -0.20 estimated by Fase and Kuné. The main conclusion of Kuipers and Wilpstra, however, was that the Dutch demand for money function in the period 1952-1976 is unstable and acceptable estimation results are only obtained with narrow concept of money, *i.e.* currency plus demand deposits rather than with the broad concept of money M2. The implication was that Dutch monetary policy may be frustrated seriously by unpredictable changes in the demand for money, especially if it is based on a broad concept of money as was the case in the Netherlands.

Since the mid-1960s the liquidity ratio, defined as the ratio of M2 and national income, was used as the main monetary indicator in the Netherlands. The aim of Dutch monetary policy at the time was to stabilise this ratio. However, in the early 1980s this liquidity ratio rose substantially, having been nearly constant for years. Kuipers and Boertje (1988) analysed the causes of this rise. Their theoretical framework was the same as that of Kuipers and Wilpstra (1978). An important novelty was the disaggregation of private sector money holdings into money held by households and firms. The monetary policy conclusion drawn by Kuipers and Boertje from their econometric analysis was that an aggregate analysis of money demand does not seem appropriate. As the money demand equation of households differs from that of the business sector, aggregation errors are likely. Another interesting conclusion was that the speed of adjustment of actual to desired money holdings was low, indicating that the buffer-stock approach should be considered in modelling the money demand. However, and interestingly enough, Kuipers and Boertje argue that the rise of the overall liquidity ratio is entirely accounted for by the business sector. The increased liquidity of the business sector in turn is the result of the fall of labour's share in businesses's value added caused by a recovery of profitability and solvability not simultaneously accompanied by a recovery of investment expenditures.

3.1.3 Demand for financial assets and portfolio modelling

The 1980s saw rapid deregulation, liberalisation and internationalisation of financial markets. In a world of perfect international capital mobility a small open economy like the Netherlands cannot control its money supply if it maintains a fixed exchange rate. These developments brought Kuipers (together with Sterken) to examine whether in the 1990s the Dutch central bank is still able to pursue both a stable exchange rate and money targeting. To examine this policy issue, Kuipers and Sterken (1990, 1995) estimated a small equilibrium portfolio model of the Dutch financial sector, based on a simple but consistent financial accounting system. They concluded that both domestic and foreign and short- and long-term assets are not perfect substitutes. Therefore, the Dutch central bank should in principle be able to pursue both goals of monetary policy. The Dutch central bank, however, has to take the resulting steepness of the yield curve and capital flows as *faits accomplis*. Should these variables also belong to the goals of monetary policy, one of the other goals has to be dropped. Given the international context, the Dutch central bank, according to Kuipers and Sterken, should drop the money supply target.

In Kuipers's view macroeconometric models are in particular an essential tool for quantitative economic policy evaluation. As outlined in several papers (see *e.g.* Kuipers *et al.* 1980; Kuipers 1983a) he has shown his expertise on constructing large empirical macroeconomic models several times, with CESAM as his crown jewel. CESAM, a macroeconometric model of the Dutch economy, has been used to generate medium-term forecasts of the Dutch economy and to analyse economic policy (see *e.g.* Kuipers and Kuper, 1990; Jongbloed *et al.*, 1990; Kuipers, 1983a). CESAM includes a fine example of portfolio modelling (Kuipers *et al.*, 1990). In 1980 Kuipers already shows his expertise as a model builder by his participation in the construction of a multi-sector model of the Dutch economy (Kuipers *et al.*, 1980).

3.2 Economic Policy in the Netherlands

3.2.1 Economic and Monetary Union

In the 1990s increasing attention has been given to the Dutch monetary policy in a European perspective. In its 62nd Annual Report the Bank for International Settlements in Basle raised the important question of whether the European Central Bank (ECB) would be able to maintain the goal of price stability in stage III of EMU. Also, it mentioned the possibility of a conflict of interest between the ECB and the ECOFIN Council, which determines the exchange rate policy, and the possibility of insufficient public support for the ECB. This urged Kuipers to express his views on this topic (Kuipers, 1992a). To his own surprise, little attention was paid to this question at that time. Kuipers argues, in addition to the critical notes of the BIS, that the Maastricht Treaty of 1992 makes only monetary policy supranational. For fiscal policy separate conditions have been agreed upon – of recent date the so-called Stabilisation Pact – but the member states of the monetary union can still formulate their own independent fiscal policy. The same holds for labour market policy, if formulated at all. This means that only monetary policy is available to maintain price stability. As stated by Kuipers, pure monetarists would argue that this is sufficient, but Keynesians and others, supported by the facts of the past decade, argued that this is overly simplistic. The interest rate sensitivity of private expenditures is small and the interest rate elasticity of money demand and money supply is relatively large. According to Kuipers it seems to be an illusion that the coordination in Europe between monetary, fiscal and labour market policy on the national and supranational level can succeed.

3.2.2 Kuipers's eclectic view on fiscal policy

From the second half of the seventies onwards, Kuipers often contributed to the debate on economic policy in the Netherlands, with the most frequent presence in the recession years of the early 1980s. His publications in this field mainly rest on two approaches, both incorporating a combination of theoretical and empirical analysis. The first is the use of simple but instructive models with a Keynesian flavour which show, for example, how opinions of policymakers crucially hinge on parameter values (Kuipers, 1979 and 1983b; Sterken *et al.*, 1995). The second approach evolved after the publication of the CESAM model (Kuipers *et al.*, 1990), presenting forecasts and policy simulations as an alternative to those presented by the CPB (*e.g.* Kuipers and Kuper, 1990). A recurring theme in Kuipers's papers on economic policy is the importance of sound public finances. This is reflected by continuous support for deficit- and debt-reducing policies (Kuipers, 1984 and 1992b). Although Kuipers did not preclude a deflationary effect, this should be put against the positive effects of a more stable public sector, lower interest rates and a reduced sensitivity of public finance to interest rate changes.

In several articles Kuipers has presented his views on stabilisation policy by confronting equilibrium and disequilibrium theories (*e.g.* Kuipers, 1982). This approach has put more structure into the debate on economic policy. Also, it illustrates Kuipers's eclectic view on stabilisation policy. This view is most clearly expressed when Kuipers (1987) summarised the monetarist and neo-Austrian approaches, as opposed to the neoclassical synthesis of mainstream Keynesians. According to Kuipers, both views would support Dutch economic policy as it has been conducted from 1982 onwards with budgetary restraint, aimed at deficit reduction; reduction of the size of the public sector, aimed at a stronger supply-side of the economy; no interference in the process of wage and price determination. However, an improved public finance situation might eventually reinforce the call for fiscal stabilisation policy. Kuipers considers the feasibility of stabilisation policy in the light of increased criticism on that matter. In his view, a market economy requires stabilisation, since prices are too inflexible to clear markets without sizeable quantity effects. Although Kuipers agreed with the monetarist view that short-run stabilisation might do more harm than good, he also argued that medium-term stabilisation of inflation, labour and capital shortage, or underutilisation is possible. In spite of Lucas's (1971) critique on policy evaluation, however, Kuipers took a pragmatic view and acknowledged that macro-econometric models could be useful to understand behaviour under disequilibrium regimes.

3.2.3 Debate on unemployment

At the end of the 1970s a vigorous debate on the nature and causes of unemployment in the Netherlands took place, focusing on the question whether unemployment was cyclical or structural in nature. Kuipers contributed to the criticism directed at the Central Planning Bureau's model of the Dutch production structure by re-estimating the model's employment equation. He showed that the effect of capacity utilisation disappeared if the period after 1975 was included in the estimation. Employment was mainly affected by stagnation in the creation of new jobs, caused by cost factors

(Kuipers *et al.*, 1978). Another important contribution of this study was that it stressed the slow adjustment of labour demand to reduced wage costs. A few years later Kuipers (1980) critically surveyed the Dutch employment debate. Characteristically, Kuipers not just recommended a policy of wage growth restraint, but added that perhaps a policy to stimulate aggregate demand, would be necessary. This should be aimed at an increase in capacity utilisation, affecting profits positively and hence private investment. The unemployment debate not only focused on the structural-cyclical distinction. Kuipers also initiated a discussion on the question which part of unemployment was caused by imperfections in the labour market (Kuipers and Buddenberg, 1978). This 'UV analysis' showed that unemployment resulting from labour market imperfection, increased only slightly during the seventies. It confirmed that structural unemployment was largely caused by quantitative job shortages and less by qualitative discrepancies between demand and supply of labour.

3.2.4 Coordination failures and income distribution

Although coordination failures are Kuipers's main argument for fiscal stabilisation policy in a market economy, another argument is given by the existence of income political views on wage determination. These two arguments, coordination failures and income distribution, respectively, occur among Kuipers's most recent and earliest scientific work. In his early work, Kuipers contributed some papers to the positive study of income policy. Tinbergen (1973) had argued that an increased supply of higher educated labour would reduce income inequality. Kuipers (1973) and Groenveld and Kuipers (1976) questioned this view, by estimating the elasticity of substitution between different income groups in the labour market.

Kuipers (1995) has recently addressed the issue of coordination failures. He questions the increasing aversion among policymakers against price rigidities and the institutions and conventions that have caused these rigidities. Reviewing the literature, he argued that general equilibrium theory is not a theory of exchange, not involving actual processes in economic reality, like markets, production, consumption, which are all affected by uncertainty. Therefore, a policy of deregulation should not be based on a general equilibrium approach, but on careful consideration of the balance between allocative efficiency and stability. Kuipers applied this view to the labour market, by reviewing the question whether there is a case for central coordination of principally decentralised sectoral wage formation (Kuipers and Kuper, 1996) and he found empirical support for his view on the base of a cross-section analysis among countries.

4. BY WAY OF CONCLUSION: A PROFILE OF SIMON KUIPERS

This article focused on Kuipers's main contributions to two important fields of scholarly interest. The first is pure macroeconomic theory with an emphasis on his work on growth theory and empirical implementation. The second is economic policy with a strong emphasis on money, empirical macroeconomic models and fiscal policy. Empirical testing, particularly in monetary matters, has played an important role. However, much more can be said about Simon Kuipers. Perhaps it is appropriate now to consider Simon Kuipers in his role as managing editor of *De Economist* for 25 years. In this capacity about 60 communications and over 500 published articles went through his hands, not to mention an even larger number of submitted but rejected papers. Kuipers very often enjoyed his editorial work, encouraging young scholars to submit their work and get it published. Moreover, Kuipers was responsible for inviting book reviewers, of which almost 1,500 were published. In today's business of scholarly rating, in particular book reviewing scores low. We may regret this, contrasting as it does with professional attitudes of, say, three or four decades ago. In view of the modern approach to the economics of information and the emphasis on the informational content of economic activities, this remarkable neglect is, to say the least, amazing. Again, as editor Kuipers discharged this information-providing responsibility with great care and enthusiasm, as for that matter he discharged all of his scholarly duties and sometimes heavy but perhaps professionally unrewarded managerial duties for *De Economist*.

The overall conclusion is as straightforward and fair as Simon Kuipers himself is. He is a true scholar with major focus on macroeconomic research but with broad economic and policy interests, with views which are imaginative and sometimes provocative, giving careful attention to the empirical underpinning of abstract views. This is precisely what could be expected of someone who has lived at least two lives. First as a scholar and prolific writer of economic books and fine articles. Second as managing editor. In this latter capacity, Simon Kuipers has been at the very centre of the board of editors of one of the oldest professional economic journals in the world for a quarter of a century. Simon has done a fine job indeed and we and our readership owe him a colossal debt of gratitude.

REFERENCES

Barro, R.J. and H.I. Grossman (1976), *Money, Employment and Inflation*, Cambridge, *etc.*.

Ewijk, C. van (1982), "Stability in Keynesian and Neoclassical Growth Models," *De Economist* 130(1), pp. 101-122 .

Fase, M.M.G. and J.B. Kuné (1974), "De vraag naar liquiditeiten in Nederland, 1952-1971," *De Economist* 122(4), pp. 326-356.

Fase, M.M.G. (1994), "Rise and Demise of Dutch Monetarism: The Schumpeter-Koopmans-Holtrop Connection," *History of Political Economy* 26(1), spring 1994, pp. 21-38.

Groenveld, K. and S.K. Kuipers (1976), "Some Further Evidence on the Substitution Possibilities between Graduate and Other Labour," *Kyklos* 29(3), pp. 531-539.

Haan, H. de and S.K. Kuipers (1967), *Onderzoek naar de invloed van monetaire factoren op het reële groeiproces in enkele traditionele theorieën van economische groei*, Rijksuniversiteit Groningen, Faculteit der Economische Wetenschappen, Groningen.

Haan, H. de and S.K. Kuipers (1969a), "Een onderzoek naar de invloed van monetaire factoren op het reële groeiproces in enkele traditionele theorieën van economische groei (I)," *De Economist* 117(2), pp. 139-160.

Haan, H. de and S.K. Kuipers (1969b), "Een onderzoek naar de invloed van monetaire factoren op het reële groeiproces in enkele traditionele theorieën van economische groei (II)," *De Economist* 117(4), pp. 381-401.

Haan, H. de and S.K. Kuipers (1969c), "Een onderzoek naar de invloed van monetaire factoren op het reële groeiproces in enkele traditionele theorieën van economische groei (III)," *De Economist* 117(5), pp. 493-510.

Hartog, H. den, Th.C.M.J. van de Klundert and H.S. Tjan (1975), "De structurele ontwikkeling van de werkgelegenheid in macro-economisch perspectief" (The Structural Development of Employment in Macroeconomic Perspective), in *Preadviezen van de Vereniging voor de Staathuishoudkunde*, Leiden, pp. 49-110.

Hartog, H. den and H.S. Tjan (1976), "Investment, Wages, Prices and Demand for Labour: A Clay-Clay Vintage Model for the Netherlands," *De Economist* 124(1), pp. 32-55.

Jongbloed, B.W.A., S.K. Kuipers, G.H. Kuper and E. Sterken (1990), "CESAM-voorspellingen voor 1990-1994," *Economisch Statistische Berichten* 75(3752), 4 April, pp. 320-323.

Kuipers, S.K. (1973), "Personele inkomensverdeling en produktiestructuur," in Vereniging voor de Staathuishoudkunde, *Inkomensnivellering: verkenning van feiten, wenselijkheden, mogelijkheden en gevolgen*, 's-Gravenhage: Martinus Nijhoff, , pp. 63-94.

Kuipers, S.K. (1973), "A Demand and Supply Model of Economic Growth," *De Economist* 121(4), pp. 553-608.

Kuipers, S.K. and B.S. Wilpstra (1973), "Over Holtrops monetaire theorie," *Maandschrift Economie* 37(11), pp. 489-511.

Kuipers, S.K. (1975), "A Vintage Model of Growth, Employment and Inflation," *De Economist* 123(4), pp. 531-558.

Kuipers, S.K. (1976), "Personal Income Distribution and Production Structure," *Economie Appliquée* 29(1), pp. 5-31.

Kuipers, S.K. (1976), "Imperfect Malleability of Capital and Economic Growth: An Attempt at Synthesis between Keynesian and Neoclassical Growth Models," *Maandschrift Economie* 40, pp. 530-542.

Kuipers, S.K. and F.H. Buddenberg (1978), "Unemployment on Account of Market Imperfection in the Netherlands since the Second World War," *De Economist* 126(3), pp. 390-412.

Kuipers, S.K., J. Muysken and J. van Sinderen (1978), "De werkgelegenheidsontwikkeling in Nederland sinds 1970: een nadere analyse," *Economisch Statistische Berichten* 63(3160), 28 June, pp. 648-652.

Kuipers, S.K. and B.S. Wilpstra (1978), "On the Estimation and Stability of Demand for Money Functions for the Netherlands, 1952-1976," *Economies-et-Sociétés* 12(10-12), pp. 1917-1942.

Kuipers, S.K. (1979), "Het verslag van De Nederlandsche Bank over het jaar 1978," *Economisch Statistische Berichten* 64(3204), 16 May, pp. 476-482.
Kuipers, S.K., J. Muysken and J. van Sinderen (1979), "The Vintage Approach to Output and Employment Growth in the Netherlands, 1921-1976", *Weltwirtschaftliches Archiv* 115, pp. 485-507.
Kuipers, S.K. (1980), "Prospects of Employment Growth in the Netherlands: A Critical Survey of Prevailing Views," in S.K. Kuipers and G.J. Lanjouw (eds.), *Prospects of Economic Growth*, pp. 117-130.
Kuipers, S.K., J. Muysken, D.-J. van den Berg and A.H. van Zon (1980), *Sectorstructuur en economische groei: een eenvoudig groeimodel met zes sectoren van de Nederlandse economie in de periode na de Tweede Wereldoorlog*, Voorstudies en achtergronden V14, Wetenschappelijke Raad voor het Regeringsbeleid, SDU, 's-Gravenhage.
Kuipers, S.K. (1981), "Keynesian and Neoclassical Growth Models: a Sequential Analytical Approach," *De Economist* 129(1), pp. 58-104.
Kuipers, S.K. and A.H. van Zon (1982), "Output and employment growth in the Netherlands in the postwar period: a Putty-Clay approach," *De Economist* 130(1), pp. 38-70.
Kuipers, S.K. (1982a), "Economisch herstel en de werking van de markteconomie," *Economisch Statistische Berichten* 67(3377), 20 October, pp. 1122-1130.
Kuipers, S.K. (1982b), "Stability in Keynesian and Neoclassical Growth Models: Reply," *De Economist* 130(1), pp. 123-130.
Kuipers, S.K. (1983a), "Macro-economische modelbouw in discussie (V): econometrische modellen - een onmisbaar hulpmiddel," *Economisch Statistische Berichten* 68(3434), 7 December, pp. 1140-1143.
Kuipers, S.K. (1983b), "Internationale en nationale stagnatie. Enkele beschouwingen naar aanleiding van het jaarverslag van De Nederlandsche Bank," *Economisch Statistische Berichten* 68(3408), 8 June, pp. 500-506.
Kuipers, S.K. (1984), "De ontwikkeling van de Nederlandse economie op middellange termijn in het licht van het gevoerde matigings- en bezuinigingsbeleid," *Maandschrift Economie*, 48(6), pp. 437-453.
Kuipers, S.K. and G.H. Kuper (1985), "Een bouwjaaranalyse van de groeivertraging in Nederland sedert het begin van de jaren zeventig," in A. van der Zwan (ed.), *Nederland in zaken. Investeren, winst en werkgelegenheid*, Utrecht/Antwerpen.
Kuipers, S.K. (1987), "Over het macro-economische beleid in de jaren tachtig," in A. Knoester (ed.), *Lessen uit het verleden: 125 jaar Vereniging voor de Staathuishoudkunde*, Leiden/Antwerpen: Stenfert Kroese, pp. 461-483.
Kuipers, S.K. (1988), "The Trade Cycle under Capital Shortage and Labour Shortage: On Witteveen's Synthesis of the Overinvestment and Underinvestment Theory of the Trade Cycle," in W. Eizinga, E.F. Limburg and J.J. Polak (eds.), *The Quest for National and Global Economic Stability*, Dordrecht, London.
Kuipers, S.K., B.W.A. Jongbloed, G.H. Kuper and E. Sterken (1988), *CESAM: het CCSO jaarmodel van de Nederlandse economie,* Groningen: Wolters-Noordhoff.
Kuipers, S.K. and B. Boertje (1988), "On the Causes of the Rise in the Liquidity Ratio in the Netherlands during the Early Eighties," *De Economist* 136(1), pp. 50-90.
Kuipers, S.K. (1990), "Stabilization Policy: A Non-Market Clearing View," in K. Groenveld, J.A.H. Maks and J. Muysken (eds.), *Economic Policy and the Market Process: Austrian and Mainstream Economics*, Amsterdam, *etc.*.
Kuipers, S.K., B.W.A. Jongbloed, G.H. Kuper and E. Sterken (1990), "CESAM: The CCSO Annual Model of the Dutch Economy," *Economic Modelling* 7(3), pp. 202-250.
Kuipers, S.K. and E. Sterken (1990), "Het Nederlandse monetaire beleid in de jaren '80: een portefeuillebenadering," in A.H.E.M. Wellink, A. Lamfalussy and S.K. Kuipers (eds.), *De*

mogelijkheden voor het monetaire beleid na de liberalisatie, NIBE, Amsterdam, pp. 77-109.

Kuipers, S.K. and G.H. Kuper (1990), "De ontwikkeling van de Nederlandse economie in de eerste helft van de jaren negentig," *Maandschrift Economie* 54(6), pp. 425-438.

Kuipers, S.K. (1992a), "Economische en Monetaire Unie," *Liberaal Reveil* 33(4), pp. 125-126.

Kuipers, S.K. (1992b), "Imbalances in Public Sector Deficits: The Dutch Experience," in D.E. Fair and C. de Boissieu (eds.), *Fiscal Policy, Taxation and the Financial System in an Increasingly Integrated Europe*, Dordrecht: Kluwer Academic Publishers, pp. 165-184.

Kuipers, S.K., H. van Ees, H. Garretsen, G.H. Kuper, E. Sterken and E. Wester (1994), *Evenwicht, conjunctuur en groei*, Utrecht: Lemma.

Kuipers, S.K. (1995), "Wanneer de veilingmeester faalt," *Economisch Statistische Berichten* 80(4028), 11 October, pp. 900-903.

Kuipers, S.K. and E. Sterken (1995), "On the Scope for Dutch Monetary Policy," *Banca Nazionale del Lavoro Quarterly Review* 48(193), pp. 173-187.

Kuipers, S.K. and G.H. Kuper (1996), "Wage Formation, Investment and Growth in the Netherlands in the Postwar Period: A Cross-Section Analysis," *De Economist* 144(3), pp. 487-495.

Kuper, G.H. and S.K. Kuipers (1996), "Minder regulering, meer prestaties?," *Economisch Statistische Berichten* 81(4084), 4 December, pp. 992-993.

Lucas, R.E. (1976), "Econometric Policy Evaluation: A Critique," in K. Brunner and A. Meltzer (eds.), *The Phillips Curve and the Labour Market*, Carnegie-Rochester Conferences in Public Policy 1, pp. 19-46.

Malinvaud, E. (1977), *The Theory of Unemployment Reconsidered*, Oxford.

Malinvaud, E. (1980), *Profitability and Unemployment*, Cambridge.

Sterken, E., J.P.A.M. Jacobs, G.H. Kuper and S.K. Kuipers (1995), "Lagere overheidsschuld, minder economische activiteit?," *Economisch Statistische Berichten* 80(4034), 22 November, pp. 1048-1051.

Tinbergen, J. (1973), "Labour with Different Skills and Jobs as Production Fators," *De Economist* 121, pp. 213-224.

Witteveen, H.J. (1956), *Structuur en conjunctuur*, Haarlem.

PART I

THEORETICAL ISSUES IN COORDINATION

Chapter 3

The Civil Society: Can It Last?

Theo van de Klundert and Fieke van der Lecq
Faculty of Economics, Tilburg University and Groningen University; Economisch Statistische Berichten, Rotterdam

Key words: Evolutionary games, Norms, Institutions

Abstract: Norms for behaviour are a well-known instrument for coordinating economic interaction. The literature on this topic indicates that economics and ethics are strongly intertwined. The chapter starts by observing that the ethics concerning the relationships between individuals and between citizens and the government are changing. One part of the citizenry becomes increasingly keen on claiming its 'rights'. However, this undermines the cooperative attitude of the other part of the citizenry. Since the claimants' lifestyle produces negative external effects, a coordination problem between socio-economic groups in society is likely to result. Will the civil society remain? In this chapter, we present a game theoretic model which illustrates the behaviour of both groups. Intragroup interaction and cultural transmission provide mechanisms by which an evolutionary development of behavioural strategies can take place. The model shows that the civil society is an equilibrium outcome, but its stability hinges upon the attractiveness of cooperation and the degree of segmentation of the population.

1. INTRODUCTION: ECONOMICS AND THE CIVIL SOCIETY

Coordination problems abound in economics. The macroeconomic coordination problem poses the question as to 'whether and how the unhampered working of the price mechanism is able to coordinate economic activities for the economy as a whole to the extent that the full-employment Pareto-efficient equilibrium is the only feasible equilibrium' (Garretsen,

1992, p. 3 and 1997, p. 4). Many coordination problems exist at the micro level of the economy. The latter type of coordination problems can be defined as situations in which the outcome of an agent's action not only depends upon his own action, but on the actions of other agents as well. Therefore, in order to determine his best action, an agent has to take expectations of other agents' behaviour into account. Depending on the mutual expectations of the actions of others, agents can end up in a situation of multiple equilibria. The question as to which equilibrium is selected and how agents coordinate their actions in order to reach that particular outcome is referred to as a coordination problem (Cooper and John, 1988).

One coordination problem in particular concerns the relationship between the individual citizen and the government. The latter is, after all, an institute created and maintained by the collective citizenry, so that individual voting decisions concerning the size and power of the government have external effects. Apart from voting decisions, other actions such as paying taxes, complying with rules and laws, and volunteering in social projects affect the necessity and cost-effectiveness of government activities. The incentive to adhere to civic virtues is often affected by the degree to which others adhere, so that society can end up in multiple equilibria.

Norms, or rules for behaviour, are helpful to form adequate expectations of others' behaviour. A norm can be defined as 'a prescribed guide for conduct or action which is generally complied with by the members of a society' (Ullmann-Margalit, 1977, p. 13). Such norms can be either self-enforcing conventions, or externally supported institutions (Van der Lecq, 1996). As long as agents comply with norms, thus being consistent with procedural rationality, coordination problems can be solved in principle. In practice, this can be seen in the many conventions and institutions which govern price and wage setting behaviour (Van der Lecq, 1998).

Two types of norms can be distinguished: behavioural norms and ethical norms. Since conformity with behavioural norms is procedurally rational, ethics can be left out from an analysis of many daily occurring coordination problems. For instance, conventions regarding driving lanes are ethically neutral. However, the situation changes once conflicts of interests occur. Then, some behaviour might be preferred above other options for behaviour from an ethical point of view. A welfare optimising behaviour may be attained via two ways. As indicated above, an institution can be created, with a punishment mechanism to enforce the behavioural norm. The alternative enforcement mechanism is a shared ethical background, which makes agents want to comply with the norm *per se*. By doing so, a group of agents can build up trust among its members, so that the conflict situation can be dealt with by means of cooperation. In the latter situation, the ethical virtues of the civil society result in an ethical norm to govern behaviour. For instance, 'being honest' is an ethical norm which economic agents can choose to comply with (see Van de Klundert, 1999, § 4).

In this chapter, the term civil society refers to a community of agents who are willing to invest part of their personal resources in the well-functioning of the society as a whole. For instance, they spend time in volunteer work with sports clubs, religious communities or The Scouts. Or they spend money and effort in managing and advising non-profit organisations. In terms of game theory, to be explained below, these investments are referred to as cooperative behaviour. Thus, by behaving cooperatively, agents are willing to reduce their direct personal income by the amount they invest in society. They may do so with the explicit aim to reap the harvests of their investment by their participation in the same society, which is brought to a higher welfare level. However, this aim is only realised if others invest as well, so that a coordination problem exists.[1] Cooperative agents may also invest without the explicit aim of attaining future benefits, simply because they consider cooperative behaviour preferable from an ethical point of view. From the economist's perspective, the two types of motivations do not differ as long as both result in higher utility.[2] By definition, the second motivation results in higher utility. However, whether cooperating from the first motivation results in higher utility depends on the fraction of people who follow suit. Here, a free-rider problem exists.

The civil society consists of a fraction of cooperators and a fraction of free-riders, or defectors in game-theoretic terms. Due to the positive externalities of cooperating, that is, contributing to the civil society, the revenues of both groups depend on the magnitude of the fraction of people who cooperate. They also depend on the extra, non-random probability of meeting an alike type of person, which is referred to as the degree of segmentation in society. The free-riders, always eager to claim their 'rights', participate without contributing time, money or effort. Lal (1998, p. 169) refers to such 'rights chatter' behaviour as an 'attack on civil society from below'. Here we focus on the question as to whether the civil society will survive in spite of 'rights chatter' by its free-riders. It is studied by means of a game theoretic model, which will be developed in Section 3. Before that, the topics of coordination problems, cooperative behaviour and segmentation are reformulated in game theoretic terms in Section 2. Section 4 draws conclusions with respect to the concept of civil society.

1 Sen (1967, pp. 114-115) refers to this issue as an 'assurance problem'.

2 For the sake of analysis, the payoff matrices are supposed to reflect utility, be it from pecuniary gains (behavioural norm) or otherwise (ethical norm), so that any motivation to cooperate can be derived from the payoff matrix.

2. CIVIL SOCIETY AND GAME THEORY

Game theory provides an instrument for analysing coordination problems. Coordination games range from pure coordination games, in which the interests of both players coincide, via mixed motive games, in which coordination and conflict are both present, to conflict situations in which the interests of parties diverge. For analysing the civil society, two types of games are relevant:

Generic form

	C	D
C	b, b	d, a
D	a, d	c, c

Prisoners' dilemma game

	C	D
C	2 , 2	0 , 3
D	3 , 0	1 , 1

$(a>b>c>d) \wedge (a+d<2b)$

Stag Hunt game

	C	D
C	5 , 5	0 , 4
D	4 , 0	2 , 2

$b>a>c>d$

Both players can choose between two strategies: 'cooperate' and 'defect', indicated by C and D, respectively. The payoff matrices indicate the rewards from both strategies to the two players, with the payoff to the left hand player given first and the payoff to the upper hand player given second. The generic form shows that the game is symmetric to both players. As the numerical examples illustrate, the games differ in the mixture of coordination and conflict elements. In the prisoners' dilemma (PD) game, defecting is the attractive strategy in terms of expected payoffs, but the Nash equilibrium (D,D) is Pareto-inferior to the cooperative outcome (C,C). Thus, the unilateral interest in defecting dominates the mutual interest in cooperating. On the contrary, in the Stag Hunt (SH) game, the mutual interest in cooperating dominates the unilateral interest in defecting. As in the PD-game, the cooperative outcome (C,C) is Pareto-superior to the strategy combination (D,D). However, the Nash equilibrium (D,D) risk dominates the Nash equilibrium (C,C), because playing D results in a higher expected payoff than does playing C (Weibull, 1995, p. 31). To sum up: the fact that players do not know the other players' actions results in both players ending up in an inferior situation even though the interests of players coincide.

Evolutionary economics studies the evolution of strategies in games which are played by randomly drawn players from a group. This implies that bilateral games are played repeatedly, but not by the same pairs of players. Different groups of players are distinguished according to the strategies they play, so that intergroup encounters and intragroup encounters result in different game outcomes. Over time, after several repetitions of the game, the group as whole can converge on an equilibrium strategy. Such equilibrium can be stable or unstable, depending on the replicator dynamics of the game (Weibull, 1995). For the games introduced above, the relevant issue is the equilibrium fraction of players who cooperate and the stability of this equilibrium fraction. PD games have only one stable equilibrium, with a zero fraction of cooperators.[3] SH-games have three equilibria, being a defectors' equilibrium, a cooperators' equilibrium and an equilibrium with a fraction of cooperators. In the numerical example, the latter would be equal to 2/3. However, the latter equilibrium is unstable. In other words, once slightly more than a fraction of 2/3 of the players cooperate, it is profitable for all players to start cooperating, while a reduction of cooperators to a fraction just below 2/3 will invoke a 'race to the bottom', thus ending up in all players defecting.

Stag Hunt game

Suppose that society as a whole faces a payoff situation that can be represented by a SH-game. Depending on the payoffs and the expected behaviour of others, agents will behave cooperatively or they will defect. The equilibrium outcome of a particular fraction of cooperators might occur, but, since it is unstable, it may be disturbed once a shock occurs. What happens next? As said above, evolutionary game theory predicts that society will end up in one of its stable equilibria, with either none or all players cooperating. However, another phenomenon can also occur: segmentation. That is, cooperators seek cooperators to deal with, while defectors seek defectors. Thus, the degree of segmentation, being the extra probability of meeting an alike type of person, increases. This behaviour of seeking alike persons is likely to be determined by tradition or culture, which induces non-random pairing. Like attracts like, until society is more or less divided in two groups, each with its own equilibrium payoff (see Bowles and Gintis, 1998).

This eventuality is fairly realistic. By way of example, one can think of groups which are very active in organising all kinds of social activities, taking care of the less well-to-do within their group, providing intellectual or social education among each other and bringing welfare within the group to a higher level. In the opposite case, one can imagine another group, which is likely to be less coherent, in which the agents simply pursue their own interests in dealing with each other and with governmental institutions.

From a policy point of view, the question as to whether government intervention would increase social welfare is relevant. If government intervention induces the defectors to comply with a cooperative norm for behaviour, such welfare increasing outcome is likely to occur. However, if government intervention would replace intrinsic motivation with extrinsic

[3] In fact, this is a corner solution, since the fraction cannot be below zero. The same would hold if the equilibrium fraction were equal to one.

motivation within the subgroup of cooperators, so that in fact the cooperators start behaving like defectors, the benefits might not outweigh the costs.[4] In the latter case, to accept segmentation might be preferable to government intervention. Even facilitating segmentation by subsidising cooperative behaviour could be welfare increasing, as the model below will show.

Prisoners' dilemma game

To a rather large extent, the same story holds if society as a whole faces a payoff situation that can be represented by a PD-game. In the numerical example given above, this is not clearly visible, since there is no equilibrium with a fraction of cooperators larger than zero. However, amendments to the game can be made, in which such positive fractions do indeed result as a stable equilibrium. From a policy point of view, the question as to how to induce agents to cooperate is relevant, as is the earlier posed question as to whether government intervention would do more good than harm. The degree of segmentation between the two subgroups of cooperators and defectors codetermines the possibility of meeting an alike agent, which feeds back on the incentive to cooperate. Moreover, the government can stimulate civil activities which induce a higher degree of segmentation, so that cooperators are more likely to meet a fellow cooperator and reach the cooperative outcome (C,C).

In the next section, an amended PD-model is developed, in which the above mechanisms are formalised. The size of the fraction of cooperators in the evolutionary equilibrium as well as the stability of such equilibrium and the degree of segmentation between the two subgroups determine whether the civil society can be considered a stable outcome.

3. THE MODEL

In the PD-game introduced above with random pairing of players the payoffs of cooperators (π^c) and defectors (π^d) are respectively:

$$\pi^c = pb + (1-p)d\,, \tag{1}$$

$$\pi^d = pa + (1-p)c\,, \tag{2}$$

where p denotes the fraction of cooperators in the population. Segmentation changes these payoffs, because matching of players is no longer random.

[4] On intrinsic motivation and extrinsic motivation, see Frey (1997).

The degree of segmentation of the population, σ, is defined as the probability that likes meet likes in an otherwise random pairing of players. Now, the probability that a cooperator will meet another cooperator is $\sigma + (1-\sigma)p$ and the probability that a defector will meet another defector is $\sigma + (1-\sigma)(1-p)$. It is assumed that σ can be influenced positively by spending effort at a level θ and at a cost $f(\theta)$. Effort is associated with the activities of cooperators in the civil society. Defectors are supposed to be passive. The payoffs of both groups can now be written as:

$$\pi^c = \sigma(\theta)b + (1-\sigma(\theta))(pb + (1-p)d) - f(\theta), \tag{3}$$

$$\pi^d = \sigma(\theta)c + (1-\sigma(\theta))(pa + (1-p)c). \tag{4}$$

To obtain closed-form solutions, we use the specifications:

$$\sigma(\theta) = \bar{\sigma}\theta, \tag{5}$$

and

$$f(\theta) = \frac{\theta^2}{2}. \tag{6}$$

Cooperators maximise π^c by choosing the optimal effort level θ^*. From the first-order condition we obtain:

$$\theta^* = \bar{\sigma}(1-p)(b-d). \tag{7}$$

Differentiating with respect to p gives:

$$\frac{d\theta^*}{dp} = -\bar{\sigma}(b-d) < 0, \tag{8}$$

because $b > d$. The more cooperators there already are, the less attractive it is to invest in activities that foster segmentation.

Replicator dynamics implies that successful players in terms of relative payoffs are imitated by others. Following Weibull (1995) the differential equation governing the evolutionary process reads:

$$\dot{p} = p(1-p)(\pi^c - \pi^d). \tag{9}$$

Substitution of the payoff relations and rearranging terms results in:

$$\dot{p} = p(1-p)\Big[-\overline{\sigma}^2(b-d)(a-c-\frac{1}{2}(b-d))p^2 + (\overline{\sigma}^2(b-d)-1)$$

$$(a-b-(c-d))p + \frac{1}{2}\overline{\sigma}^2(b-d)^2 - (c-d)\Big]. \quad (10)$$

There are two roots at the corners $p = 0$ and $p = 1$. Whether or not these are stable solutions depends upon other possible roots. Because of the quadratic expression there are at most two interior roots in the domain $0 < p < 1$. If there are two interior roots, one will be stable and the other will be unstable. The differential equation can be simplified substantially in the case of a symmetric PD-game with parameters:

$b = t,$
$a = t + \lambda,$
$c = s,$
$d = s - \lambda,$
$(t > s).$

Substitution of these parameters in equation (10) gives:

$$\dot{p} = p(1-p)\left[-\frac{1}{2}\overline{\sigma}^2(t-s+\lambda)^2 p^2 + \frac{1}{2}\overline{\sigma}^2(t-s+\lambda)^2 - \lambda\right]. \quad (11)$$

The unique interior root (p^*) can now easily be obtained:

$$p^* = \sqrt{1 - \frac{2\lambda}{\overline{\sigma}^2(t-s+\lambda)^2}}, \quad (12)$$

under the condition:

$$\overline{\sigma} > \frac{\sqrt{2\lambda}}{t-s+\lambda}.$$

If the returns on investment are too low no interior equilibrium can be established. In the special case without segmentation ($\overline{\sigma} = 0$) the differential equation reduces to:

$$\dot{p} = -\lambda p(1-p). \quad (13)$$

This gives the familiar result that cooperators are completely driven out by defectors in the long run ($p = 0$).[5] This is shown in Figure 1 below:

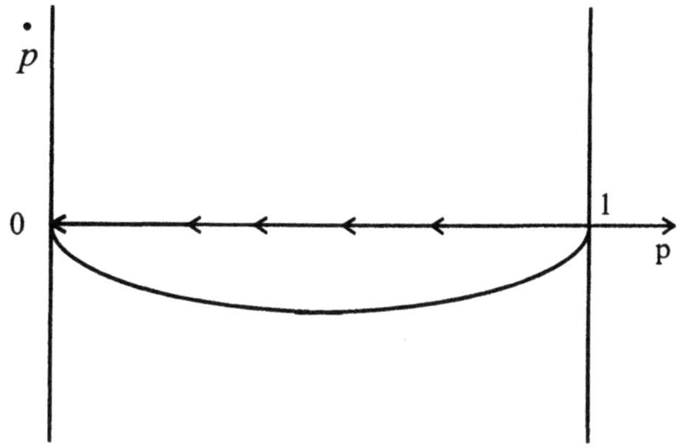

Figure 1. No interior equilibrium in the long run ($p = 0$).

Segmentation gives rise to a stable interior equilibrium at $p=p^*$. At $p=p^*$ we have $d\dot{p}/dp < 0$. This result is illustrated in Figure 2.

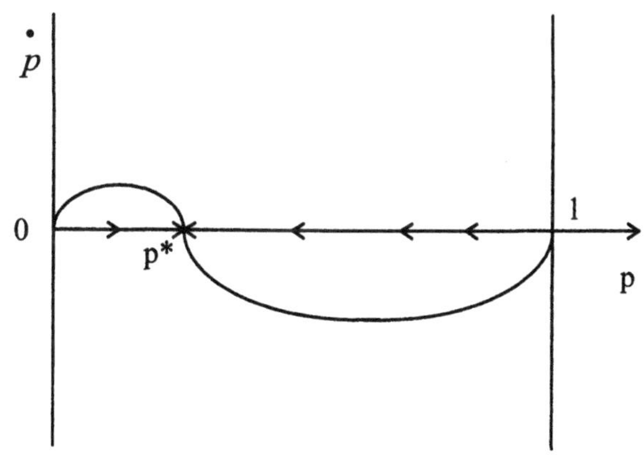

Figure 2. A stable interior equilibrium at $p = p^*$.

For high values of p defection is relatively attractive and investment in activities fostering segmentation by cooperators is relatively unattractive. Therefore, cooperators are driven out by defectors. Gradually however,

[5] See for instance Weibull (1995).

investment becomes more rewarding and segmentation increases. At some point, cooperative players break even and a long-run equilibrium with both groups coexisting is established. Starting from a low value of p, a similar line of reasoning applies.

Comparative static results are easily found:

$$\frac{dp^*}{d\overline{\sigma}} > 0, \quad \frac{dp^*}{d(t-s)} > 0, \quad \frac{dp^*}{d\lambda} < 0.$$

The equilibrium fraction of cooperators is higher, the higher is the return on effort, the higher is the difference in payoffs between reciprocal cooperation and reciprocal defection, and the lower is the reward of cheating.

The segmentation model exhibits positive externalities. Cooperative players investing in segmentation do not take into account that other players benefit from their activities. A higher degree of segmentation favours all cooperative players, but defectors are less well off. However, an increase in segmentation induces a higher fraction of cooperators in the population, which is favourable to both groups. Therefore, to improve welfare for both players the government should stimulate segmentation, which can be done by subsidising investment. The revenues required to subsidise cooperative players can be obtained by a lump sum tax, which has no impact on decisions in the margin. Denoting the subsidy on unit cost by ρ we can write:

$$f(\theta) = (1-\rho)\frac{\theta^2}{2}, \qquad 0 \leq \rho \leq 1. \tag{14}$$

The optimal effort level in case of a symmetric PD-games now reads:

$$\theta^* = \frac{\overline{\sigma}}{1-\rho}(1-p)(t-s+\lambda). \tag{15}$$

The long-run solution for the fraction of cooperators equals:

$$p^* = \sqrt{1 - \frac{2\lambda(1-\rho)}{\sigma^2(t-s+\lambda)^2}}. \tag{16}$$

As appears from these results players benefit from a subsidy that is at its maximum. However, very high levels of ρ may lead to distortions which are not taken into account in the model. Fully reimbursing investment cost may induce problems like fraud, which should be dealt with in determining the optimal subsidy rate.[6]

Numerical example

To illustrate the role of subsidies in the present model we introduce numerical results for different values of ρ in Table 1. The payoffs are taken from the symmetric PD-game introduced before. Moreover, we assume $\bar{\sigma} = 0.75$. The results in Table 1 refer to the long-run outcomes for different values of the subsidy rate. Social welfare (w) is defined as the weighted average of payoffs corrected for the investment costs accounted for by the government:

$$w = p\pi^c + (1-p)\pi^d - \frac{1}{2}\rho\theta^2 .$$

In the long run equilibrium payoffs of cooperators and defectors are equalised: $\pi = \pi^c = \pi^d$. Then, social welfare can be written as:

$$w = \pi - \frac{1}{2}\rho\theta^2 .$$

Table 1. Long-run solutions

	Subsidy		
Variable	$\rho = 0$	$\rho = 0.1$	$\rho = 0.9$
p	0.3333	0.4472	0.9545
θ	1.0	0.9213	0.6822
$\sigma(\theta)$	0.75	0.6910	0.5117
$f(\theta)$	0.5	0.3820	0.0233
π	1.1667	1.2764	1.9322
w	1.1667	1.2340	1.7228

In the long run, subsidising the costs of cooperation results in a lower level of investment and a higher fraction of cooperators in the population. Effort (θ) rises on impact of the shock, so that the degree of segmentation (σ) increases. Cooperation becomes more attractive as the chance of meeting a defector declines. Defectors are also thrown back on their own group, but as payoffs change in favour of cooperation they will revise their strategy. As a result the fraction of cooperators in the population rises gradually. There is then less need to spend effort aimed at fostering segmentation. Ultimately,

6 See for a similar comment Nyberg (1997).

the degree of segmentation (σ) is lower than without subsidy, because there is less need for from the vantage point of cooperators. Subsidies raise social welfare, as appears from the last row in the table.

4. CONCLUSIONS

Now that the model is presented, we can return to the question as to whether the civil society can survive in spite of defectors who claim their rights without investing in society. Fortunately, the outcome of the model suggests that this is likely to be the case.

The PD-model with players who cooperate and players who defect, shows that the long-run solutions of the evolutionary dynamics point towards the beneficial impact of segmentation. By increasing the probability that likes meet likes, the rewards to cooperative behaviour increase, so that more agents are willing to invoke the costs of behaving cooperatively. Thus, the civil society is a stable equilibrium outcome.

From the first order conditions, it follows that such investment is strictly rational. This implies that ethics need not to be introduced as an exogenous factor in the analysis: ethical behaviour pays off.

The model also shows that the government can increase social welfare by subsidising cooperative behaviour. In the long run, the costs of the subsidy are outweighed by the benefits of the higher number of cooperators and the degree of segmentation.

Beyond the model, some reflection upon behavioural norms and ethical norms as discussed in the introductory section leads to the following observation. A trade-off between segmentation and cooperation may exist. If a society has little segmentation, then relatively many defectors will meet a cooperator. Profitable as such encounter may be to the defectors, this may make them reflect upon the virtue of their defective behaviour and may perhaps even make them change their strategy. Of course, the relatively many cooperators who meet defectors may change their strategy as well, albeit for pecuniary rather than ethical considerations. However, once the degree of segmentation is higher, fewer changes in strategy occur. The remaining defectors will get stuck in their attitude, because they are less often confronted with the alternative strategy.

REFERENCES

Bowles, S. and H. Gintis (1998), "The Moral Economy of Communities: Structured Populations and the Evolution of Pro-Social Norms," *Evolution and Human Behaviour* 19, pp. 3-25.

Cooper, R. and A. John (1988), "Coordinating Coordination Failures in Keynesian Models," *Quarterly Journal of Economics* 103, pp. 441-463.
Frey, B.S. (1997), *Not Just for the Money*, Cheltenham: Edward Elgar.
Garretsen, J.H. (1992), *Keynes, Coordination and Beyond; The Development of Macroeconomic and Monetary Theory Since 1945*, Cheltenham: Edward Elgar.
Garretsen, J.H. (1997), *Terug naar 1937?*, Inaugural Address, University of Nijmegen.
Klundert, Th.C.M.J. van de (1999), "Economic Efficiency and Ethics," *De Economist* 147(2), pp. 127-149.
Lal, D. (1998), *Unintended Consequences*, Cambridge: MIT Press.
Lecq, S.G. van der (1996), "Conventions and Institutions in Coordination Problems," *De Economist* 144(3), pp. 397-428.
Lecq, S.G. van der (1998), *Money, Coordination and Prices*, PhD Thesis, University of Groningen.
Nyberg, S. (1997), "The Honest Society: Stability and Policy Considerations," *Journal of Public Economics* 64, pp. 83-99.
Sen, A.K. (1967), "Isolation, Assurance and the Social Rate of Discount," *Quarterly Journal of Economics* 81, pp. 112-124.
Ullmann-Margalit, E. (1977), *The Emergence of Norms*, Oxford: Clarendon Press.
Weibull, J.W. (1995), *Evolutionary Game Theory*, Cambridge: MIT Press.

Chapter 4

Coordination and Communication

Piet Keizer[1]
Department of Economics, Maastricht University

Key words: Coordination, Communication, Socio-economics

Abstract: This chapter is about the interrelationship between processes of coordination and communication in an economy. Economics as a theoretical perspective focuses on the explanation of processes of coordination between demand and supply decisions of individual subjects. Sociology as a theoretical perspective, however, focuses on the explanation of processes of communication between the principal groups that constitute society, including the economy. It will be shown that coordination will be less efficient in cases of ineffective communication. On the other hand, it is difficult to communicate fruitfully when the processes of coordination are inefficiently organised.

[1] The analysis is made in honour of my former master Professor Simon Kuipers, who has confronted me time and again with his rigorous economic theory. But, besides his quite orthodox views on the paradigmatic and analytical level, his economic-political and social views must be interpreted as a *conditio sine qua non* of the results of orthodox analysis. In terms of macroeconomic policy his views are moderately Keynesian and his social points of view are revealed by his monthly travels to the Social Economic Council. The Council is the principal symbol of the sociological consensus view. This approach is based on the axiom that processes of economic coordination can only be efficient if the most powerful groups in the economy agree upon the basic principles of distribution of everything that is of value: income, wealth and decision-making power. This chapter tries to show that the work of the SER-member Simon Kuipers is a necessary condition for the usefulness of the analyses of the economist Simon Kuipers.

1. INTRODUCTION

Many economists see Adam Smith as their intellectual father. His brilliant analyses of the functioning of a free market economy are considered to be the beginning of economics as an independent science. But as we will see in the following sections, economics has developed into something quite different from what our "father" was involved in more than two hundred years ago. Now we call his approach the classical political economy, while the so-called neoclassical approach has become known as the typical and orthodox economic approach. While the classical economy is about the economy as a real life system, the neoclassical economic approach is about the economy as an aspect-system of our real life society.[2] By focusing on an explanation of the economic aspect of human behaviour, the research strategy of the neoclassical approach differs significantly from the classical approach that pretended to give an explanation of real human behaviour in the economic system of transactions exchanging goods for money.

This evolution of economics took place in about the same period as other social scientists developed sociology. The theoretical perspective developed by people like Comte, Durkheim and Weber can be interpreted as an explanation of the social aspect of the real life society. Many sociologists consider Comte, who was the first to attempt to formulate social laws, as their intellectual father. After him Durkheim and Weber developed different frameworks of analysis in their attempts to characterise and explain social development, not only of society in general, but also of the economy in particular.

Each group, the economists as well as the sociologists, pretended to explain developments in the real life economy and society respectively. We must be aware that the real life economy is a subsystem of the real life society. This means that both economists and sociologists explain the functioning of the economy, although quite independently of each other. They operate like rivals, while their theoretical perspectives focus on different aspects of the *same* real life phenomenon. This means that both approaches need each other. This chapter will develop the arguments for this point of view.

In the following section we will define the problem of disciplinary integration more precisely. In a third section we will sketch the historical development of both theoretical perspectives. During the second half of the twentieth century both disciplines showed developments that deviated from their orthodox hard core. A short characterisation of these developments will

2 The terminology used is in compliance with the so-called general systems approach as it is used in many sciences. In the next section we will explain the application of the typical systems concepts to our problems more explicitly.

make clear that the interrelationships between the different theoretical perspectives within social sciences must be made more explicit in order to get a more realistic framework of analysis of the economy and society viewed as a real life system. In a last section, under the heading of "socio-economics", we will show that there are promising developments on the paradigmatic and analytical level. The message of this emerging paradigm is that economic coordination and social communication are highly interrelated, while its mission is to clarify and explain the existence and evolution of trading processes, taking both aspects into account.

2. THE PROBLEM OF INTEGRATION

To clarify the problem of integration of the two different fields, economics and sociology, we will formulate the character of both disciplines in their orthodox form. As a result we will be able to understand why they are unfit to explain (sectors of) real life. As already said the use of the language of the *systems approach* is helpful in this respect. Especially the distinction between an aspect-system and a subsystem is of the utmost importance.

In the systems approach several distinctions play a role. In the first place, we can distinguish between *reality* and a *real life system*. The first concept refers to what people experience as real and must be explained. By explaining it we hope to gain control over our reality to make life more meaningful. Reality itself is only an unstructured thing. To get control over it we must make a simple structure of it. This structure must reflect the most important relationships. This simple structure reflecting the essence of reality is called a real life system.

Once we have a whole or *general* system of our real life, we can distinguish between different *subsystems*, each of them structuring more *specific* sectors of our life. Thus, we can consider society as a real life system and the sector "families" or the sector "firms" or the sector "economy" as a subsystem. Being a subsystem of a more general system means that specific actors of the general system are taken into account and that other actors are ignored. However, all aspects of the relationships that are accounted for in the general system are included in the analysis of the specific sector.

While a general system can be split up in specific subsystems, a whole or *integral* system can also be divided into different *aspect-systems*. Then all actors of the whole system are taken into account. But in an aspect-system not all aspects of the relationships are taken into account; only one aspect, *i.e.* one sort of relationship. Thus, a real relationship is considered to be too complex to analyse integrally. To make a simple start we must first distinguish between different aspects of a particular relationship. For instance, we can distinguish between the economic aspect, the social aspect and the political aspect. An economic aspect-system frames the scarcity dimension, while a social aspect system focuses on the status aspect. A political aspect-system, however, is about the control aspect that plays a role with respect to all elements of the system. In Figure 1 we present a picture that clarifies the difference between an aspect- and a subsystem. When we have developed a series of aspect-systems, we must find a way to get these systems integrated. As long as we are not able to construct an integral analysis, it is impossible to have a real life system that can form the theoretical basis for empirical research.

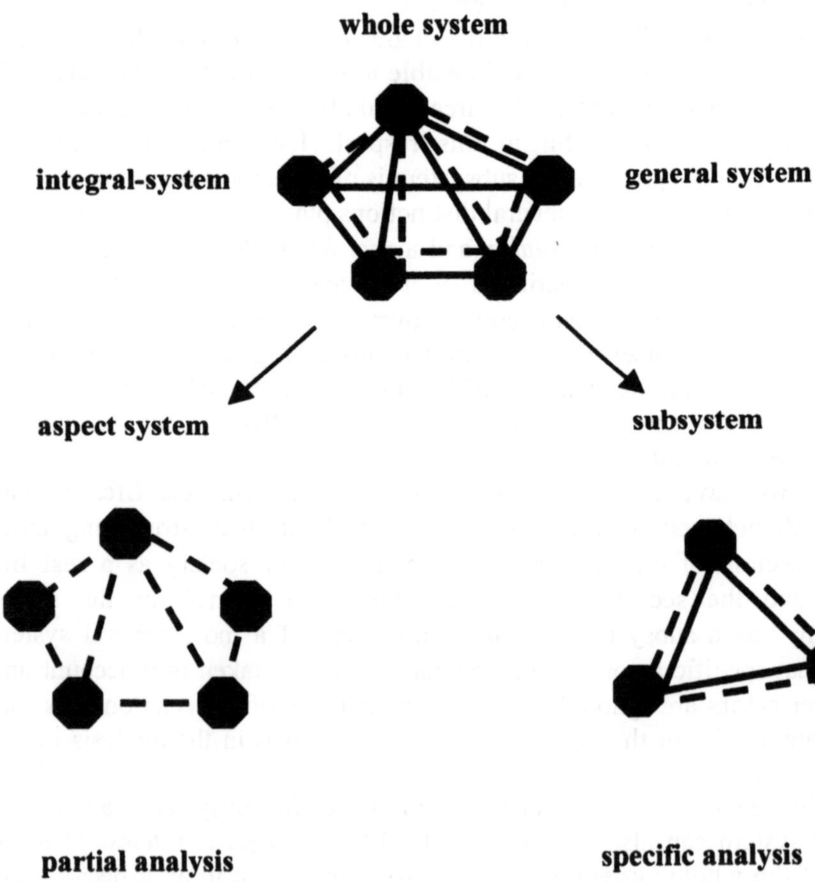

Figure 1. The difference between an aspect system and a subsystem

Figure 1 shows different structures of relationships between a number of elements. The first structure can be considered as a whole system, in our case a closed system, because there are no relationships between the system and its environment. If we consider this system to be too complex to be analysed at once, we can divide this system into pieces that are studied separately.

There are two main procedures to follow when we want to specialise ourselves. The first way is to call the whole system an integral system and to distinguish between several aspects of the system. This means that all real life relationships between the elements are studied, but from the perspective of one aspect only. Such analysis is called a *partial* analysis (being part of a more *integral* analysis). Orthodox economics is an example of such an aspect system. Orthodox sociology is another example. In Figure 1 we have pictured such an aspect-system in the lower left panel. We have illustrated the integrated system by drawing three lines between the elements. The number taken (three) is arbitrary; the lines reflect the different aspects that can be distinguished. If we take the global society as our whole and integrated system as an example, then the three lines can be interpreted as the political, the social and the economic aspect of the behaviour of all elements in the global society, which is a real life system in our interpretation. The second way is to call the whole system a general system and to distinguish between different subsystems. This means that only a part of the whole real life system is studied. However, the relationships that are studied are taken as they are in real life. Business administration is a field of study that pretends to be about a subsystem of a real life system, namely economy or society. Their analyses are called *specific* analyses, being part of a more *general* analysis. In the reality of our scientific development we see a large number of specialisation fields. Most of the fields are a mix of aspect- and subsystems. For instance, agrarian economics is a subsystem (agriculture) of an aspect-system (economics). When we look at this field as it functions in practice, it appears not to be a perfect aspect-system. Social and political factors are playing, although mostly *ad hoc*, a role. So with industrial economics, development economics, industrial sociology and family sociology: they are all mixes of different kinds of systems with a large amount of *ad hoc* solutions. For the development of a sound scientific foundation of our knowledge, however, knowledge of the character of our knowledge systems is of the utmost importance.

In the next section we will give a short historical overview, which will show that the evolution in economics has given us a strong paradigm and analysis. But the character of this system is definitely of an aspect kind. This historical overview will also show that the analysis developed by the orthodox sociologists must be interpreted as of an aspect kind. After that, we will show that more recent developments and adjustments within both sciences can be interpreted as important attempts to find the necessary interdisciplinary relationships.

3. HISTORICAL DEVELOPMENTS

3.1 Moral Philosophical Foundation

Social science has its origin in the moral philosophy that developed from the seventeenth century onwards. Thomas Hobbes (1651) is one of the first philosophers of the modern era. After him Locke (1689) and Rousseau (1745) played an important role in the definition of the nature of society. With hindsight these three philosophers can be considered as the forerunners of three well-known social and political views, namely *the conservative, the liberal* and *the socialist view.*

While philosophy is about the nature of things, science is about the functioning of things. They need each other in the sense that one has no function without the other. Philosophy without science is only speculation, while science without philosophy cannot be interpreted in a meaningful way. Moral philosophy is about the human condition and is called moral because these philosophers considered the moral capacity of humans as their basic distinction from animals, plants and other inspired material. It functions as the basis of social science, whose mission it is to explain the functioning of society.

3.2 From Moral Philosophy to Political Economy

Adam Smith was a famous moral philosopher who analysed the forces that keep society together. In his *Moral Sentiments* (1759) he developed a social system on the basis of the concept of moral sentiments; a concept he borrowed from David Hume. In this book he explains which mechanism in a free society is responsible for a stable and just order. He sketched an "inner man" inside each of us who functions like an "impartial spectator". This spectator can be imagined as an arbitrator who decides upon what is fair and what is unfair. In his second major book, namely *The Wealth of Nations* (1776), Smith analysed a system of a free market economy, assuming the presence of a social system based on moral sentiments. This book was a defence of free trade; if society would leave manufacturers and traders free to act in their self-interest, society as a whole would profit. Civil society would automatically organise a minimum of care for the poor, while a free production system would maximally profit from specialisation as a main source of wealth.

After Smith other scientists also analysed the functioning of a free market economy as a subsystem of the real life society. Now we call this the Classical School of Political Economy. Their belonging to one school of thought results from some similarities in their approach in explaining the free market economy. With respect to former schools of thought their analyses were of a more positive type. With respect to the schools that followed they focused especially on long run production and distribution.

3.3 From Political Economy to Neoclassical Economics

The most important difference between the classical school on the one hand and its successor, the neoclassical school, on the other hand, is of a methodological nature. It implies a move from an explanation of a real life economic system towards the explanation of an economic aspect-system. Economists such as John Stuart Mill, Stanley Jevons and Carl Menger focused their analysis on the scarcity aspect of human life.[3] They tried to find theoretical laws that determined human behaviour as far as the scarcity problem is concerned. They constructed the so-called economic motive, saying that every individual always maximises his utility under the constraints of a limited amount of resources. So given the preferences of individuals being ranked in order of priority and given the limited amount of resources, economic subjects are motivated to maximise their utilities. This economic force sets people in motion. We cannot observe this force. A human person's behaviour is a vector of different forces, of which the economic force is only one. A comparison with Newton's law of gravity is clarifying in this respect. Only if there are no counter-forces we can see an object fall to the ground. So, too, with the economic force; only if there are no other forces human behaviour is fully determined by economic force. While in physics laboratory experiments make the effect of a particular force observable, in economics there is no such thing as a laboratory. Economists can only make analyses and build models that are logically consistent.

The ideal-type situation, reflecting the operation of the economic force in isolation is called *perfect competition*. Subjects are supposed to be economic

[3] The classic on neoclassical methodology is L. Robbins (1932). This book functions as a kind of bible for orthodox economists. It did not only function as a justification of the work of neoclassical economists up to then. It also laid the philosophical foundation for the large extension in the application of the economic paradigm to fields of study other than the free market sector. This process took place after the Second World War.

subjects. This means that they do not make an explicit distinction between the economic and the social aspect of relationships between people. The world is interpreted as consisting only of scarce goods having value and price. The subject is constantly producing, investing, trading and consuming. He plays the role of supplier and demander. The location where suppliers and demanders are meeting each other is called market. It goes without saying that this market is very different from markets, as we know them from real life. Here humans are driven by more than only the economic motive.

3.4 The Social Factor

Another motive is the desire to reach a status as high as possible. By status we mean the position in the social hierarchical ranking. It is related to the amount of prestige in the eyes of other people. This motive implies that individuals compare themselves with other individuals. In sociology individuals are supposed to have social identities; a person belongs to the group of males or females, young or old, whites or blacks, Christians or Muslims. Individuals are supposed to be aware of what is their own group ("US") and what is their opponent ("THEM"). Most of the time it is quite clear to people which group distinctions dominate the social struggle. Prestige can be derived from the difference in status between the "US"-group and the "THEM"-group. (Bauman, 1990).

If we build this motive into the economic analysis, we have made an important paradigmatic shift towards a socio-economic approach of our real life system "economy" or "society". To clarify this we will first explain precisely what we mean by the orthodox economic paradigm.

4. THE ORTHODOX ECONOMIC PARADIGM

As has already been said the economists who build a theoretical framework want to find universal theoretical laws. Therefore they abstract from factors that could lead to differences in human behaviour in the various real life economies and societies. They focus on something that all societies have in common, that is their struggle against the omnipresent scarcity phenomenon. By defining carefully what scarcity is, they hope to get that universal picture.

Scarcity can be defined as the relationship between needs and the resources that can satisfy those needs. A lower level of scarcity can be realised by decreasing the level of needs and/or by increasing the level of valuable resources. The first option, the decrease in the level of needs, is a Buddhist type of strategy. The second option fits modern Western culture.

By increasing our technical knowledge we can improve the relationship between the necessary inputs on the one hand and the level of output that results from a transformation process on the other.

Part of the goods might be represented by the services of other people. But also in such cases these "goods" are only valued in terms of the scarcity of their services. This means that there is no difference between social and economic relationships. All relationships are of an economic character. To isolate the scarcity phenomenon from other kinds of problems, the strategy of the orthodoxy was to construct a perfectly rational individual. This is an individual who knows his preferences and can rank them in order of priority. This person has reflected upon these preferences time and again and now they are stable and do not change in the face of unexpected experiences. Because the person has already experienced much before reaching the stage of perfect rationality, all alternatives are already considered. A person who has considered all alternatives and extensively reflected upon it, is called an economically rational person.

To understand why the fathers of the neoclassical economic paradigm constructed this picture of man, it is illuminating to see that this economic man is a person without any psychic and social problem. By leaving psychic problems to psychologists and social problems to sociologists, they created a kind of niche on the market of scientific knowledge, focusing their analyses on just the problem of coordination between activities of psychically perfect and socially completely independent subjects. This person is framed as being surrounded by resources. The state of production technology determines the relationship between inputs and outputs. Thus, given the inputs, technological progress determines the pace of economic growth and the speed with which the scarcity problem can be solved. If we take the biological-psychological laws determining the satisfaction of needs on the one hand and the physical-chemical laws determining the production of valuable resources on the other hand, the economists can derive their laws about the processes of coordination.

Pareto and Walras became famous neoclassical economists by formulating conditions for a maximum of economic efficiency. When all economic agents are free in taking their decisions, an equilibrium system of markets that produces an optimal allocation of scarce resources exists. The framework is an isolated abstraction, which means that as long as persons are economically rational, a free market system will induce a perfectly optimal system of allocation.[4]

[4] Pareto did not only work on problems from a neoclassical theoretical perspective. He became also a well-known sociologist, analysing society from a social point of view. Walras called his system "*économie pure*", to distinguish it from the real life system "economy". His famous law is about the general equilibrium of a system of markets.

This research strategy presumes a labour division between different sorts of scientists. While economists fully admit that increasing control over physical-chemical processes leads to an increase in wealth, they are at a loss for a reaction on developments in knowledge of a psychosocial kind. The assumption of perfection with respect to the self-control of persons (perfect reflection) and the human understanding of each other (perfect communication) are far from realistic. Recognition has far-reaching consequences for the explanation of the real life economy and society.[5] The next section will show what happened when sociology was developed as a separate science.

5. THE ORTHODOX SOCIOLOGICAL PARADIGM

When, during the second half of the nineteenth century, classical political economy was transformed into neoclassical economics, other scientists started searching for what they called *social laws* that must explain the historical development of society. The first sociologist was Auguste Comte, who wanted to formulate empirical-scientific laws.[6] Later scientists like Durkheim and Weber did a lot of work, establishing what we now can call orthodox sociology. The methodological interpretation of their work is quite difficult. While neoclassical founders discussed their methodologies and agreed upon its character, sociologists disagree sharply when it comes to a methodological interpretation. They agreed upon the subject matter, namely the explanation of the main characteristics of society as a real life system. But in terms of philosophy as well as in terms of the method of analysis there were sharp differences. With the knowledge of the sociological discussions during the twentieth century, however, we can discover what apparently is typical for the orthodox approach to the problems of society.

General economists are used to call an analysis of one market a partial analysis, while calling an analysis of all markets together a general analysis. They deviate in this respect from the use of the systems language used in other sciences. When applying common usage economic analysis is a partial analysis. Within this partial analysis we can distinguish between a partial specific analysis (one market) and a partial general system of markets. So the general equilibrium analysis based on Walras's law is still a partial analysis. To make this analysis more integral we have to introduce systematically psychological and social factors into this partial general system. See for an expose of modern developments in the world of general equilibrium analysis Herings (2000).

5 See for a sophisticated treatment of the methodological discourse on realism in economics Lawson (1997).

6 For an extensive and well-documented introduction into the field of theoretical sociology the book by Ritzer (1996) is highly recommended. In an Appendix, Ritzer gives an overview of the latest methodological discussions among sociologists.

In the first place, it is based on the paradigm that all human behaviour is determined by the characteristics of the group to which one belongs. In other words, behaviour is (socially) learned behaviour. Especially during their childhood human beings learn how to behave (*socialisation*). Parents, family, teachers, priests and governments teach people about what they should and what they should not do. We all are taught about the basic values and norms and about the principal symbols that reflect our unity.

In the second place, the relationships between the important groups in society can be characterised by *conflict* or by *harmony*. Some sociologists consider conflict as a necessary trigger for progressive development. Other sociologists, however, consider conflict resolution and the establishment of consensus as a necessary condition for progress. So they differ in their explanation of how social development takes place.

In the third place, orthodox sociologists have their *historical approach* in common. Technology is regarded as the exogenous variable. Our growth in knowledge is an irreversible process. It affects the functional structure of the economy and the relative political power of the different economic groups. According to some sociologists the trend is basically characterised as a process of rationalisation (Weber, 1922), although others see a trend of increasing secularisation (Comte, 1866). But technological progress and economic growth is the undeniable outcome of development.

In the fourth place, social theory is characterised by methodological collectivism. It means that an explanation of collective phenomena must be sought on the same collective level. Durkheim's explanation of suicide is exemplary in this respect. He explained the fluctuations in time series of suicide rates by fluctuations in what he called *anomie*, that is, norm uncertainty. In other words, suicide is not the outcome of an individual choice, but a social phenomenon caused by social developments.

When we take all these characteristics together, we can agree upon the fact that in the sociological explanation of developments in economy and society, the economic and biological/psychological aspect are completely absent. Social theory is only about relationships between important groups in economy and society. Theories differ in the way in which criteria determine intra- and inter group structure. Moreover, they differ with respect to the possibility of creating solidarity or whether rivalry is unavoidable or even necessary for progressive development.

When trying to typify orthodox sociology in terms of the systems theory, we must conclude that it is, like orthodox economic theory, an explanation of the functioning of the social aspect-system and developments in the characteristics of it. It is not about society as a real life system. Therefore the economic and the psychological factors have to be taken into account. Actually orthodox sociologists are far away from their scientific ideal of discovering scientific social laws, if they exist at all. But their results can be used as a partial social theory, which might contribute to the construction of a social science of a more integral type.

In the next section we will pay attention to developments within economics during the twentieth century. Thereafter we will deal with some important developments within sociology during the same period.

6. TWENTIETH CENTURY ECONOMICS

For our subject there are two developments of the utmost importance. In the first place this is the introduction of the assumption of imperfect information. In the second place, this is the application of the economic paradigm to other areas than the subsystems "free market" and "free market economy".

The first development, the attempt to make economic theory more realistic by recognising that information is also a scarce good, had far-reaching consequences. Preferences cannot be given by assumption and market structures are not necessarily competitive. Moreover, economic analysis of a system of markets shows that long-term disequilibria are a possibility, when assuming imperfect information. Keynes did not only introduce uncertainty as an important characteristic of subjects on financial markets in depression. He also introduced rigidity in wage structures because of the presence of social relationships on the labour market. These two pieces of analysis made the outcome of Keynes's analysis of the economy as a real life system quite different from the outcome of orthodox analysis of the economy as an aspect-system (Keynes, 1936).

The second development, the application of the economic paradigm to areas other than free markets is perfectly in line with the fact that economic orthodoxy is about the economic aspect of all human behaviour. In this way, the behaviour of families and individuals within a family context, the behaviour of governments and churches became subject to economic analysis. This was a shocking affair for many scientists who considered themselves experts in those respective fields. Political scientists and sociologists were confronted with a rival who invaded their territory.

The first development has made economic theory more realistic. The introduction of uncertainty and risk appeared to be a nice way to introduce some psychology into economic analysis. Individuals, who are free to choose, but lack relevant information with respect to what their needs actually are and which goods have the capacity to satisfy their needs, hesitate to choose. Without the necessary information it is difficult to be rational. From existential philosophy we know that individuals can start to panic, if they do not know what to do. Fortunately, individuals are not alone in this world. There are fellow travellers. But this discovery means a disciplinary border-crossing activity. In a strictly orthodox world there are no fellow travellers. Other people are only resources that can satisfy the needs of people who are well informed about their needs and the needs-satisfying capacity of the goods available. But in a situation of existential fear people need each other, not only as resources, but also as people who recognise each other as *human* beings. This makes it important to make the distinction between human resources and non-human resources. With the first it is possible to have a social relationship. With the second it is only possible to have an economic relationship. From this we can conclude that the introduction of imperfect information opens the door for an introduction of the psychical and the social factor.

7. TWENTIETH CENTURY SOCIOLOGY

As explained in Section 5 orthodox sociology is based on methodological collectivism. Individual behaviour is completely determined by the relevant group to which they belong. Social relationships change under the influence of changes, especially in production technology. But orthodoxy did not give any explanation of the logic of social action. Individuals were adjusted to the culture of the group and if culture changed, all individuals automatically adjusted to the new culture. What was lacking was a micro-oriented explanation of the existence of social ties. If psycho-sociology would give an answer to that problem, changes in the character of social ties could also be explained, namely by referring to changes in the environment of these ties.

This is exactly what happened in sociology. Sociologists like Herbert Mead and Irving Goffman developed a social theory on the micro level of direct human interaction (Ritzer, 1996). Where people have face-to-face contact with each other, especially with people with the same characteristics, they recognise each other as human beings and as equals. They start a communication process and develop common values and norms. This process creates a safe environment for the people involved and makes their social environment more predictable. Mead made the distinction between two parts of the individual Self. The first part is the "ME"-part. This is the area within the individual that functions as a store of the values and norms that constitute the culture of the group to which the individual Self belongs. The second part is the "I"-part. This is a kind of decision-making centre, where the Self takes decisions about the degree of adaptation to the social environment. The "I" can also decide to deviate. If a deviant has many followers, a change in culture can take place. So if production technology changes and makes particular functions superfluous and some norms that belonged to the function inefficient, there must always be an individual who starts a process of adjustment. So-called cultural entrepreneurs play an important role in cultural change. These changes play an important role in creating the necessary room for the implementation of new technologies in the production process.

Such an explanation of the existence of social ties makes it possible to explain social developments on the collective level, by referring to actions that take place on the individual level. The methodology that is based on such a procedure is called methodological individualism. The sociological approach just set out is called the micro-interactionist approach and it opens the black box of the individual to explain the existence of social ties.

A more recent development in sociology is the rational choice-approach. Already in the fifties some sociologists approached social relationships in terms of exchange relationships. But, in contrast to orthodox economics, exchange theorists did not consider every exchange as a result of deliberate action. They interpreted every social action as an exchange in order to find out what costs and benefits apparently played a role in human behaviour. Suppose a person is very loyal to a church or to a political party. To understand a phenomenon like loyalty it could be useful to search for benefits that people derive from their being loyal. The costs are clear in this particular case. If the church is not preaching the same message as before, but the views or preferences of the people have remained the same, then the exit option is a rational one. Staying while being dissatisfied is not very rational. The exchange-theorists hoped to find hidden benefits for loyalists by following these search procedures. Nowadays the so-called rational choice-approach has become popular among sociologists. Under the influence of economics and its strong analytical apparatus, sociologists have introduced the concept of rationality in their analyses. Being member of a group or moving towards another group is considered the result of deliberate and rational choice. Every social action is based on a weighing of costs and benefits, given the information that individuals have. This means that human communication, too, is a matter of coordination. However, there is an important difference between sociological rational choice and economic rational choice. When analysing a situation on the basis of an economic rational choice framework we assume a rational individual who is confronted with a limited amount of resources. These resources can consist of land, material goods, capital services or human services. An economic analysis abstracts from differences between these types of resources and focuses on what they have in common, namely their scarcity. This means that all relationships between individuals and resources are of a strictly economic kind.

When analysing a situation on the basis of a sociological rational choice framework, however, we assume a set of rational individuals who are confronted with a limited amount of resources and with each other. A sociological analysis explicitly recognises the possibility of social relationships that are of a different kind compared to economic relationships. What makes a relationship a social relationship is the mutual recognition of each other's "being human". Such recognition has a significant effect on the character of the actual relationships. In general we can say that social relationships can be positive as well as negative. In the case of a positive relationship it is characterised by solidarity; in case of a negative relationship it is characterised by rivalry. Of course the strength of the social ties differ according to place and time. But wherever people are together, the social aspect of the relationship cannot be denied.

Thus, a sociological framework of rational choice gives outcomes that are quite different from the economic framework of rational choice. One of the most remarkable differences is the *transfer of authority* that regularly takes place in the social world. People appear to be prepared to transfer their "rights-to-act" to other agents or create a conjoint authority, *i.e.* a government (Coleman, 1990). The sociological government has real authority, a phenomenon that does not exist in an economic framework.

During the twentieth century psychology and economics has influenced orthodox sociology increasingly. In the following section we will see whether developments within economics and sociology has given us the tools to construct a new socio-economic paradigm.

8. TOWARDS A SOCIO-ECONOMIC PARADIGM

In conclusion, orthodox economics emerged from political economy when economists tried to formulate the omnipresent phenomenon of scarcity. This attempt was meant as a division of labour. Economists analyse the scarcity aspect of human behaviour, leaving other aspects to other disciplines. Economics is about the tension between the biologically/psychologically explained (control over) needs on the one side and the physically/chemically explained (control over) natural processes on the other side. The basic paradigm in this respect is the statement that all individuals maximise the utility they derive from the consumption of goods, given limited resources. The situation of perfect competition is the ideal type of a scarcity situation. The constructors of this picture never meant to construct a realistic picture of human behaviour. They left other relevant factors out of the analysis on purpose. They pretended to have developed a pure theory of exchange. Some of them thought they had developed a useful tool to analyse free markets.

Their construction could function as an ideal to strive for. But others were of the opinion that even for the explanation of the functioning of free markets the so-called institutional setting was very important.

In conclusion, orthodox sociology is an attempt to explain changes in the social structure over time. Most of the orthodox sociologists agreed upon the fact that social structure always adapts to economic structure, which itself changes under the influence of the prime mover in society, namely technology. Growth in knowledge is considered the only genuinely irreversible factor. The principal debate was about the way social change takes place. In particular, the question whether or not social conflict is a necessary and efficient phenomenon for triggering economic progress was central. The development in the control over natural processes was considered to be the prime source of progress. Given an efficient mechanism of coordination of economic decisions, sociologists analysed the dynamics of social change.

Both the orthodox economists and orthodox sociologists have the same research strategy. Given the processes analysed by other sciences economists/sociologists analyse their subject matter. They sketch an ideal-type of solution and compare "reality" with their ideal. On the basis of the outcome of this difference they advise policies that are assumed to change "their" processes in such a way that they lead, in their ideal-typical situation at least, to an improvement of that situation. When we realise that both groups are analysing only one aspect of the same practical problem, that is the functioning of the real life economy and society, then we know that this is not a very fruitful approach. Actually we have to construct a common paradigm and take this as the frame of analysis of real processes in economy and society.

When constructing such a paradigm we can take advantage of the attempts of both sides to become more realistic. Economists started to introduce the assumption of imperfect information. In previous sections we set out that this strategy made the introduction of psychological and sociological factors possible. The introduction of sociological analysis into orthodox economic analysis may transform economic theory into a theory of the economy, being a real life system. Sociologists started to introduce psychology in their social analysis to get a genuine micro-foundation for the existence of social ties. Besides that, economic concepts like exchange, rational choice, benefits and costs were introduced. That makes the construction of a more integral analysis much easier.

A promising development in both fields is the discussion concerning the role of *institutions* (Rutherford, 1994). In economics the assumption of imperfect information has led to an explanation of institutions being information cost saving methods. A subject cannot base every action upon a deliberate calculation of costs and benefits. So, intuition and experience are playing an important role in the economic decision making process. Human behaviour consists of series of habits, routines and conventions. These 'institutions' make life more transparent and predictable. For economic agents these institutions are economically efficient patterns of behaviour. In orthodox sociology, however, institutions are socially motivated solutions to the social problem of rivalry (Wrong, 1994). Institutions in sociological theory must make the mechanisms of social change more effective.[7] These institutions concern the adoption of values and norms by the group, whether it is a firm, a branch or a state.

In a heterodox sociological rational choice framework, institutions play an important role as well. But in this framework, institutions are not only socially motivated but also economically motivated patterns of behaviour. This means that these institutions are not isolated abstractions like the ones used in the orthodox versions. They refer to regularities in the behaviour of individuals and groups in the real life economy and society. These institutions are based on a mix of an economic and a social motive.

Now we must find a method that makes it possible to analytically distinguish between the social aspect of human communication and the economic aspect of coordination. We can distinguish between different *analytical stages*.[8] In Stage One communication takes place between the social agents, leading to a continuation or a change in the socially motivated institutions. On the basis of the results, in Stage Two, coordination takes place leading to a continuation or a change in the buying and selling decisions of the same, but now economic, agents. In Figure 2 we have presented these two analytical stages. Now we can imagine an evolutionary development, described by a series of two-stage periods. Here decisions are not taken on the basis of an implicitly assumed ideal solution to the other aspect of the problem. All period decisions are taken on the basis of the institutional context as it functions at that particular moment in time.

7 There is a fast growing field in sociology focused on the analysis of the economy. White (1981) and Granovetter (1985) are important contributions in this respect. Fligstein (2001) deals with the emergence, stability and decline of markets. It offers a political cultural explanation of the functioning of markets and market economies.

8 Compare this procedure with the neoclassical distinction between the short and the long term. This is also an analytical rather than an empirical distinction.

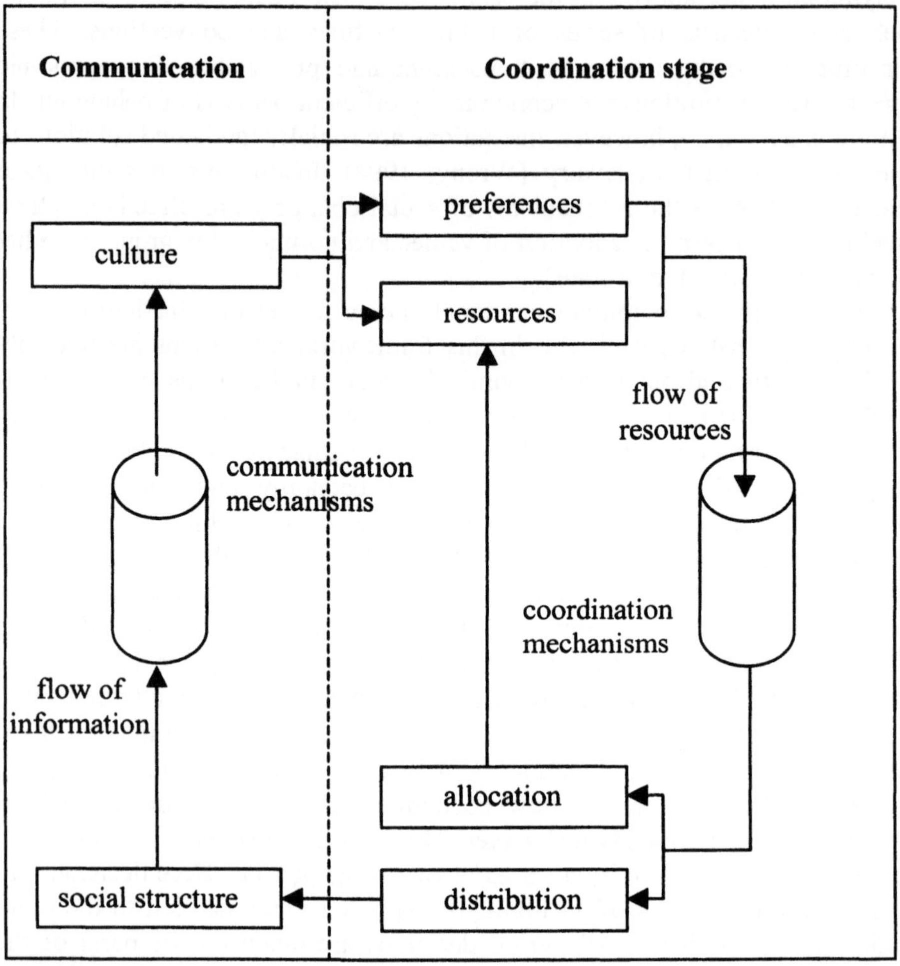

Period One

Stage One:

Given the allocation and distribution of resources there is a society-large debate going on about the performance; the communication takes place in numerous ways and is basically about the social ranking (=structure), the preference we (ought to) have and about our resources (=rights-to-act).

Stage Two:

Given the preferences and the distribution of resources economic decisions are coordinated in different ways – command, democratic voting, collective bargaining, price mechanism. This results in a particular allocation and distribution.

Period Two

etcetera

Figure 2. Communication and coordination

Now it has become clear that stable and predictable socially motivated institutions "decided upon" in Stage One, make it easier for economic agents to decide upon what to buy and what to sell. These stable and predictable institutions are not the same as constant and rigid institutions. Moreover, it does not mean that all economic behaviour is determined by sets of norms and values that are shared by all parties. Institutions are about the rules of the game making it probable that actual distributions of everything that is of value are the result of power relationships. These power battles are regulated games; not perfectly free fights. So by carefully communicating about the rules it is possible that all parties accept the outcome as unavoidable if not desirable. In such cases the institutional context is a stable one, making economic calculations relatively easy. Such predictable contexts are highly beneficial for a long period of prosperity.

REFERENCES

Bauman, Z. (1990), *Thinking Sociologically*, Oxford: Blackwell Publishers.
Coleman, J. (1990), *Foundations of Social Theory*, Cambridge: The Belknap Press of Harvard University Press.
Comte, A. (1866), *System of Positive Philosophy*, Reprinted in 1976, New York.
Fligstein, N. (2001), *The Architecture of Markets*, Princeton: Princeton University Press.
Granovetter, M. (1995), "Economic Action and Social Structure: The Problem of Embeddedness," in M. Granovetter and R. Swedberg (eds.) (1992), *The Sociology of Economic Life*, Westview Press.
Herings, J.J. (2000), *Van alle markten thuis*, Maastricht.
Hobbes, T. (1651), *Leviathan*, London: Penguin Books.
Keynes, J. M. (1936), *The General Theory of Employment, Interest and Money*, London: MacMillan.
Lawson, T. (1997), *Economics and Reality*, London: Routledge.
Locke, J. (1689), *An Essay Concerning Human Understanding*, Reprinted in 1975 by Oxford: Clarendon Press.
Rousseau, J.J. (1983), *Vertoog over de ongelijkheid*, Boom, Originally: *Discours sur l'origine et les fondements de l'inégalité*, Paris: Gallimard, 1755.
Ritzer, G. (1996), *Sociology*, MacGraw Hill, Third Edition.
Rutherford, M. (1994), *Institutions in Economics*, Cambridge: Cambridge University Press.
Robbins, L. (1932), *An Essay on the Nature and Significance of Economic Science*, Oxford.
Smith, A. (1759), *The Theory of Moral Sentiments*, Reprinted in 1982 by Liberty Fund.
Smith, A. (1776), *An Inquiry into the Nature and Causes of the Wealth of Nations*, Reprinted in 1994 by Random House Inc.
Weber, M. (1922), *Economy and Society*, Reprinted in 1976 by Berkeley: University of California Press.
White, H.C. (1981), "Where Do Markets Come From?," *American Journal of Sociology* 87(3), pp. 514-547.
Wrong, D.H. (1994), *The Problem of Order*, Cambridge: Harvard University Press.

PART II

ECONOMIC POLICY

Chapter 5

Wage Cost Moderation and Employment Growth in the Netherlands

Bas B. Bakker[1]
International Monetary Fund, Washington DC

Key words: Employment, Wages, Netherlands

Abstract: Since the mid-1980s, the Netherlands seems to have shifted from a European pattern of rapid wage growth and low employment creation, to a more Anglo-Saxon pattern of low wage growth and high employment growth. The shift towards moderate wage costs growth was partly the result of a change in union behaviour, but cuts of taxes and social security contributions, and the rapid increase of the labour force (driven in large part by increased participation of women) also played a role. However, while employment creation has been rapid, this has mainly benefited new entrants on the labour market; hidden unemployment remains very high and has fallen only recently.

1. INTRODUCTION

The pace of employment creation in the Netherlands in the past decade and a half has been striking. Between 1983 and 2000, employment grew by 40 percent, compared to 10 percent in Germany, and 1 percent in Italy (Figure 1).[2] At the same time, real wage costs grew very slowly. Between 1983 and 2000, they rose only ½ percent annually, compared with 4½ percent annually in the 1970–78 period.

[1] The views expressed here are solely those of the author and do not necessarily reflect those of the IMF staff or Executive Board. Comments of Robert Ford and Ydahlia Metzgen on a previous version are gratefully acknowledged.

[2] Employment growth in full-time equivalents was also 40 percent.

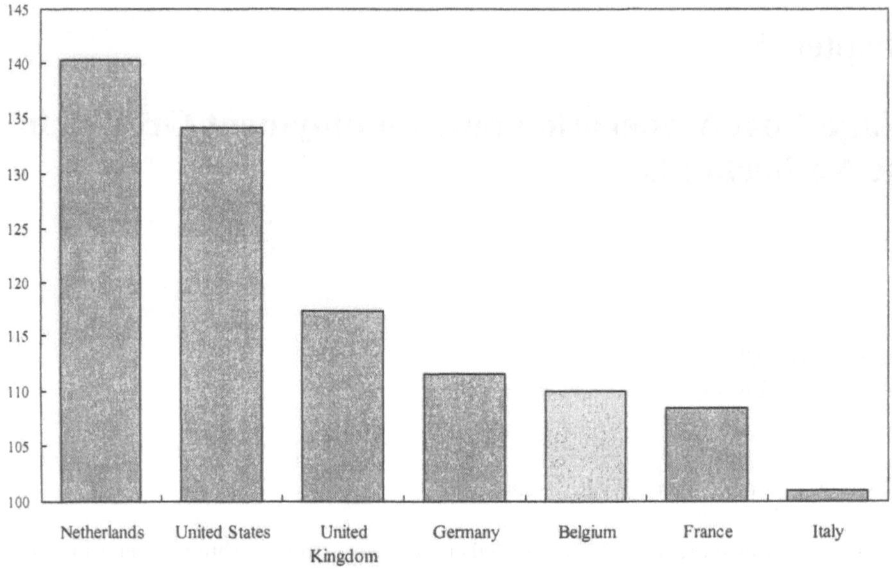

Figure 1. Netherlands: Employment Creation, 1983-2000 (1983=100)

This chapter will argue that slow wage growth and rapid employment growth were linked. Moderate growth of wage costs, and the perception of employers that the behaviour of unions had changed and that this moderation would continue, resulted in a shift from a European pattern of rapid wage growth and low employment creation, to a more Anglo-Saxon-like pattern of rapid employment growth and lower wage growth. The chapter will also delve into the causes of wage moderation. It will argue that while a change of behaviour of unions may have played a role, government policy was also important: it restrained wage growth by cutting taxes and social security contributions, which allowed net incomes to rise, in the absence of increases of gross wages. Wage moderation was also favoured by a rapid increase in the labour force, driven in large part by increased participation of women. These newcomers on the labour market were the principal beneficiaries of the new jobs: employment creation was not very successful in reducing the number of social security benefits recipients.

2. WHY WAS WAGE COST GROWTH MODERATE?

The initial consensus on the necessity of wage moderation appears to have resulted from experiences in the 1970s. The combination, in the early 1970s, of substantial GDP growth and stagnating employment had cast doubt on the view that unemployment was a Keynesian problem, and stimulated the idea that persistent unemployment was caused not by insufficient effective demand but by a lack of profitable opportunities to produce. This idea was underscored by the introduction by the CPB (Netherlands Bureau for Economic Policy Analysis) of a new generation of models, which contained supply side, as well as demand side elements (Den Hartog and Tjan, 1974). According to these models, the excess growth of real wage costs over the rate of technical progress affected employment in two ways: it led to accelerated scrapping of old labour intensive vintages of capital; and it implied lower profitability, which resulted in lower investment, slower growth of the capital stock, and fewer new jobs.[3]

The gradually emerging consensus on the necessity of a different strategy on wages was formalised in November 1982, when labour unions and employers reached the "Wassenaar agreement" — an understanding to pursue moderate wage growth to stimulate employment creation. While wage growth had slowed in the 1970s, the slowdown had been insufficient to prevent a sharp increase in the labour-income share, which reached the unsustainable level of 95 percent in 1981. Wage moderation went into effect from 1983 and continued after the economy began to recover from recession; the beneficial impact on employment creation was widely felt and recognised. By the late 1980s, wage moderation had become a virtually unchallenged policy recipe among labour unions, employers, and political parties in the Netherlands.

The Wassenaar agreement abolished automatic price indexation. As in many sectors collective labour agreements for 1983 had already been concluded, a special law was passed in December 1982 that suspended automatic price indexation and declared all concluded labour agreements void. By 1985, automatic price indexation had virtually disappeared; only 10 percent of all collective labour agreements still included it.

Another element of the 1982 agreement was the decentralisation of wage bargaining. Before 1982, unions and employers' organisations sought agreement at the national level, thereafter negotiations only took place at the sectoral level. The degree of change in the process of decentralisation is debatable however. Although agreement was always sought at the national level before 1982, negotiations were often unsuccessful and ended up at the sectoral level anyway. Moreover, after 1982, there was a high degree of coordination within labour unions and employers' organisations at the national level.

[3] See also Kuipers and Bosch (1976) and Kuipers and Van Zon (1982).

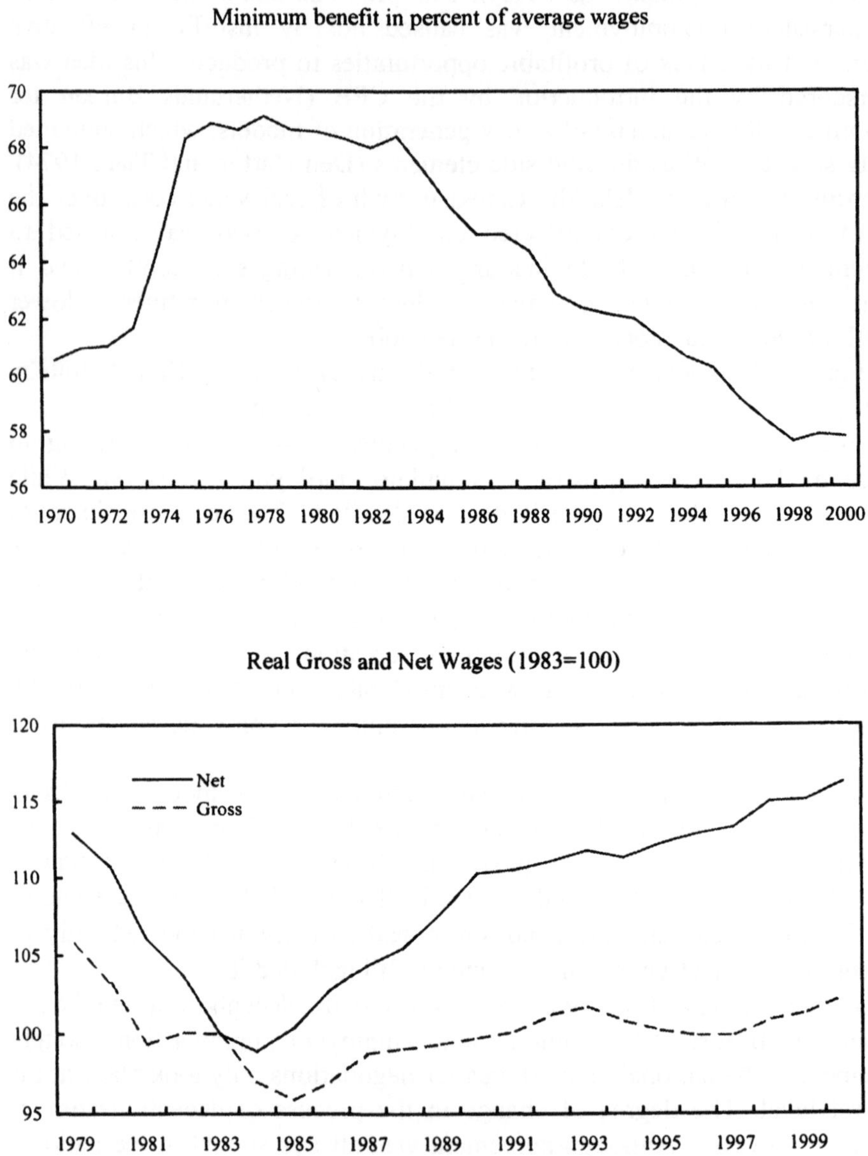

Figure 2. Netherlands: Labour Market Policy

The government encouraged wage moderation in several ways. First, the legal minimum wage was reduced significantly in real terms. The nominal minimum wage for adults was frozen during most of the 1980s and 1990s. In 1984, the minimum wage was reduced by 3 percent; subsequently it was frozen until 1990, and then again from 1993 until 1996. As a result, the gross *real* minimum wage declined substantially, and by 1997 was 22 percent lower than in 1979. The youth minimum wage was twice cut substantially (at the beginning of 1981 and mid-1983), at other times it followed the nominal freeze of the minimum wage for adults. Second, because of its link to the minimum wage, the gross minimum social benefit declined in real terms by more than 20 percent (and the net minimum benefit by some 12 percent), thus strengthening incentives in the labour market (Figure 2, top panel). Third, partly with a view to encouraging wage moderation, taxes and social security contributions paid by employees were cut substantially. The reduction of taxes and social security contributions allowed for an increase in disposable income even in the absence of real gross wage increases, thereby reducing wage demands. The impact of cuts in taxes and social security contributions was quite substantial; whereas the real gross wage of the average production worker increased by only 2.2 percent over the 1983–2000 period, the corresponding real net wage went up by 16.2 percent (Figure 2, bottom panel). Expenditure restraint on the side of the government thus played an important role in containing wage costs, as it made possible to simultaneously cut taxes and reduce the deficit.

Other factors that favoured wage moderation included a rapid rise in the participation of women, and a strong increase in the working age population: with a sizeable increase in labour supply, wage pressures were less likely to emerge. Indeed, without the reforms on the demand side of the labour market, unemployment would clearly have risen steeply. There may also have been an indirect influence in the other direction: wage moderation, through its positive impact on employment creation, is likely to have induced participation and thus a higher effective labour supply.

To what extent did the Wassenaar agreement result in larger wage moderation than could be expected on the basis of high unemployment and tax cuts? Analysis of the determinants of Dutch labour costs by the IMF tends to confirm that the moderation of wage growth relative to productivity growth in the 1980s was triggered by underlying fundamentals, while its continuation was aided by government policy.[4] Dutch labour costs are in large part determined by three factors: productivity growth, the change in taxes and social security contributions, and the change in unemployment.[5] A

[4] See Bakker and Halikias (1999).

[5] This would suggest that workers in the Netherlands are more concerned about an *increase* in unemployment than about the level of unemployment itself. This could perhaps be

change in taxes and social security contributions has a pronounced impact, with an increase in taxes and contributions of 1 guilder leading to an increase of labour costs of 0.7 guilders. The impact of unemployment is also significant, with each percentage point rise in the unemployment ratio leading to a reduction in real wage growth of 0.6 percentage points. The rapid increase in unemployment in the early 1980s reduced real wage growth; subsequent cuts in taxes and social security contributions helped keep wage growth moderate.

The Wassenaar agreement, however, probably played a crucial role, by changing employers' expectations of future wage growth. Becoming convinced that future wage increases would be moderate, employers felt much less incentive to substitute capital for labour, and to continue shedding labour. As a result they have stopped substituting capital for labour, and the previously strong growth in the capital-labour ratio has levelled off (Figure 3). With a slowdown of the capital-labour ratio increase, labour productivity growth slowed down as well. However, this slowdown in labour productivity did not negatively affect output growth. On the contrary, as investment was now used predominantly for expansion, rather than for replacement of labour, it was associated with an acceleration of GDP growth. Overall, the Netherlands thus seem to have switched from a European kind of labour market "equilibrium" in which rapid wage increases lead to a strong increase in labour productivity (fuelled by a continuous increase in the capital-labour ratio) but weak growth of employment and output, to a more US-type equilibrium, in which wages grow slower, the capital-labour ratio does not rise as fast, and employment and output growth is faster.[6]

Seen in this way, the change in union behaviour may have played a role in creating a more labour-intensive growth pattern. Such a shift would be hard to detect in an empirical wage-costs equation, since it is reflected in a simultaneous reduction in productivity and wage growth. In this view, while it is likely that the change in employers' expectations was not triggered by a single event, such as the Wassenaar agreement, the continuous support of labour unions for wage moderation is likely to have been important.[7]

---

explained by the fact that large-scale dismissals typically only take place when unemployment is rising (rather than when it is high), and there is not much competition on the labour market between those already employed, and those without a job.

6 As is well known, productivity growth in the United States has been very strong in recent years, which would suggest a break with the past pattern of low productivity growth. However, as this coincided with very strong GDP growth, it is not yet clear to what extent this productivity increase was cyclical, rather than structural.

7 This long-run substitutability between capital and labour is in accordance with putty-clay vintage models, in which the labour-intensity of each new vintage depends on real wages. In such models, a prolonged period of wage moderation would result in much smaller increase of the capital-labour ratio. See Kuipers and Van Zon (1982).

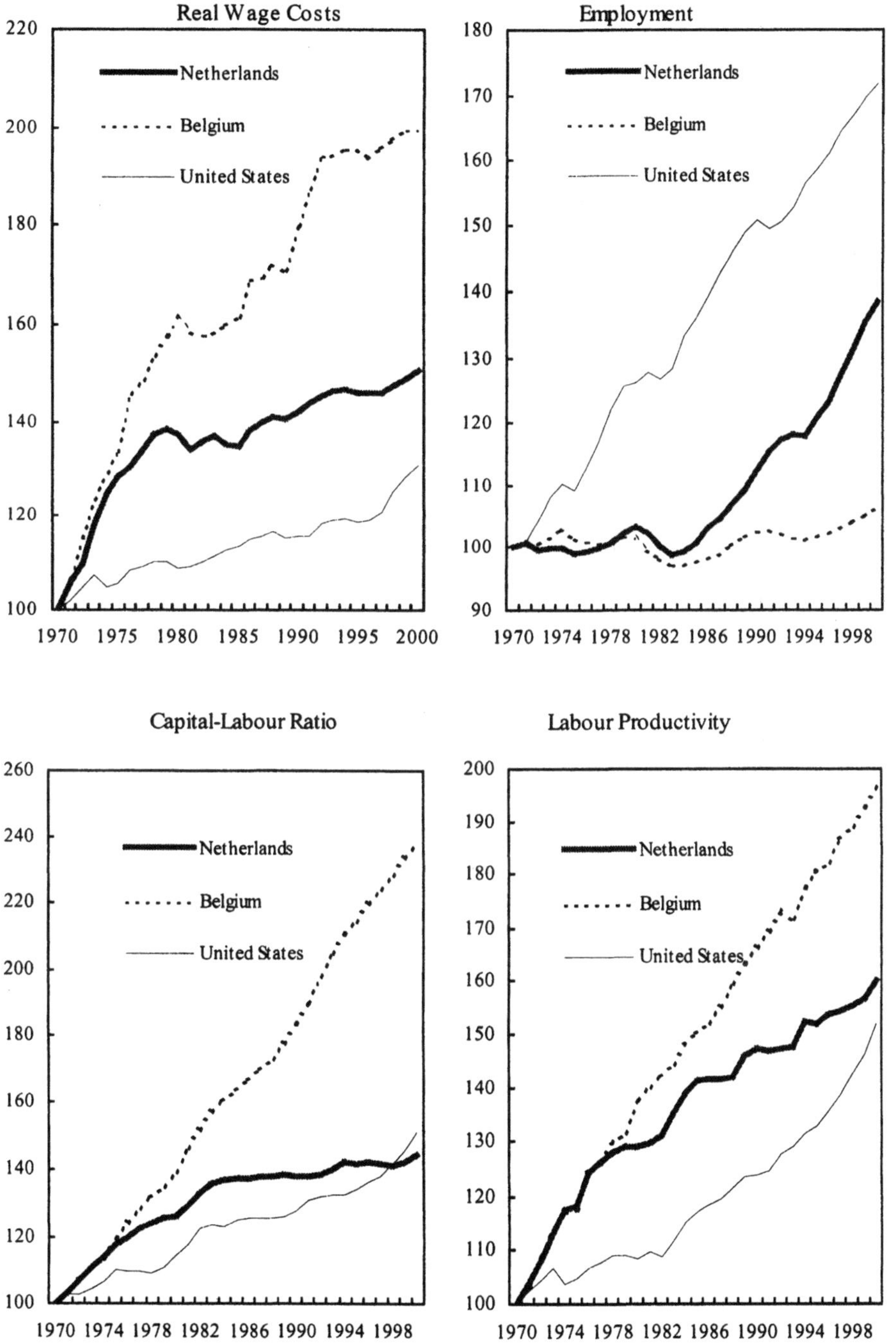

Figure 3. Labour market data for the Netherlands, Belgium and the United States

3. THE IMPACT OF WAGE COST MODERATION ON EMPLOYMENT GROWTH

The idea that wage cost moderation has played an important role in employment growth no longer seems very controversial in the Netherlands. The importance was confirmed by a study of the CPB Netherlands Bureau for Economic Policy Analysis in 1991. This study analysed why the employment performance in the 1983-90 period (a gain of 500 thousand jobs) was so much better than during 1975-82 (a loss of 250 thousand jobs). The study concluded that the much better employment performance was mainly the result of a more favourable development in wage costs. If the labour income share had remained at its 1979 level, real wage costs would have been 22 percent higher, and employment in persons would been 380 thousand persons lower. The increase in part time work also played a role, but other factors were not very important. Estimates at the IMF also tend to confirm the idea that the long run impact of higher wages on employment was quite important, with a 1 percent higher real wage associated with a little less than ½ percent lower employment.[8]

According to the CPB, the impact of lower wage costs on employment was not through its impact on production, but mainly through its impact on labour intensity. If the labour-income share had not declined, the impact on production in the market sector would have been modest (a decline of 2 percent, with lower exports and investment compensated by higher consumption), but enterprises would have reacted to higher wage costs by shedding more labour, and employment would have declined commensurately.

While wage cost moderation initially led to a sharp drop in the labour income share, in the 1990s it was associated with a shift to a more labour intensive growth pattern. The labour-income share declined from 95 percent in 1981 to 81½ percent by 1989, but did not decline further in the 1990s, although wage growth continued to be moderate. Instead, productivity increases seem to have adjusted to lower wage increases, leading to a new equilibrium of more labour intensive growth.

A comparison with other countries shows that GDP growth in the Netherlands is much richer in employment growth than that in many other industrial countries. Growth is now also more employment intensive than two decades ago. Whereas in the 1970-82 period a growth rate of 2.5 percent was just sufficient to keep employment from falling, in the 1990-2000 period a only slightly higher average growth rate (3 percent) generated an annual employment growth rate of 2¼ percent.

[8] See Bakker and Halikias (1999).

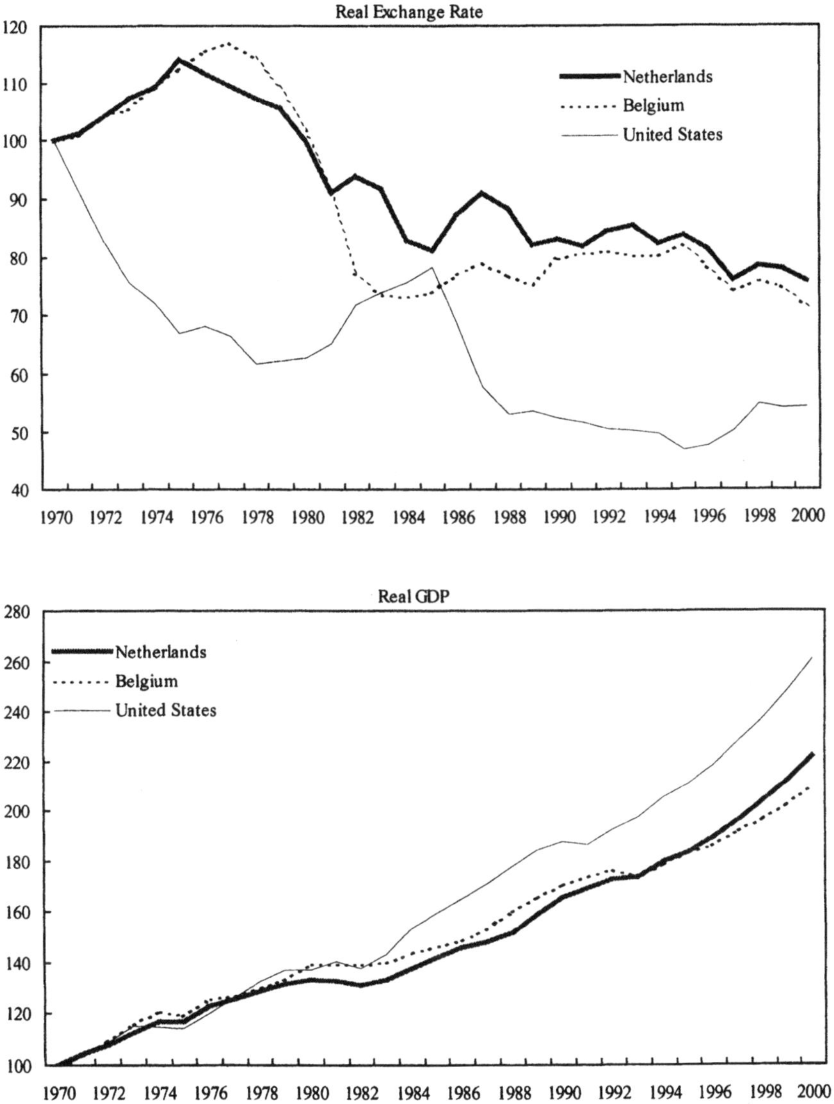

Figure 4. Netherlands: Competitiveness and GDP

The better performance in employment does not seem to result from an improvement in competitiveness—or at least not only. A comparison with Belgium illustrates this point: Belgium's real exchange rate depreciated more than that of the Netherlands (Figure 4), but employment in Belgium was essentially flat, while employment in the Netherlands grew strongly. Moreover, while competitiveness did indeed improve from the late 1970s onward, this was in large part a reversal of an unsustainable appreciation that occurred during the 1960s and 1970s; and since the mid-1980s, the real exchange rate has not changed much.

Not only is growth more labour intensive, growth is also higher. This does not reflect higher exports, but stronger domestic demand (Table 1). Strong domestic demand growth is partly the result of rapid employment growth, not only through its effect on income, but also through its impact on consumer confidence. Domestic demand is also stimulated by developments in the housing market. Real housing prices doubled between 1990 and 2000, and the corresponding wealth gains are likely to have boosted consumption.

An important question is whether wage moderation mainly stimulated employment growth because it contained average wage growth or because it slowed, as a by-product, the growth of the minimum wage. A priori, there are arguments for both. The moderation of average wage growth helped to restore profitability of firms and corporate investment and to reduce the excessive substitution of capital for labour, thereby stimulating employment growth. Alternatively, in an environment where greater wage differentiation was not feasible for political and cultural reasons, the slowdown in overall wage growth may have been the only feasible way to reduce wage growth at the lower end of the wage spectrum. To the extent that wage costs were a more serious constraint for low-skilled workers, the main impact of wage moderation would have been on jobs for the lower skilled, with much less effect on jobs for the higher skilled.

Table 1. Growth of GDP, Exports, and Domestic Demand, 1990-2000 (Average growth rates, in %)

	GDP	Exports	Domestic demand
United States	3.2	7.2	3.5
Netherlands	3.1	5.9	2.7
Germany	2.2	5.2	2.1
Belgium	2.2	4.9	1.9
United Kingdom	1.8	5.5	2.1
France	2.0	6.4	1.5
Italy	1.5	5.8	1.4

Source: OECD Economic Outlook Database

CPB data on employment creation by skill level of employees show that in the 1980s and early 1990s employment creation accelerated for both high and low skilled workers. The contrast between the 1970s and the late 1980s is particularly marked. Between 1972 and 1977, employment in full time equivalents decreased on average by 1.1 percent a year, as a large decline in low skilled employment (contributing 2.0 percentage points) was only partially compensated by an increase in high skilled employment (contributing 0.9 percentage points). Between 1986 and 1991, employment increased by 2.3 percent, as the contribution of high skilled employment creation became much stronger (2.6 percentage points) and the decline in low skilled employment became much less pronounced (0.3 percentage points). Interestingly, these data show that the changes in employment in skilled and unskilled employment were of similar magnitude. Intuitively, this suggests that the impact of wage moderation did not arise from its impact on low skilled wages but was an across-the-board effect.

Employment growth in lower-*paid* jobs was much faster than overall employment growth. Between 1985 and 1989, low-paid employment (in persons) grew by almost 4 percent annually, compared with almost 2 percent for overall employment; between 1989 and 1994 the corresponding figures were 3 percent and 1 percent. It might seem puzzling that low-paid employment grew faster than overall employment, while low-*skilled* employment grew slower. Part of the explanation is that many new jobs were low-paid, part-time jobs, which were occupied by high-skilled, often part-time working women or students. Also, many of the new higher-skilled workers were young and therefore had a relatively low wage. However, this puzzle is not yet entirely understood. For instance, why did high-skilled women not find high-paid jobs? Are the kind of jobs that lend themselves well for part-time, typically less well-paying jobs?

Overall, low-wage employment increased strongly, and employment of lower skilled declined much less than before. Thus, wage moderation was clearly beneficial low-wage employment. On the other hand, lower paid jobs were increasingly held by higher skilled, rather than low skilled workers, and this substitution suggests that wage differentials may have been a problem (see section 5 below).

4. THE RISE IN FEMALE LABOUR FORCE PARTICIPATION

The substantial growth of employment since the mid-1980s would not have been possible without a marked rise in labour force participation. Following a decline in the 1970s (from 63 percent in 1970 to 61 percent in 1982), the participation rate rose strongly in the 1980s and 1990s, to 73 percent in 2000.[9] With unemployment and low labour force participation concentrated among the unskilled, the expansion of employment that took place in skilled

[9] The participation rates mentioned here are as a percent of the population between 20 and 64.

jobs was only made possible by younger, relatively skilled, workers entering of the labour force.

The increase in the participation rate was entirely due to higher participation by women: female participation increased from 39 percent in 1982 to 61 percent in 1998, while male participation remained stagnant at some 84 percent.

Determining the role that government policies have played in increasing female participation is difficult. While a positive impact of government policies is plausible, it should be noted that the increased participation in the women labour force was not notably different from that observed during the 1970s; the participation rate of women aged between 20 and 64 increased from 31 percent in 1970 until 39 percent in 1982, and from 39 to 48 percent between 1982 and 1994. The observed increase is likely to have been largely the result of shifts in cultural patterns that have been observed in other countries also; and the sharp increase in the female participation rate observed in the Netherlands was basically a catch-up to the European average.

Government policies are likely to have played a role in ending the decline in the male participation rate. The drop (from 95 percent in 1970 to 80 percent in 1985), in large part associated with an increase in early retirement and disability benefits, but also with an increase in educational participation, ended in the mid 1980s; ever since the rate has been virtually stable. Government policies stimulated participation in several ways. Social security benefits were lowered and eligibility was tightened, which made leaving the labour force for social security benefits less attractive. The percentage of the working age population receiving disability benefits slowed from the mid 1980s onward, and from 1993 onward, declined. The difference between minimum benefits and the effective minimum wage was progressively widened. While both the official minimum wage and minimum benefits were delinked from contract wages, the lowest wage scales moved until recently in line with contract wages (resulting in a widening gap between wages and benefits).

Participation may also have been stimulated by strong employment growth. Many women who previously were not in the labour force may have been encouraged to look for a job, and the use of early retirement and other exits of the labour force as an alternative to unemployment is likely to have been reduced under the influence of a strong labour market.

Supply-side policies were only partially successful: although they managed to attract newcomers to the labour market, they did not succeed in reintegrating those who had dropped out of the labour market (other than through public employment programs). Thus, the male participation rate did not recover to its earlier levels, and participation among the elderly remained minimal.

Overall, the main cause of the participation increase seems to have been cultural factors that led to increased participation by women; but government policy may also have played a role, especially in bringing to a halt the decline in participation by men.

Viewed in this way, the initial conditions in the early 1980s of low female participation were ideal for an expansion of employment. If in the early 1980s, female participation had already been at elevated levels, the observed strong increase in employment would probably not have continued as long. Moreover, if the increase in female participation were to taper off in the future, labour supply growth would decline, and employment could only continue to grow at the same rate if workers in categories or age cohorts that typically dropped out of the labour force in the past could be reactivated.

5. THE PROBLEM OF THE LOW-SKILLED

Although employment has grown rapidly in the past decade and a half, this has not substantially reduced the number of benefits recipients. Official unemployment has dropped significantly, and is now at a low level (3½ percent in 2000, according to CPB figures). The number of unemployment benefits recipients declined less, and the gap between official unemployment and unemployment benefits recipients widened progressively. The decline in the level of nonemployment was even smaller, if the rise of the number of disability benefits recipients is taken into account. The percentage of the working age population that is on either unemployment or disability benefits kept rising throughout the 1980s and reached an all-time high in 1994 (18.3 percent). It has since declined, but its 2000 level (14.7 percent) is not very different from that in 1990 (16.4). Thus, employment creation mainly served to absorb the growth in the population of working age and increased participation by women; it contributed little to reducing the part of the working age population receiving benefits.

What explains the poor performance in reducing the number of benefits recipients? One important factor may have been the decrease in wage differentials between high and low-skilled workers. Somewhat surprisingly, wage dispersion between high-skilled and low-skilled labour has decreased since the early 1980s. According to CPB data, the ratio of wages of low-skilled workers to high-skilled workers increased in both the sheltered and exposed sector; in the sheltered sector from 0.71 in 1982 to 0.82 in 1993, and in the exposed sector from 0.73 to 0.92. Thus, while real wages of high-skilled workers remained stable, those of low-skilled workers continued to increase. The decline in wage differentials between high-skilled and low-skilled workers has also been documented by other authors. Salverda (1998) found that the wage premium of university educated workers over those with only primary education decreased from 73 percent in 1979 to 50 percent in 1989.

From a demand-side perspective, the decline in wage differentials is somewhat surprising, as technological progress has increasingly reduced demand for low-skilled workers. This shift in demand from low-skilled to high-skilled labour has also been observed in other OECD countries, and a common view is that it has led to rising wage inequality in the United States, and to rising unemployment among the low-skilled in Europe (Freeman, 1995). The Netherlands would seem to fit in well with the rest of Europe in that wage differentials have not increased, resulting in high inactivity among the low skilled.

The narrowing of wage differentials in the Netherlands becomes more understandable if supply is also taken into account. The supply of skilled workers increased strongly, caused by a sharp increase in the participation rate of young, skilled women and by an increase in education among young people in general. Wages of high-skilled workers adjusted to the large inflow of skilled workers, and the strong increase in relative supply of high-skilled workers reduced wage differentials. At the lower end, wages did not decline despite a reduced minimum wage and high unemployment; with replacement rates at low wage levels often close to 100 percent, the incentive to search for a job may not have been very strong, and with a reservation rate well above the minimum wage, employers found it very difficult to attract workers at wage levels close to the minimum wage.

The declining wage differentials among skill categories were probably detrimental to employment for low skilled workers. According to the CPB, low-skilled and high-skilled labour are good substitutes: if wage costs for low-skilled labour are decreased by 10 percent, employment of low-skilled workers increases by 15.4 percent, and employment of high-skilled labour decreases by 8.1 percent (Drapers and Manders, 1997).

This breakdown of employment growth by skill puts the performance of the Dutch labour market in some perspective. While it performed well in absorbing high-skilled newcomers to the labour market, it performance poorly in reabsorbing the low-skilled unemployed.

6. SUMMARY

Since the mid 1980s the Netherlands seems to have shifted from a European growth pattern of rapid wage growth and low employment creation, to a more Anglo-Saxon-like pattern, that is, a more labour intensive growth pattern, resulting in low productivity but high employment growth. This shift is likely the result of the very moderate growth of wage costs, and the perception of employers that the behaviour of unions had changed and that this moderation would thus continue. Government policy played an important role in wage moderation. By reducing taxes and social security contributions it allowed net incomes to rise, in the absence of increases of gross wages. Expenditure restraint on the side of the government played an important role in containing wage costs, as it made possible to simultaneously cut taxes and reduce the deficit. Unique initial conditions on the supply side of the labour market clearly amplified the impact of wage cost moderation, although they could have exacerbated unemployment in the absence of strong job creation. These conditions included a low labour force participation rate, with relatively few women in the work force; rapid demographic growth, which underpinned wage moderation; and an excessively high labour income share, reduction of which triggered rapid employment growth. This was a propitious setting for wage cost moderation to be effective; in more typical circumstances, even stronger labour supply-side measures would have been needed to foster such strong employment growth. Moreover, while employment creation has been rapid, this has mainly benefited new entrants on the labour market. Hidden unemployment remains very high and has fallen only recently.

REFERENCES

Bakker, B.B. and I. Halikias (1999), "Policy Reforms and Employment Creation," in C.M. Watson, B.B. Bakker, J.K. Martijn, and I. Halikias (eds.), "The Netherlands, Transforming a Market Economy," *Occasional Paper* 181, International Monetary Fund, Washington.

CPB Netherlands Bureau for Economic Policy Analysis (1991), "De werkgelegenheid in de jaren tachtig," *Werkdocument* 41, The Hague.

Draper, D.A.G. and A.J.G. Manders (1997), "Structural Changes in the Demand for Labour," *De Economist* 145, pp. 521–546.

Freeman, R.B (1995), "Are Your Wages Set in Beijing?," *Journal of Economic Perspectives* 9(3), pp. 15–32.

Hartog, H. den and H.S. Tjan (1974), "Investeringen, lonen, prijzen en arbeidsplaatsen," CPB Netherlands Bureau for Economic Policy Analysis, *Occasional Paper* 2.

Kuipers, S.K. and H.F. Bosch (1976), "An Alternative Estimation Procedure of a Clay-Clay Type of Vintage Model: The Case of the Netherlands, 1959-1973," *De Economist* 124(1/2), pp. 56-82.

Kuipers, S.K. and A.H. van Zon (1982), "Output and Employment Growth in the Netherlands in the Postwar Period: A Putty-Clay Approach," *De Economist* 130(1), pp. 38-70.

Salverda, W. (1998), "Incidence and Evolution of Low-Wage Employment in the Netherlands and the United States, 1979-1989," in S. Basen, M. Gregory and W. Salverda (eds.), *Low-Wage Employment in Europe*, Cheltenham: Edward Elgar, pp. 25-62.

Chapter 6

From a Job-Rights to a Job-Search Labour Market in Poland and Hungary

Jouke van Dijk and Ruud Dorenbos
Department of Spatial Sciences, University of Groningen; NEI, Rotterdam, Division of Labour and Education, and World Bank Institute, Human Development Division

Key words: Wage determinants, Human capital, Transition economies

Abstract: Before 1989 the centrally planned economies in Poland and Hungary provided employment opportunities for all members of the potential labour force. Although there was hidden unemployment and labour hoarding, open unemployment did not exist by definition. Because workers were assured of a job (job rights) they had little practical experience in matters of job-search. This implies that the interaction between supply and demand was nearly absent as a coordination mechanism to match workers and jobs in an efficient way. From 1990 onwards the labour market changed from a job-rights to a job-search economy. The main aim of this chapter to investigate to what extent human capital variables were able to explain wages differentials between individuals immediately after the transition. The empirical analysis is based on micro data for Poland and Hungary on wage information in January 1992.

1. INTRODUCTION

One of the most dramatic outcomes of the transformation process in Central and Eastern Europe was the high unemployment. With the exception of the Czech Republic the unemployment rates were within a period of hardly four years higher than 10%. The expectation was that the growing number of private firms could absorb most of the newly unemployed. This appeared not to be the case. The private employers preferred employees directly coming from the state sector, thus, without an intervening period of unemployment. Private employers were also looking for young and high educated starters on the labour market (Boeri, 1994a, 1994b; Jackman, 1994). The politically and economically more advanced countries like Hungary and Poland underwent the same developments. In 1989, unemployment did not officially exist in both countries. However, the structural adjustments in both countries caused high unemployment in both countries, mounting to 15.9% in Poland and 12.2% in Hungary in 1993 (OECD, 1994).

This reallocation process has now been underway far a decade. Both from a social and scientific point of view, it is interesting to get better insights into the processes that took place on the labour market during the transformation process. Aggregated data are not only seldom, they also give limited information. Individual data offer more opportunities. These data can be derived from the project *Social Stratification in Eastern Europe after 1989* (Treiman, 1994). Former research based on these data gave detailed information about all kind of labour market transitions between the labour market states 'employment, unemployment, and inactivity' but also on job-to-job transitions (Dorenbos, 1999). Besides changes in labour market stage it is also very likely that the transformation process affects the wage structure. The evolution of the wage structure acts as an important labour market signal (Rutkowski, 1996). Huber suggest that from the institutional point of view Eastern and Central European countries have adhered the system of the continental European countries. He suggests that the labour market adjustments take place via participation decisions, while wage flexibility and migration are much less important (Huber, 1999). However, several recent studies based on micro-data show that nowadays wage equations based on human capital theory show for Central- and Eastern European outcomes which are highly comparable with studies for western countries (see Plánovský, 1999 and references in that paper). Wages vary systematically with education, work-experience, gender *etc.* which can be seen as indicators reflecting differences in (potential) productivity. A general conclusion from these studies is that the labour market in the former communist countries tend to behave now more and more like the labour market of a market economy. However, not much is known about to what extent wages already varied systematically with these human capital variables in the initial stage of the transformation process.

The main aim of this chapter is to examine to what extent individual characteristics like gender, education, marital status, work experience *etc.* as well as job characteristics like sector, organisation and number of subordinates affected the individual wages of Hungarian and Polish employees in the initial stage of the transformation process.

The structure of this chapter is as follows. In Section 2 a wage equation will be derived on the basis of personal- and job characteristics, in which the human capital theory will serve as basic assumption. Moreover, the variables used and their expected impact on the individual wage will be discussed. In Section 3, the data used and the estimation results will be commented. In Section 4 conclusions are derived and the results in this chapter are compared with results of western countries and of studies of Eastern and Central European countries in a later stage of the transition process.

2. THE WAGE EQUATION: THE VARIABLES

2.1 The Human Capital Concept

The human capital theory assumes a positive relation between education and the future wage. According to the neoclassical theory, the marginal productivity of the employee equals the real wage rate. By means of schooling, the marginal productivity of the employee increases and, consequently, the wage of the employee increases. The decision to invest in human capital depends on the expected net return. The decision of economic rational individuals to continue schooling depends on the consideration between the expected wage increase (as a result of a higher level of education) and the costs of schooling (De Grip, 1987).

The availability of data concerning personal earnings (labour) together with information of other individual characteristics have resulted in an abundance of empirical studies that attempted to test alternative hypotheses regarding the determinants of personal earnings. In the literature this kind of research is better know under the name *earnings functions* (Psacharopoulos, 1987). The independent variables that have been used in empirical studies are extensive. Table 1 shows the most commonly used variables classified into two groups: personal- and other variables. Another distinction is between individual-dependent and individual-independent variables.

The majority of the *earnings functions* use labour income as dependent variable. Labour income comprises the greater part of total income. That's why can be assumed that all aspects that explain labour income also explain the greater part of total income. Often the logarithm of labour income is preferred as dependent variable above the labour income in absolute terms. This facilitates the interpretation of the effects of the individual variables (in terms of percentage increase of earnings). Besides, also the human capital school mentions theoretical reasons for the use of the logarithmic scale (see Mincer, 1974).

Table 1. Most commonly used variables in *earnings functions*

Personal characteristics		
Individual independent:	Gender	
	Age	
	Ethnicity	
	Intelligence	
	Family-background (social class)	
	Motivation	
Individual-dependent:	Profession	
	Marital status	
	Number of children	
	Working experience	
	Human capital:	Number of years schooling,
		Quality of education
		Experience and *on-the-job*-training
		Return of education
		Migration
Environmental- and institutional aspects		
Geographical location		
Economic sector		
Organisation-level		
Monopoly, monopsony		
Discrimination		

Source: Psacharopoulos (1987).

2.2 Wage Equation

The standard human capital *earnings function* as developed by Mincer (1974) reads:

$$\ln Y = \beta_0 + \beta_1 s + \beta_2 t + \beta_3 t^2 ,$$

where Y is the hourly wage, s the years of schooling and t years of working experience. The education coefficient β_1 gives an estimation of the return on schooling. The concave shape of the observed income-course is displayed by the quadratic terms for working-experience, t and t^2 if the expected signs of the coefficients β_2 and β_3 are, respectively, positive and negative. This equation is often used in research efforts as a standard equation to examine the impact of other factors, as it will in this chapter. By using the data from the project "Social Stratification in Eastern Europe" most of the variables mentioned in Table 1 could be used. Besides, a number of job-specific variables has been included like the number of subordinates, sector, type of organisation, and membership of the Communist Party. In the end this resulted in the following selection of variables: gender, number of years of education, marital status, propensity to migration, number of children, social status parents, type of organisation, sector, number of job changes, number of subordinates, membership Communist Party, tenure, working experience. Besides, the quadratic tenure-term and the quadratic working-experience term are included as well. Also the interaction-term of both is included. Before the estimation results of this equation will be presented, in the next section the expected impacts of the above-mentioned variables will be discussed on the basis of theoretical insights.

Gender

The general opinion is that men earn higher wages. The thought behind this view is that, as a result of pregnancy- and maternity leave, house-keeping activities *etc.*, women are for a shorter period available on the labour market (Mincer and Polachek, 1974). Besides, in Hungary and Poland, the retirement age for women is lower than for men, which strengthens this effect. This means that employers have fewer incentives to invest in women, but also women are less prepared to invest in themselves. Probably also discrimination plays an important role in the realisation of the wage differences between men and women. Discrimination theories try to give explanations for the fact that – despite equal productivity – men earn higher wages than women. However, it is difficult to ascertain discrimination (Schippers, 1987). Nevertheless, we expect that the income profiles of Hungarian and Polish women will be less steep than the income profiles of Hungarian and Polish men. Since the position of Hungarian women on the labour market is somewhat stronger (lower unemployment) than the Polish women (Dorenbos, 1999), we expect that for Hungarian women the wage differences with their male counterpart will be lower.

Marital status and number of children

Employers see being part of a family as an indicator for stability and reliability (Nickell, 1979). This could mean that married men and women have a stronger position on the labour market compared to singles. Indeed, there is empirical evidence that married men have a stronger position on the labour market in the sense that they earn higher wages than single men. A possible explanation is that married men have an extra incentive to earn (the greater part of) the family income and, consequently, are more prepared to invest in themselves. The fact that singles are more to be found in so-called secondary jobs[1], where the wages are generally lower than for jobs in the primary sector, strengthens the expectation that married men earn higher wages than singles. However, empirical results show that married women earn lower wages than single women. This is mainly because married women take for the greater part the responsibility to take care of the house keeping activities and raising the children. This could mean that their effort on the labour market is less (Van der Meer, 1993). Married women are over-represented in the secondary segment of the labour market (Schippers, 1987), which points to lower wages.

As for the number of children, the same train of thought can be followed. After all, it is still often the case that in a family with children women are not working or working part-time. In case the women are working full-time, they often earn a lower wage. Besides, they also bear the greater responsibility regarding bringing up the children (Van der Meer, 1993). This means that men have to take care for the greater part of the income which is an extra incentive to invest in themselves. The expectation is that men (with children) will earn more than men without children, whereas women with children are expected to earn less than women without children. With respect to the more specific situation in Hungary and Poland we expect that for Polish married women (with children) the situation will be less rosy because of their relatively weak position on the labour market.[2]

Social class

In the literature also the social class of the parents is to be considered as an important factor on the wage level of the child (Brown, 1977). The higher the social class the parents are in[3] the higher the educational level of the children. The explanation of this is that, among other things, parents from the higher social classes possess over more financial resources to let their children be educated in better schools. Also in Hungary and Poland the social status determines to a high extent the educational careers of their children (Ganzeboom, 1993). However, probably this will be to a lesser

[1] Unmarried men only have to take care of themselves and, consequently, do need less means. Married men share a large part of their means with their partner (and children). Therefore, it is expected that the effort of married men will be higher than of unmarried men. Married men will, *ceteris paribus*, end up in higher paid jobs than unmarried men (Van der Meer, 1993).

[2] In Hungary there is no secondary labour market as there is in, *e.g.* the United States. In Hungary one speaks of a marginal labour market which can to some extent be compared with the secondary labour market (Mihok, 1992).

[3] It is assumed that parents who have studied for a longer period of time, have better job positions and, consequently, earn higher wages. In this chapter this means that these parents belong to the higher social classes.

extent compared to the situation in Western countries since the costs of following education are less high.[4] It also appears that parents from higher social classes keep a closer eye on the progression of the study of their children. In addition, they have certain social contacts that may help the career of their children. On the basis of this, the expectation is that also in Hungary and Poland the children of parents from the higher social classes earn higher wages. The differences will be less big in comparison to the Western countries since the costs related to following education are not so high.

Years of schooling

In the human-capital approach, an employee with a higher level of education has a higher (marginal) productivity in contrast to an employee with a lower level of education. This means that the higher educated is able to earn a higher wage. By investing in education, employees can increase their wage level. Indeed, empirical research shows that the number of years of schooling has a positive impact on the productivity, and consequently on the wage level. The impact of the number of years of schooling will be probably less strong in Hungary and Poland since the education followed before the start of the transformation process has lost at least part of their value because of technological and organisational changes. Besides, the educational system was considered to be the most powerful mechanism to decrease the inequality. The idea was that by making the accessibility for all social classes equal, also the distribution of professions and income could be influenced (Peschar, 1992). However, the modernisation process demands a flexible and highly educated workforce, that must be able to adjust to the new needs of the market. That is why Polish and Hungarian employers will reward specific knowledge and skills by paying a higher wage. In the early years of the transformation, the educational system has not yet developed towards an institution that takes the newly demanded knowledge and skills into account. Besides, in our analyses only those persons will be analysed who were already on the labour market in 1988. Based on the foregoing, the expectation is that wages will be higher with the number of years of schooling, but the returns of schooling will be lower than compared to the returns in Western countries.

4 As mentioned before, the educational system during the communist era was directed towards a decrease in inequality. By making education equally accessible for all social classes, this would also influence the distribution of jobs and wages.

Previous working experience and experience in current job

Research for a number of Western countries showed that both tenure and total working experience have a positive impact on the individual wage (Hartog *et al.*, 1994). The expectation is that this also holds for Hungarian and Polish workers, but to a lesser extent. Although those employees who have many years of working-experience possess over much (obsolete) human capital, the rapid developing new labour market demands other types of knowledge and skills. The modernisation of the production structure involves the need of extra training to deal with the changing job-structure. In case we assume that in the current job extra attention has been paid to firm-specific training (on-the-job training) – to deal with the modernisation of the production structure – the experience in the current job will have a bigger impact on the individual wage than experience obtained in the previous job.

Number of job changes

In the wage-equation also the number of job changes between 1988 and 1992 is included. It concerns job changes without an intervening period of unemployment. Also promotions or transfers are considered as job changes, as well as a job change within a firm. It was not possible to distinguish between a real job change and a promotion or transfer. We expect that those who have made a job change (or more) between 1988 and 1992 earn higher wages compared to those who did not. Hungarian and Polish job changers may have the disposal of more valuable human capital and, thus, earn higher wages because of their higher marginal productivity. However, empirical research for the Netherlands and Sweden shows that job changes do not have a significant impact on the wages (Van Dijk and Folmer, 1992; Björklund and Holmlund, 1989).

Migration

The human capital theory can also be applied to the decision to migrate or not. Here, the decision to migrate is seen as decision to invest where the returns of migration (for example a higher wage) will be compared with the costs associated to migration. In the event the returns are expected to be higher, the decision to migrate will possibly be made. On the basis of this we expect that workers who have been emigrated in the past will have higher wages compared to the workers who did not move in the past. Empirical evidence shows a positive relation between migration and the post-move wage (Van Dijk and Folmer, 1992; Holmlund, 1984). It must be mentioned that nowadays the geographical mobility of the Hungarian and Polish people is very limited (even more limited than during the communist era) due to the situation on the housing market and the increasing costs of public transport (ILO, 1994; Ruttkay, 1995). This would mean that those who migrated, despite the impediments mentioned, would probably earn (much) higher wages. In other words, we expect that the individuals who have moved earn higher individual wages compared to those who have not moved.

Membership Communist party

The early phase of the transformation process was characterised by mass privatisation. Often it took the form of spontaneous privatisation that means that state enterprises can be transformed – on their own initiative – into a partnership, after which the shares of the enterprise can be sold. However, the sensitivity of practising fraud in this type of privatisation is high and led to a situation in which the old management (the communists) took the opportunity to buy the ownership rights for less than the market price. Since the enterprises obtained – in the course of the years – a certain degree of autonomy – the governments were less able to lead the privatisation in an effective and efficient way (Laky, 1994; Hoen, 1995). This means that the membership of the Communist Party (CP) was of importance before the transformation process started, in particular when a high office was hold. Research showed that (old)-members of the Hungarian Communist Party were under-represented in the group of persons who became unemployed in the early phase of the transformation process. There were no significant results found for (old)-members of the Polish Communist Party (Dorenbos, 1995). A possible explanation is that the Polish regime was more strict than the Hungarian regime, which led to a situation where the (old)-members of the CP in Hungary have a relatively better position on the labour market than their Polish counterparts. Based on this, we expect that (old-)members of the Hungarian CP hold higher offices which means that they earn higher wages compared to non-members of the Hungarian CP. For the Polish situation we do not expect significant differences.

Organisation

In the wage equation also a variable is included distinguishing between the state sector and private sector. The size of the private sector increased sharply in Hungary and Poland. Poland already had an extensive private sector before the transition, although almost all private initiative took place in the agricultural sector. In Hungary the private sector was also relatively large (as compared with other Central and Eastern European countries) but here it concerned mainly the small self-employed (Laky, 1994). After 1989, employment in the state sector declined rapidly, whereas employment in the private sector grew. The growth of the private sector was not enough to absorb all the unemployed people coming from the state sector.

The general situation is that in Western-European countries state employees earn lower wages than private employees. State employees working in lower-educated jobs earn more than their private counterparts but the state employees in the higher-educated jobs earn less than in the private sector. Since the private sector is relatively young in Hungary and Poland we expect to detect only some small differences in wage level. Besides, the share of private employees who are employed in the Polish agricultural sector is still very high (Frenkel, 1994), which has a onerous impact on the individual wage in the private sector. However, in case a connection is laid between profitability of firms and the wage level it could be expected that young private firms make high profits (particularly during the first phase of the transformation process) and, consequently, pay higher wages. Therefore, the expectation is that employees employed in the private sector earn a higher income than state employees.

Sector

Wage differences between sectors can be explained by, on the one hand, differences in job specific characteristics and, on the other hand, differences in institutional barriers between sectors. Possible institutional barriers can be, for example, unions and legislation. The wage-negotiating process between employers and employees will be affected by the way unions are cooperating and organised. Well-organised unions are to be expected to obtain higher wages because of the so-called *insider-effect*.[5] Also the *efficiency-wage* theory gives an explanation regarding the existence of wage differences between sectors. By paying higher wages the employers try to increase the working moral and, thus, their productivity. Besides, they expect that by doing this the number of personal mutations and the costs of hiring new employees will decline. Probably, the employers will increase their effort because of the higher wages (Summers, 1990). It is to be expected that also for Hungary and Poland the wages between sectors will differ. As for the 10 distinguished sectors in Hungary and Poland, the expectation is that the fastest growing sector (the financial sector) will pay the highest wages. Also the impact of foreign investments could have a

[5] In the extreme case the wage negotiating process takes place only between the employees (insiders) and the employers, "insiders" will negotiate in such a way that their own position will not be endangered. This means that the position of the outsiders (the unemployed) will not or hardly be taken into account. This may lead to a situation which generates sustainable unemployment (Summers and Blanchard, 1990).

positive impact on the wage level. The knowledge-intensive financial services are a sector – both in Hungary and Poland – where modernisation is taking place rapidly. In the first year of the transformation process, the service sector attracted 40% of the investments, particularly the banking- and insurance companies as well as the trade sector. These sectors are searching for high-educated professionals who can easily respond to new technologies and skills. Consequently, the wages that are being paid are high.

Because of the relatively high share of Polish private farmers in the total private sector, the wages in the Polish agricultural sector are probably less low compared to the Polish service sector than in the case of Hungary. Foreign investors invest mainly in the industrial sector. In 1994, 55% of all investments ended up in the industrial sector (Pronk, 1994). The potentially big market and the lower wages – as compared to the wages in Western Europe – made in particular the car industry a popular investment destination. Since employees who were working in the heavy industry – already during the communist era – received higher than average wages[6], the expectation is that this situation will be continued.

Supervision

As for the variable 'supervision' the expectation is that individuals who have supervision over a number of subordinates will earn a higher wage. After all, having a number of subordinates means having a certain degree of responsibility that is reflected in their wage level.

Besides the discussed variables, it would also be interesting to look at variables like unemployment duration. Unemployment duration has not only a negative impact on the search for another job[7], it is also likely that having a certain unemployment duration lowers the offered wage. Employers see unemployment as a negative indicator for labour productivity, and, consequently, will offer a lower wage. Besides, being unemployed for a while means also having a great deal of leeway to make up. As noticed in the introduction, most Polish and Hungarian (private) employers prefer to hire employees directly coming from the state sector (thus without having an unemployment history), as well as starters on the labour market (Boeri, 1994a, 1994b; Jackman, 1994). However, the number of individuals who have been unemployed between 1988 and 1992 but at January 1992 were employed again is very low in our database. Therefore, we can not examine whether our expectations were correct or not.

[6] In particular the mining sector in Hungary pays above-average wages, partly as compensation for the bad working-conditions (KSH, 1994).

[7] The long-term unemployed lack recent working-experience. The unemployed are probably also stigmatised by employers.

3. DATA AND RESULTS

We have used the data from the project "Social Stratification in Eastern Europe after 1989".[8] Sample surveys have been carried out in 1993 and 1994 in six countries: Bulgaria, the Czech Republic, Poland, Russia, Slovakia, and Hungary. For every country *national probability samples* of approximately 5000 adults have been interviewed. Only one questionnaire was used for all countries. By means of retrospective questions, information was gathered regarding labour market transitions between 1988 and 1993.

The sample size of the total Hungarian survey consisted of 4,977 respondents. These respondents consist of 2,657 women (53.4%) and 2.320 (46.6%) men. Only individuals who were born before 1976 were interviewed. In behalf of Poland, multistage random samples were taken from the National Register of Polish citizens (PESEL). The sample frame covers the whole population of Poland. The sample size for Poland consisted of 3,520 respondents, of whom 1,840 were women (52.3%) and 1,680 men (47.7%). The Polish survey only included people who were between 20 and 69 years old at the time of interview.

To examine the impact of the number of job changes on the individual wage we designed a sub-sample. This sub-sample consists of the number of respondents who were in January 1988 employed or unemployed and who were employed in January 1992. The observations that were incomplete, for example with regard to the variables used in the analyses, as well as the self-employed and part-timers, were excluded. This resulted in a research-population of 1,878 Hungarians and 1,072 Poles.[9]

3.1 Results

The dependent variable in the wage equation is the natural logarithm of the net monthly wage in dollars the respondents earn when being employed (in their most important job). The independent variables used have been discussed in the previous section. Table 2 shows the OLS results for the whole population in both countries. In case there are significant differences between the results for men and women these will be discussed separately (see Appendix B and C). The value of the adjusted R^2 is between 0.3 en 0.4, which is reasonable for this kind of models.

The results for the variables sex and years of schooling are in accordance to the theoretical expectations. Women and the lower educated earn a significantly lower wage as compared to what they earn in Western countries. Polish women earn on average almost 12% less than Polish men.

8 For more information regarding this project, see Treiman (1994).

9 For an overview of the sample characteristics, see Appendix A.

Table 2. The estimation results regarding the impact of individual characteristics on the individual wage Hungary and Poland (* significant on a 10%-level.)

	Poland		Hungary	
	coefficient	*t*-value	coefficient	*t*-value
Constant	2.0937	58.325*	2.1713	102.810*
Female	-.1152	-10.042*	-.0927	-13.087*
Married	.0194	1.369	-.0105	-1.180
Number of children:				
No children	-	-	-	-
1-2 children	.0344	2.522*	.0083	1.037
More than 2 children	.0153	.873	.0098	.736
Education parents:				
Mother studied ≤ 8 years	-.0255	-1.786*	-.0083	-.863
Father studied ≤ 8 years	-.0184	-1.508	-.0185	-2.490*
Years of education:				
≤ 8 years	-	-	-	-
9-11 years	.0604	3.937*	.0264	2.794*
12-14 years	.1171	6.794*	.0903	8.898*
≥ 15 years	.2206	10.735*	.1946	16.587*
Job changes between 1988 and 1992	.0182	1.055	.0216	1.961*
Experience in current job (A)	.0046	1.812*	.0061	3.426*
$(\text{Experience in current job})^2$	-.0305	-.504	-.0764	-1.690*
Previous working-experience (B)	.0015	.550	.0033	2.521*
$(\text{Previous working-experience})^2$	.0398	.521	-.0396	-1.451
A×B	-.0210	-.194	-.0369	-.604
Migration	.0053	.357	.0155	2.165*
(Old-)member CP	-.0125	-.862	.0032	.323
State sector	-.0419	-2.438*	-.0138	-1.304
Sector:				
Agriculture, Fishery	-.0574	-3.208*	-.0469	-4.334*
Industry	-	-	-	-
Construction	-.0415	-2.055*	-.0107	-.747
Public utility services	.0675	2.570*	.0208	.921
Transport, Communication	.0008	.962	.0262	2.090*
Wholesale- and retail trade, Restaurants	-.0680	-3.129*	.0081	.683
Education, Culture, Social services, Health care	-.0813	-4.973*	-.0258	-2.471*
Financial services	.0727	2.083*	.1065	3.874*
Other services	-.0626	-2.483*	-.0095	-.671
Public administration, Social security *etc.*	.0225	1.048	.0310	2.101*
Supervision:				
No	-	-	-	-
1-9 persons	.0648	4.193*	.0746	6.091*
More than 10 persons	.1320	6.676*	.1139	9.087*
Standard error of regression		.1595		.1371
Adjusted R^2		.3695		.3950
Number of observations	1072		1878	

As we expected, for Hungarian women this is a little less worse: Hungarian women earn 9% less than Hungarian men. In contrast to the situation in Hungary, in Poland the return on additional schooling increases after primary school. The following return of additional schooling shows a more or less similar pattern. The results for women and men separately (Appendixes B and C) show remarkable results in the sense that the return of schooling for women is higher than for men. In a similar research for the former Soviet Union, Katz (1995) also found higher returns for women. Probably the difference in wage between lower educated men and lower educated women is higher, which causes the return on additional schooling to be higher for women. However, also the difference between average-educated women and higher educated women is larger compared to men.

Marital status does not have a significant impact on the individual wage level. In case of Poland, married people earn a higher wage but the difference with unmarried people is not significant. As for the number of children in the household, Polish employees with 1 or 2 children have a higher wage of more than 4% than employees without children. This is in accordance to our theoretical expectations. In case we look at the results for men and women separately, Polish men with 1 or 2 children have a higher wage of more than 8% compared to Polish men without children. Polish men with more than 2 children earn 6% more than men without children. Polish women with children earn less than Polish women without children, but this difference is not significant. In Hungary, for all groups no significant differences were found. On the basis of these results, it can be concluded carefully that – for Hungarian employees – being a member of a family is not seen as an indicator for reliability and stability, which is expressed in the result that married Hungarians with children do not earn a significantly higher wage than Hungarians without children.

The number of years of education of the parents (social status) of the respondents also appeared to be of influence on the individual wage level. It is remarkable that Polish employees, of whom the mother has studied for a less long time, earn a significantly higher wage (more than 20%), whereas for Hungarian employees the lower number of years of education of the father has a significantly negative impact on the individual wage (almost 2%). The results for men and women separately show that in Poland in particular the lower status of the father has a negative impact on the individual wage of the male child, whereas in Hungary the lower social status of the father negatively affects the individual wage of the female child.

(Old-)members of the Communist Party earn in Poland less than non-members. In Hungary the opposite holds, although for both countries the results are not significant. However, the impact of the (old-)membership on the individual wage is in Hungary a positive one for men (a higher wage of around 2%). For Hungarian women, the opposite holds, they earn significantly less. A possible explanation is that in particular male communists held high offices during the communist regime. In contrast to female (old)-party members, they got – as a result of the process of spontaneous privatisation – the opportunity to obtain the property rights for less than the market price. In Poland both men and women (old-members of the CP) earn less, but this result is not significant.

Hungarian employees who have been migrated in the past earn a significantly higher wage. Although we do not know whether these employees migrated because of a new job, these results are in accordance to our theoretical expectations. However, when the model is estimated separately for men and women, the *t*-values for migration are slightly below the level of 10%-significance (see Appendixes B and C). Also the expectation that employees who changed jobs between 1988 and 1992 will earn a higher wage is confirmed by the results, although only in the case for Hungary. Also here the results are just below conventional significance levels when the model is estimated for women and men separately.

The coefficients of the variables tenure and previous experience as well as the interaction-variables show in most cases the expected directions. Nevertheless, income increases just slightly for each year of additional working-experience. As expected, the results show that experience in the current job is of more importance for the individual wage than the experience in the previous job. This may point to the fact that recent firm-specific training is more valued since it will lead to a better adjustment process to the modernised production and organisation structure. In Hungary, the returns of working-experience are higher than in Poland. The coefficients with regard to tenure and previous working experience as well as the interaction variable show the expected signs for Polish women and Hungarian women and men: these variables have a positive impact on the individual wage. For Polish men, the signs of the coefficients of these variables are not in accordance to the expectations, but the results are not significant.

Workers employed in the state sector earn a lower wage than workers employed in the private sector. In Poland the wages in the state sector are on a 4%-lower level than the wages in the private sector. In Hungary, employees in the state sector do not earn significantly less than employees working in the private sector. The results for men and women separately show that the wages are in all cases lower in the state sector. However, this result is only significant for Polish men. Polish private employees earn a 7% higher wage than Polish men working in the state sector

The results regarding the variable 'supervision' are in accordance to the theoretical expectations. Employees who have 1-10 subordinates earn a wage that is around 7% higher than employees without subordinates. In the event the number of subordinates is higher than 10, Polish employees earn a wage that is 14% higher than employees without subordinates. The separate results for men and women show almost the same picture. Female and male employees with subordinates earn a significantly higher wages than without subordinates. It is again striking that Hungarian women are in a better position than Polish women. In the event female Hungarian employees have more than subordinates they earn – compared to the reference group – an equally higher wage as their male counterparts.

The results also show that the sector in which one is employed is of big relevance for the wage level. In Poland it appears that employees employed in the public utilities services or in the financial services earn a significantly higher wage (about 7%) than employees employed in the industry. In particular in the social services, health care, and education sector, employees earn significantly less than in the industry sector. Also in the agricultural sector, construction, wholesale- and retail trade, and restaurants employees earn a significantly lower wage. These results are in accordance to the expectation that in industry and in the financial services the wages are relatively higher. This can partly be explained by the very fast developments in these sectors, as well as the impact of the foreign direct investments.

In Hungary only in the financial services and the transport and communication sector employees earn significantly higher wages in comparison to the industry sector. Employees working in the financial services earn a 11% higher wage than the reference sector (industry). The sectors agriculture, social services and health are also in Hungary the sectors where the wages are significantly lower than in the industry sector. In contrast to the situation in Poland, the sector consisting of the wholesale, retail trade and restaurants do relatively well.

The results for men and women separately show that the results regarding Polish men agree with the results for the whole Polish population. The only remarkable exception regards the result that male employees working in the financial services earn less – although not significantly – than the male Polish employees of the industry sector. Polish women working in the financial services earn almost 11% higher wages than women working in the industry. Polish women working in the industry earn significantly higher wages than Polish women working in the sectors education, social services, health care, wholesale and retail trade.

As for the situation in the financial services in Hungary, Hungarian men employed in this sector earn significantly higher wages (27%!) than men working in the industry, whereas for Hungarian women the wage difference is only 4%. Finally, Hungarian women employed in agriculture earn a significantly lower wage than women employed in the industry sector (3%).

Only in public administration and social security women earn a significantly higher wage (6%) than women who are employed in the industry.

4. CONCLUSIONS

We examined to what extent individual characteristics influence the individual wage of Hungarian and Polish employees in the initial stage of the transformation process. For that purpose a wage-equation has been estimated on the basis of data derived from the project *Social Stratification in Eastern Europe*. The net monthly individual wage has been used as the dependent variable.

The results are for the greater part in accordance to our expectations. Women and the lower educated earn lower wages than men and the higher educated, which is also true for the Western European countries. Besides, as was suspected, in Hungary the income of women differs less compared to Hungarian men than in the case of Poland. Marital status did not have a significant impact on the individual wage, but also in similar research efforts marital status appears to be of no significant impact. It was expected that Polish men with children would earn significantly more than Polish men without children. However, for Hungary there were no significant differences found. Possibly, having a family is not valued in Hungary as an indicator for stability and reliability.

Hungarian employees who have been moved appeared to earn significantly higher wages than Hungarian who did not move. This result was in line to our expectations. Despite the bad housing situation and the rising costs of public transportation, these people were not discouraged to move. Probably because they had a higher wage in prospect. Similar results for Western countries also show a positive relation between migration and income. However, for Poland no significant results were found. Perhaps the costs of migration are lower for Hungary (or the wage increases higher) which makes the decision to migrate easier. Also the results with regard to the social status of the parents are in accordance to the expectations. A lower social status of one of the parents (measured on the basis of their educational level) has a negative impact on the wage level of their child. It is striking that – for Poland – the lower social class of the mother has a significant negative impact on the individual wage, whereas for Hungary the social class of the father is of significant importance

Also in accordance to the expectations were the results concerning the type of organisation. Polish employees working in the state sector earn less than Polish employees working in the private sector. In Hungary the differences between the state sector and private sector were less striking. The (old)-membership of the Polish Communist Party did not have a significant impact on the individual wage. However, in Hungary this variable appeared to be significant for both men and women. Male employees who were (or still are) member of the Hungarian Communist Party earn a significantly higher wage than non-members. For Hungarian women the opposite holds. A possible explanation is that male employees who were member of the Hungarian CP held high offices whereas for Hungarian women this is true to a lesser extent.

Hungarian employees who made at least one job change between 1988 and 1992 have a significantly higher wage than Hungarian employees who were constantly working in the same job. In Poland no significant results were found for job mobility. Similar studies for the Netherlands and Sweden show no significant differences. The fact that in this study also promotions and transfers were taken into consideration can be mentioned as a possible explanation that in the case of Hungary significant differences were found.

The coefficients of the variables experience in the current job and previous experience as well as the quadratic terms and interaction term appear to show – in most cases – the expected sign. Experience in the current job had a bigger impact on the individual wage in comparison to the previous working experience. This supports the view that after the economic restructuring recent job experience is of greater value than skills obtained under the old economic system.

The variable 'supervision' appears – as expected – to have a strong positive impact on the wage level. For all distinguished groups, having subordinates led to a significantly higher wage – varying in the range of 4-14% – compared to employees who do not have subordinates. Also in Western countries, having subordinates has a positive impact on the individual wage level. As we expected, the individual wage differences between the industrial sectors were strong. The financial service sector appeared to be sector where the wages are the highest, although for Polish men the industry sector appeared to pay be the highest wages. The sectors agriculture, health care, education, social services, wholesale- and retail trade, and restaurants, appeared to be – in almost all cases – the sector where the individual wages are (significantly) lower than in the industry sector.

Our results indicate that even in this early phase of the transition process human capital variables are already important determinants of the differences in wages. It is remarkable that these results are more or less similar to results found in studies concerning Western countries. Since the data used refer to the situation at the beginning of 1992, it might even be true that already before the transformation the relation between wages and productivity was much more in line with the situation in western economies than should be expected under the communist regime.

APPENDIX A – SAMPLE CHARACTERISTICS

The sample characteristics for Poland and Hungary, 1992

	Poland		Hungary	
	Average	Std. Dev.	Average	Std. Dev.
Female	.454	.498	.455	.498
Married	.806	.396	.806	.396
Number of children:				
No children	.244	.430	.278	.448
1-2 children	.594	.491	.642	.480
More than 2 children	.161	.368	.080	.272
Education parents:				
Mother studied ≤ 8 years	.797	.403	.836	.370
Father studied ≤ 8 years	.679	.467	.613	.487
Years of education:				
≤ 8 years	.178	.383	.217	.412
9-11 years	.365	.482	.307	.461
12-14 years	.297	.457	.267	.442
≥ 15 years	.160	.367	.209	.407
Job changes between 1988 and 1992	.771	.421	.707	.455
Experience in current job (A)	10.849	9.030	9.816	8.652
(Experience in current job)^2	.199	.299	.171	.267
Previous experience (B)	10.817	7.996	13.220	9.297
(Previous experience)^2	.180	.243	.261	.362
A×B	.095	.102	.102	.105
Migration	.857	.350	.695	.460
(Old-)member CP	.162	.369	.133	.339
State sector	.882	.322	.874	.332
Sector:				
Agriculture, Fishery	.104	.305	.136	.343
Industry	.285	.452	.315	.465
Construction	.078	.269	.059	.253
Public utility services	.040	.196	.021	.144
Transport, Communication	.090	.287	.081	.274
Wholesale and retail trade, Restaurants *etc.*	.071	.257	.096	.295
Education, Culture, Social services, Health care	.192	.394	.160	.366
Financial services	.022	.148	.014	.119
Other services	.046	.209	.061	.240
Public administration, Social security *etc.*	.071	.257	.056	.230
Supervision:				
No	.786	.410	.842	.365
1-9 persons	.131	.337	.078	.268
> 10 persons	.083	.276	.080	.272
Number of observations	1072		1878	

APPENDIX B – ESTIMATION RESULTS FOR MEN

The estimation results concerning the impact of individual characteristics on the individual wage for men, Hungary and Poland, 1992 (* significant on a 10%-level)

	Poland		Hungary	
	Coefficient	*t*-value	Coefficient	*t*-value
Constant	2.1860	42.908*	2.1993	76.503*
Married	.0239	.948	-.0145	-.951
Number of children:				
No children	-	-	-	-
1-2 children	.0832	3.844*	.0144	1.177
More than 2 children	.0625	2.359*	.0212	1.143
Education parents:				
Mother studied ≤ 8 years	-.0316	-1.482	-.0088	-.667
Father studied ≤ 8 years	-.0342	-1.927*	-.0098	-.968
Years of education:				
≤ 8 years	-	-	-	-
9-11 years	.0425	1.921*	.0209	1.554
12-14 years	.0889	3.362*	.0655	4.167*
≥ 15 years	.1899	5.999*	.1658	9.298*
Job changes between 1988 and 1992	.0134	.540	.0214	1.384
Experience in current job (A)	-.0032	-.833	.0055	2.212*
$(\text{Experience in current job})^2$	.0924	1.020	-.0871	-1.413
Previous experience (B)	-.0031	-.728	.0013	.741
$(\text{Previous experience})^2$	.1067	.934	-.0070	-.176
A×B	.2532	1.541	-.0081	-.098
Migration	.0077	.359	.0150	1.515
(Old-)member CP	-.0036	-.186	.0228	1.795*
State sector	-.0697	-2.830*	-.0126	-.893
Sector:				
Agriculture, Fishery	-.0665	-2.834*	-.0614	-4.427*
Industry	-	-	-	-
Construction	-.0653	-2.568*	-.0207	-1.247
Public utility services	.0588	1.774*	.0136	.516
Transport, Communication	.0042	.176	.0177	1.145
Wholesale and retail trade, Restaurants *etc.*	-.0934	-1.871*	-.0106	-.525
Education, Culture, Social services, Health care	-.1020	-3.381*	-.0374	-2.063*
Financial services	-.0410	-.556	.2701	5.348*
Other services	-.0931	-2.578*	-.0166	-.888
Public administration, Social security *etc.*	.0261	.850	.0094	.478
Supervision:				
No	-	-	-	-
1-9 persons	.0842	3.825*	.0885	5.569*
More than 10 persons	.1402	5.436*	.1170	7.415*
Standard error of regression		.1711		.1387
Adjusted R^2		.3088		.3386
Number of observations	585		1024	

APPENDIX C – ESTIMATION RESULTS FOR WOMEN

The estimation results concerning the impact of individual characteristics on the individual wage for women, Hungary and Poland, 1992 (* significant on a 10%-level)

	Poland		Hungary	
	Coefficient	*t*-value	Coefficient	*t*-value
Constant	1.8496	35.735*	2.045	65.232*
Married	.0135	.826	-.0041	-.366
Number of children:				
No children	-	-	-	-
1-2 children	-.0161	-.932	.0045	.403
More than 2 children	-.0364	-1.524	.0017	.087
Education parents:				
Mother studied ≤ 8 years	-.0153	-.826	-.0097	-.684
Father studied ≤ 8 years	.0013	.082	-.0310	-2.836*
Number of years education:				
≤ 8 years	-	-	-	-
9-11 years	.0767	3.708*	.0197	1.428
12-14 years	.1443	6.696*	.1091	8.212*
≥ 15 years	.2539	9.769*	.2188	14.009*
Job changes between 1988 and 1992	.0087	.368	.0182	1.147
Experience in current job (A)	.0111	3.365*	.0067	2.574*
(Experience in current job)^2	-.1174	-1.496	-.0447	-.643
Experience in previous job (B)	.0079	2.100*	.0070	3.672*
(Experience in previous job)^2	-.0641	-.643	-.0971	-2.583*
A×B	-.3146	-2.277*	-.1227	-1.317
Migration	.0056	.279	.0160	1.555
(Old-)member CP	-.0208	-.965	-.0292	-1.724*
State sector	-.0047	-.192	-.0196	-1.204
Sector:				
Agriculture, Fishery	-.0399	-1.390	-.0302	-1.717*
Industry	-	-	-	-
Construction	.0276	.764	.0084	.262
Public utility services	.0595	1.305	.0299	.656
Transport, Communication	-.0108	-.363	.0332	1.504
Wholesale and retail trade, Restaurants *etc.*	-.0489	-2.051*	.0241	1.609
Education, Culture, Social services, Health care	-.0641	-3.361*	-.0179	-1.353
Financial services	.1076	2.897*	.0381	1.174
Other services	-.0493	-1.401	-.0093	-.429
Public administration, Social security *etc.*	.0167	.573	.0602	2.677*
Supervision:				
No	-	-	-	-
1-9 persons	.0441	2.059*	.0545	2.799*
More than 10 persons	.1150	3.368*	.1176	5.453*
Standard error of regression	.1401		.1332	
Adjusted R^2	.2867		.3647	
Number of observations	487		854	

REFERENCES

Björklund, A. and B. Holmlund (1989), "Job Mobility and Subsequent Wages in Sweden," in J. van Dijk *et al.* (eds.), *Migration and Labour Market Adjustments*, Dordrecht/Boston/London: Kluwer Academic Publishers, pp. 201-216.

Boeri, T. (1994a), "Labour Market Flows and the Persistence of Unemployment in Central and Eastern Europe," in *Unemployment in transition countries: Transient or persistent?*, OECD, Paris.

Boeri, T. (1994b), "Transitional Unemployment," *The Economics of Transition* 2(1), pp. 1-25.

Brown, H.P. (1977), *The Inequality of Pay*, Oxford: Oxford University Press.

Dijk, J. van and H. Folmer (1992), "The Impact of Personal and Regional Unemployment on Individual Wages in the Netherlands," in C.H.A. Verhaar and L.G. Jansman (eds.), *On the Mysteries of Unemployment*, Dordrecht/Boston/London: Kluwer Academic Publishers, pp. 110-128.

Dorenbos, R.J. (1995), "Labour Mobility in Hungary and Poland between 1988 and 1993," forthcoming in *Studia Demograficzne*.

Dorenbos, R.J. (1999), *Labour Market Adjustments in Hungary and Poland*, PhD Thesis.

Frenkel, I. (1994), "Economic Activity and Rural Unemployment in Poland," Paper presented at the CURE-congres, Ameland, 11-14 October 1994.

Ganzeboom, H.B.G. (1993), "The Intergenerational Transmission of Cultural and Material Status in Eastern Europe in a Period of Transition: A Research Proposal," Workshop Transformation Processes in Eastern Europe, Proceedings, 16-17 December.

Grip, A. de (1987), *Onderwijs en arbeidsmarkt: scholingsdiscrepanties*, Amsterdam: VU-uitgeverij.

Hartog, J., R. van Opstal and C.N. Teulings (1994), "Loonvorming in Nederland en de Verenigde Staten," *Economische Statistische Berichten* 79, pp. 528-533.

Hoen, H.W. (1995), "Tsjechië: het knapste jongetje van de klas?," *Tijdschrift voor Politieke Ekonomie* 18(2), pp. 60-77.

Holmlund, B. (1984), "Labor Mobility-Studies of Labor Turnover and Migration in the Swedish Labor Market," The Industrial Institute for Economic and Social Research, Stockholm.

Huber, P. (1999), "Labour Market Adjustments in Central and Eastern Europe: How Different," Paper presented at the 11th annual EALE conference, 23-26 September 1999, Regensburg, Germany (File P-6-1-1 on the CD ROM with conference papers).

ILO- International Labour Organisation (1994), *Labour Market Developments in Hungary*, Central and Eastern European Team (CEET), Budapest.

Jackman, R. (1994), "Economic Policy and Employment in the Transition Economies of Central and Eastern Europe: What have We learned?," *International Labour Review* 133(3), pp. 327-345.

Katz, K. (1995), "Were there any Returns to Education in the USSR? Controversies, Concepts and Estimates," Paper presented at the 7th Annual Conference of the European Association of Labour Economists, 7-10 September, Lyon.

KSH-Központi Statisztikai Hivatal (Central Statistical Office) (1994), *Labour Costs in Hungary*, Budapest.

Laky, T. (1994), "Characteristics of Privatisation in Hungary and Some of Its Social Effects, Szociológiai Szemle, *Review of Sociology of the Hungarian Sociological Association*.

Meer, P. van der (1993), *Verdringing op de Nederlandse arbeidsmarkt: sector- en sekseverschillen*, Interuniversity Center for Social Science Theory and Methodology (ICS), Groningen.

Mincer, J. (1974), *Schooling, Experience and Earnings*, New York: Wiley.

Mincer, J. and S. Polachek (1974), "Family Investments in Human Capital: Earnings of Women," *Journal of Political Economy* 82, pp. 76-108

Mihok, B. (1992), "Socio-Ethnic Stratification in Hungary," Workshop Transformation Processes in Eastern Europe, Proceedings, 3-4 December.

Nickell, S.J. (1979), "Estimating the Probability of Leaving Unemployment," *Econometrica* 47(5), pp. 1249-1264.

OECD (1994), *Employment Outlook*, Paris: OECD.

Peschar, J. (1992), "Change and Continuity in Central Europe: Education and Social Reproduction in Comparative Perspective," Workshop Transformation Processes in Eastern Europe, Proceedings, 3-4 December.

Plánovský, J. (1999), "Wage Developments in the Post-Transitional Slovak Economy," Paper presented at the 11th annual EALE conference, 23-26 September 1999, Regensburg, Germany (File P-18-2-3 on the CD ROM with conference papers).

Pronk, C.J.E. (1994), "Buitenlandse investeringen in Oost-Europa," *Economisch Statistische Berichten* 79, pp. 1024-1027.

Psacharopoulos, G. (1987), *Economics of Education, Research and Studies*, Pergamon Press.

Rutkowski, J. (1996), *Changes in the Wage Structure during Economic Transition in Central and Eastern Europe,* World Bank Technical Paper, No. 340, Social Challenges of Transition Series, The World Bank, Washington.

Ruttkay, E. (1995), "Borders and Border Regions (A Case Study: Hungary)," Paper presented at the 35th European Congress of the Regional Science Association, Odense (Denmark), 21-25 August 1995.

Schippers, J.J. (1987), *Beloningsverschillen tussen mannen en vrouwen; een economische analyse*, Groningen: Wolters-Noordhoff.

Summers, L.H. (1990), "Why is the Unemployment Rate so very high near Full Employment," in *Understanding Unemployment*, Cambridge/London: MIT Press, pp. 286-328.

Summers, L.H. and O.J. Blanchard (1990), "Hysteresis and the European Unemployment Problem," in *Understanding Unemployment*, Cambridge/London: MIT Press, pp. 227-285.

Treiman, D.J. (1994), *Social Stratification in Eastern Europe after 1989: General Population Survey*, Provisional Codebook (Revised).

Chapter 7

European Tax Coordination in the 21st Century: A Brief Inquiry

Sijbren Cnossen, Casper van Ewijk and Ruud de Mooij
Erasmus University Rotterdam and Maastricht University; CPB Netherlands Bureau for Economic Policy Analysis, Tinbergen Institute and University of Amsterdam; CPB Netherlands Bureau for Economic Policy Analysis and OCFEB

Key words: European Union, Tax competition, Tax coordination

Abstract: This chapter examines the choices between tax competition and tax harmonisation in the European Union. The choices are highlighted on the basis of the trade-offs that can be made between diversity and scale, and between incentives and cooperation. The authors conclude that greater diversity appears feasible with respect to VAT rates, but that greater coordination seems to be required for capital income taxes and the excises. Labour income taxes can be left to the discretion of the member states.

1. INTRODUCTION

Coordination problems arise at many points in the economy. Coordination problems at the micro-level – *i.e.* between individual agents – may have major effects at the aggregate level. Keynes convincingly demonstrated this in his *General Theory* (Keynes, 1936), when he laid down the basis of macroeconomics. Coordination problems are the *raison d'être* of modern macroeconomics. This has been developed further in the New Keynesian theory, according to which economies of scale and "thick market" externalities are important causes of coordination failures (*cf.* Shleifer 1986). Coordination problems may also occur at the government level, *e.g.* between national authorities. We again have Keynes to thank for pointing this out, warning for the risk of beggar-thy-neighbour policies, when national authorities try to hive off their problems to other countries with potentially deleterious consequences for the international economy.

Coordination problems at lower decision levels are often used as an argument for control at a higher level. However, control has its price. Often, there is not enough information to act effectively, so that the optimum result remains beyond reach. Control also does not do justice to the diversity of preferences at the micro-level. Furthermore, control creates administrative cost (bureaucracy) and may result in political distortion (government failure).

In choosing the right level of decision-making, the principle of subsidiarity is an important guideline: economic decisions should always be taken at the lowest possible level. Only for compelling reasons can coordination be placed at a higher level. The advantages of coordination must be confronted with the cost of control. If the cost of control is higher, autonomy at the lower level must be respected. This principle applies both to the choice between coordination through hierarchy or market (Williamson, 1975), *i.e.* between price mechanism and bureaucracy, and to the choice between policy coordination and policy competition.

In this contribution we focus our attention on the latter choice. In particular, we concentrate on the question of tax coordination within the European Union (EU). Has undesirable tax competition occurred? To what extent is tax harmonisation desirable? Following a brief description of the two fundamental "trade-offs" in policy competition, namely that between incentives and cooperation, and that between diversity and scale (Section 2), attention is paid in turn to coordination problems in Europe with indirect taxation (Section 3) and direct taxation (Section 4).

2. TAX COMPETITION OR COORDINATION

There are two fundamental trade-offs that play a role in the debate on tax coordination. Firstly, that between diversity and scale; secondly, the trade-off between incentives through tax competition and the advantages of coordination.

2.1 Trade-off 1: Diversity versus Scale

Diversity

Subsidiarity means that member states should in principle be permitted to make their own choices when setting up a tax system and more generally when choosing the optimum mix of tax and the provision of public goods. Tax autonomy caters for the differences in preferences amongst member states. To what extent should income redistribution be pursued through the tax system? To what extent should tax instruments be used to correct distortions in the economy? Preferences in these areas reflect differences in economic and social structures, differences in views on the role of taxation, differences in the acceptability and the practicability of various taxes and, more fundamentally, differences in preferences regarding the level of the tax burden and the extent to which income should be redistributed through the budget.

Scale

Subsidiarity is, however, not synonymous with diversity. It implies, in fact, that tax coordination may be desirable, *e.g.* in the case of positive effects of scale. As an example, multinational companies at present have to cope with diverse rules for calculating taxable profits, which entails high compliance costs. Greater uniformity could reduce these costs.

2.2 Trade-off 2: Incentives versus Coordination

Incentives

Another advantage of tax autonomy is that it makes tax competition possible. This is attractive if it disciplines governments in performing their public tasks. After all, according to *public choice* theory, governments are not ideal representatives of the public interest but a collection of bureaucrats, politicians and pressure-group representatives who are influenced not only by the public interest but also by their own interests. Accountability is usually insufficient to discipline governments so that government failure occurs. Brennan and Buchanan (1980) suggest that centralised policy leads more rapidly to government failure than decentralised policy on account of the reduced *accountability*. Centralised policy offers a *Leviathan* government more space in which to pursue its own interests – instead of the voter's interests – which generally involves excessive government expenditure and a corresponding high tax burden. Tax competition can reduce this natural expansionist tendency because the threat of factor flight has a disciplinary effect on extravagant politicians. Tax competition is a complement as it were to the disciplinary influence of democratic control by the citizen.

Cooperation

Tax competition can also have a disruptive effect. Sinn (1997) argues that government must in principle act where markets fail. However, competition between policies may undermine such government action by the backdoor and consequently result in inefficient policy. When governments compete they fail to take account of the consequences of their policies on the welfare of other countries. This produces cross-border, external effects for policy, a kind of beggar-thy-neighbour situation that may potentially justify policy coordination.

External effects may result in the social functions of taxes being undermined. Regulatory levies on activities that pollute the environment lose their effectiveness when these activities can simply be transferred abroad. A similar problem arises with ordinary taxation. The tax yield may, for example, fall when mobile factors – such as capital or highly trained people – migrate to another member state. This puts pressure on the supply of public goods or the ability-to-pay principle. In addition, the "user pays" principle can be undone, *e.g.* when economic subjects can benefit from public goods provision in countries with high taxes but do not pay for them because they can shift their tax base to countries with low taxes. In either of these cases, governments can more effectively guarantee the social functions of their tax systems if these systems are coordinated. Coordination in fact reduces the welfare loss of levying taxes – the so-called marginal cost of public funds – for an individual country because tax avoidance between countries is reduced.

Large and small countries

According to theory, small countries benefit particularly from tax competition while large countries benefit from coordination (Bucovetski, 1991). In practice we see a small country like Ireland adopting relatively low rates and being consequently able to attract capital successfully. Model calculations by the International Monetary Fund in the early 1990s similarly indicate that small countries will not benefit from tax harmonisation within the EU, while the EU as a whole is proceeding with it on account of the favourable consequences for the large member states (Fuente and Gardner, 1990).

Besides, one must realise in the trade-off between incentives and coordination that capital is mobile not only within the borders of the EU but also beyond them. Most tax havens are consequently situated beyond the EU's boundaries, so that European coordination will have relatively little effect on the overall reallocation of profits. Switzerland, for example, is a favourite location outside the EU for savers who wish to conceal their assets for the tax authorities. In the absence of a world tax administration, European coordination must then be conceived of as a second-best solution for the external effects of tax competition.

3. INDIRECT TAXES

When considering the choice between tax competition and tax coordination, we draw a distinction between indirect taxes and direct taxes. We shall deal with indirect taxes first. These taxes can be divided into general taxes on goods and services, such as VAT, and selective taxes or excise duties on specific goods and services, such as alcohol, tobacco, energy and motor vehicles. VAT has an exclusively budgetary function. The aim of this tax is to generate income for the government as efficiently as possible by minimising the economic and operational costs of the tax per euro of revenue. Selective taxes, in addition, are aimed at incorporating the social or external cost associated with (excessive) consumption into the price (internalisation).

3.1 VAT

VAT has been largely harmonised within the EU. The agreed tax base and administrative procedures are laid down in the Sixth Directive, which has been incorporated into the national laws of all member states. Agreement has also been reached on a minimum standard rate of 15% and a minimum reduced rate of 5%. The so-called deferred payment system applies to intra-Community transactions, meaning that VAT is levied on imported goods not at the border but at the level of domestic purchaser. The border has been shifted, as it were, to the accounts of the taxpayers. We shall explain the background to harmonisation on the basis of the two trade-offs, between incentives and cooperation and between diversity and scale.

Diversity versus scale

The harmonisation of VAT results from the objections against the cumulative sales taxes that were levied in most member states at the time the European Economic Community was founded. A fundamental objection to these taxes was that they could be used for protectionist purposes, because the refund on export and compensating levy on import could not be precisely calculated. As a result, a country could, for example, levy more tax on imports than on similar home-produced articles, in order thereby to protect domestic output. On export, a country could refund a higher amount than corresponded to the taxes levied in the previous stages of production and distribution and so promote exports. These objections do not apply to VAT, because the refund on export corresponds to the tax shown on the sale invoices of suppliers and the tax credit mechanism for VAT means that imports are subject to the same tax as goods produced within the country.

An argument that could justify harmonisation of VAT rates (in the form of minimum rates) is cross-border shopping. Empirical studies concerning shopping behaviour in South Limburg, South Denmark and Northern Ireland, however, show that the extent of cross-border shopping reduces sharply with distance. It is true that its scope is not negligible within the border regions themselves, but it is small within the national context. In addition, we find that some 70% of cross-border shopping is attributable to excise duties. With some additional measures (taxation of specified consumer durables in the country of registration, tax levied on mail order firms and exempt entities on the basis of the destination principle) it seems unlikely that cross-border shopping will increase greatly if the differences in the VAT rates were to be increased – not even with the rise of the Internet. In brief, external effects are not a convincing argument for far-reaching restriction of freedom in national policy on VAT, as is currently the case.

Incentives versus cooperation

An objection to far-reaching harmonisation is that it may lead to locked-in tax systems. Individual countries have few incentives – or opportunities – to improve their tax system and to adjust it to changing circumstances. And for the EU legislative innovation is difficult, because this requires the consent of all member states. The Sixth Directive, which dates back to 1977, is therefore becoming outdated. One example are the VAT exemptions, which apply to certain services that were formerly government tasks but are now for the most part privatised. As a result of these exemptions, unfair competition may occur when taxed services, such as circus shows, have to compete with other – exempt – cultural performances. Exemptions may also result in cumulative features of the old sales tax system nonetheless slipping into VAT. After all, VAT on purchases from exempt entities cannot be passed on to taxpaying customers, such as companies that place their research with exempt hospitals or universities.

These problems arise especially for services in such areas as housing, culture, health, education, banking, insurance, and communication which are at present exempt but should ideally be included in the tax base. VAT in Canada and New Zealand, for example – countries that were able to learn from the EU's errors – have a much broader tax base. Typical in this connection is that Austria – which used to tax rents and health services – was forced to exempt these services on joining the EU. In addition, special schemes for agricultural firms and small traders are ripe for reconsideration.

These examples indicate that the present form of harmonisation in the EU (under the Sixth Directive) stands in the way of improvements in the system. More national autonomy would benefit diversity and so leave more room for improvement. Generally speaking, it would be advantageous if member states could improve their VAT more rapidly than the Sixth Directive at present permits.

3.2 Other Indirect Taxes

Harmonisation is certainly an obvious step for excise duties and some regulatory energy and environment levies where there is a clear international dimension.

The external cost of excessive consumption of alcohol and tobacco is generally higher than corresponds to the yields from duty. However, higher tax rates can be relatively easily evaded (by smuggling) because they are levied on products that match a high retail value with small volume. Harmonisation of excise duties is therefore of greater importance than harmonisation of VAT.

However, the diversity of interests prevents this for the time being. Viniculture and tobacco growing are undertaken chiefly in the southern member states where higher taxes do not appeal to producers (and consumers). Certain member states even charge no wine duty at all and tobacco duty is levied mainly on the basis of an *ad valorem* duty (low-priced inferior tobacco then means less tax). However, where duties are aimed at internalising the external cost of excessive consumption, specific tax rates adjusted for inflation are preferable to *ad valorem* tax rates.

Energy and environmental levies are aimed at making the polluter pay. In the case of cross-border pollution or relocation of production, levies at EU level should be coordinated with those in third countries. This applies especially to a world-wide public "bad", such as carbon emissions.

4. DIRECT TAXES

Whether policy coordination is necessary for direct taxes depends above all on the international mobility of the tax base. Wide differences exist on this point between taxes on labour and taxes on capital. Taxes on labour are not the subject of tax coordination within the EU, with the exception of an arrangement for cross-border workers. Tax autonomy for taxes on labour accords with the subsidiarity principle: because the mobility of labour is small, there are virtually no external effects.

The position is different with taxes on capital. Especially, the source-based corporation tax is important. This tax is imposed on business profits after deducting the cost of debt (interest). In addition to this tax at business level, capital income is also taxed at the personal level. Here the residence principle applies. Personal capital income is taxed in different ways in Europe. Certain countries have a (final) withholding tax on interest, while other countries tax interest received under their income tax. Scandinavian countries have a dual income tax under which capital income is taxed at a flat rate, separately from labour income. The new Dutch income tax taxes the income from specified assets at a flat rate applied to a presumptive yield.

4.1 Corporation Tax

Corporation tax is levied in the country where production takes place (source principle). The tax base can be reduced by diverting profits abroad through the manipulation of transfer prices or royalty payments. These forms of tax evasion become more widespread as enterprises become more internationally intertwined. Empirical research provides various indications as to the existence of this reallocation of profits. We find that firms in countries with high tax rates relatively frequently finance their investments through debt obtained from countries with low taxes. In addition, multinational companies with a subsidiary in a so-called *tax haven* pay less tax than those that do not have one. Furthermore, the gross yield from capital in countries with low taxes is significantly higher than in countries with high taxes, although economic theory suggests that capital mobility should result in equalisation of net yields.

Corporation tax can additionally be avoided by shifting real investment to other countries. Empirical research in the US indicates that the effective tax burden on corporate profits is certainly important to the international allocation of investments; a drop in the effective rate by one percentage point would result on average in an increase in inbound investment by some 1.5% (Hines, 1996).

Incentives versus cooperation

Because capital and profits are sensitive to tax differences, governments can make use of this by competing in attracting real investment and paper profits. Looking at the international trends in capital taxation, the indications certainly point towards tax competition. The statutory corporation tax rates have fallen in the past fifteen years and the spread amongst countries has also been reduced. The fall in the statutory rates was not, however, accompanied by lower effective tax rates on corporate profits on account of the broadening of the tax bases in many countries (Chennells and Griffith, 1997). A possible explanation of this is that physical capital is less sensitive to tax differences than paper profits are. Because physical capital reacts to effective tax burdens and accounting profits to the statutory tax rates, tax competition could well become more manifest in the latter.

Avoidance of corporation tax can be prevented by agreeing on (minimum) rates within the EU. Agreement on such rates is more necessary than agreement on the rules for determining profits. A minimum rate avoids the yield from mobile capital escaping the tax authority. However, rules for determining profits with regard to depreciation, stock valuation and similar matters, concern relatively immobile physical capital, such as buildings, plant and stocks. Unlike financial capital, physical capital is less easily moved as a result of differences in tax treatment. This makes it less necessary to impose restrictions on the tax autonomy of member states regarding this aspect of determining profits.

Scale versus diversity

Coordination of the tax base may well be desirable with an eye to the advantages of scale resulting from the compliance cost of corporation tax for international enterprises. A far-reaching solution to coordination of the tax base urged by the business world is the introduction of *unitary taxation* with *formulary apportionment*. Under unitary taxation, applied by many American states, the profits of an enterprise with EU-wide activities would be ascertained on the basis of uniform rules. The profits thus determined would be assigned to the member states where the enterprise pursues taxable activities. In the United States, such allocation is mainly made on the basis of the so-called *Massachusetts formula* where equal weights are attached to sales, payroll and capital in the various states. Each state can then make corrections to the allocated profits and apply its own rate. Of course, formulary apportionment means that the corporation tax becomes a tax on the factors that go into the formula.

A form of coordination that offers more opportunities for diversity is that where multinational enterprises are taxed according to the rules and the tax rates in the country where the head office of the enterprise is established. The tax yield is then distributed amongst the countries where the multinational is active according to a specified formula. Under this proposal, countries retain their freedom with regard to fixing their own tax base but recognise each other's systems for the taxation of multinationals. A disadvantage of this proposal is that the choice of head office may become sensitive to differences in the tax systems.

A third way of coordinating the corporation tax base is by agreeing on a minimum tax rate applied to a simplified, harmonised tax base. The ensuing amount forms a minimum tax payable, *i.e.* if the tax under the national system turns out lower, an enterprise will still have to pay this minimum. This system leaves more room for diversity and seems to be an acceptable way of achieving some corporate tax harmonisation in the EU.

4.2 Income Tax

Income from portfolio investments and savings is subject to tax on the basis of the residence principle. Because it is often difficult to obtain all the information on income earned on these financial investments when made abroad, taxes based on the residence principle are more easily evaded than source-based taxes. The widespread use of savings deposits in countries with banking secrecy, such as Luxembourg and Switzerland, supports this assertion. The more financial markets in Europe are integrated and the EMU gets completed, savings and investments will internationalise more and the information problem will become more pressing for the tax authorities.

Scale versus diversity

The mandatory provision by banks of information to the tax authorities is the most direct solution in coping with this information problem, although tax evasion outside the EU would continue to pose problems. Strict requirements are imposed on the information in this case because it must serve as the basis for imposing tax in the country where the individual saver resides. If this information exchange proves possible, it is an attractive option because it offers room for diversity; countries have the autonomy to tax the yield from debt as they wish. Because the mobility of citizens between countries is fairly small, external effects of this diversity will not be particularly great.

Cooperation versus incentives

Information exchange is politically a bone of contention, especially because certain countries have acquired an attractive position in competition with others. To limit this competition, the introduction of minimum withholding taxes on interest could offer an attractive alternative. However, there is a risk that this will come down to a tax on small savers because interest paid to non-residents is not subject to a withholding tax. This allows residents with high incomes to behave as non-residents so that the interest received by them will not be taxed, either.

4.3 Towards Fundamental Reform: CBIT and DIT

Solving the problem of information for income tax still leaves us some way from home. The problems are more deep-seated and often require a more fundamental change of system, where both corporate tax and tax on personal capital income are involved.

One of the essential problems is that arising through the unequal treatment of debt and equity. At present, income from debt is hardly taxed, if at all, because interest is deductible and the recipient (pension fund, non-resident) is generally not subject to tax. The large-scale substitution of equity by debt, also known as *thin capitalisation*, means that an appreciable loss of revenue occurs. Moreover, the distribution of the total burden is probably less progressive than would otherwise have been the case. Studies with regard to the United States and various Scandinavian countries show that little or no tax was imposed on capital income in the 1980s. The deductibility of interest, together with the substitution of equity by debt, makes the corporate tax akin to the proverbial sieve. Any kind of positive yield amounts either to tax on work performed in closely-held companies or proprietorships but taxed as profits, or tax on rents.

If the government really wishes to tax the returns on equity and debt, it should consider no longer permitting interest to be deducted or subjecting it to a withholding tax. By no longer permitting interest to be deducted from profits (as proposed under the *comprehensive business income tax* or CBIT devised by the American Treasury), interest is treated on the same footing as dividend which is also non-deductible. Tax on all modes of finance is then taxed at enterprise level. Under CBIT, interest and dividend are no longer taxed at the level of the recipient. In addition, exempt entities and non-residents are not entitled to a refund of the tax (implicitly) levied at business level.

The same result can be achieved by subjecting interest to a withholding tax at corporate level, which may be offset against income or corporation tax by the recipient. If the recipient pays no tax because he/she is a non-resident or an exempt entity, the tax withheld is not refunded. Under this approach, which is associated with the dual income tax (DIT) applied in the Scandinavian countries, interest and retained and distributed profits are also treated equally in principle. Profits are subject to corporate tax, interest is subject to a withholding tax. Basically, CBIT and DIT differ only with respect to the treatment of labour income. Under CBIT labour income is taxed at the same rate as capital income; under DIT labour income is taxed at a higher, progressive rate. The only other difference between CBIT and DIT is that a withholding tax can be more easily phased in and incorporated in existing tax treaties.

Tax treatment of dividend and interest under the CBIT or DIT implies a choice for the source principle. All returns to capital are taxed by the source state where the enterprise is located, irrespective of whether the returns are paid to residents or non-residents. In principle, the state of residence levies no further tax on the capital supplier. This means that no information on interest and/or dividend payments needs be exchanged either. To that extent, the source principle is appreciably simpler to apply than the residence principle. The source principle is also more effective because there is no longer any point in placing a *tax haven* between the company and the ultimate recipient.

The effective taxation of interest by eliminating the deduction under the CBIT or by introducing a withholding tax which is not refunded to non-residents under the DIT means an increase in capital tax burdens on business. This may result in enterprises shifting their taxable activities to countries where interest is deductible or is not subject to a withholding tax. In principle, therefore, the aim should be for the EU-wide introduction of CBIT or DIT. In addition, the tax should be coordinated with the United States and Japan. In any case, it should be possible to introduce a withholding tax up to the level of the transaction costs associated with shifting investment activities.

5. CONCLUSION

Coordination or competition? There is no clear answer to this question. The advantages and disadvantages of each type of tax must be determined separately. Figure 1 shows the present situation in the EU along an axis running from strong competition to strong harmonisation. We also see in what direction the system would have to develop to match the arguments in this chapter. The arrow shows the movement from the present position to the optimum position for each type of tax. In conclusion, we believe that the tax autonomy of member states should be respected where possible and coordination should therefore take place only where strictly necessary. Experience in federal states, such as the United States, Canada and Switzerland, shows that a large degree of tax diversity is still compatible with the existence of one internal market. The tax systems in the United States and Switzerland are patchworks of federal, regional and local levies, without this impeding the functioning of the domestic market. The Canadian tax system, on the other hand, is largely coordinated, although most provinces are economically more integrated with their American than with their Canadian neighbours. The challenge in Europe is therefore to aim to maintain as much tax diversity (subsidiarity) as is compatible with the functioning of the internal market (neutrality). This probably demands steps towards greater coordination in the area of excise duties and taxes on capital income. In exchange, greater diversity could be permitted in VAT.

	Tax competition	tax harmonisation
Indirect taxes		
VAT		←
Excise duties	→	
Environmental duties	→	
Direct taxes		
Labour income tax	X	
Corporate profits tax	→	
Investment income tax	→	

Figure 1. Desirability of greater or less tax coordination

REFERENCES

Brennan, G. and J. Buchanan (1980), *The Power to Tax: Analytical Foundations of a Fiscal Constitution*, Cambridge: Cambridge University Press.

Bucovetsky, S. (1991), "Asymmetric Tax Competition," *Journal of Urban Economics* 30, pp. 167-181.

Chennells, L. and R. Griffith (1997), *Taxing Profits in a Changing World*, Institute for Fiscal Studies, London.

Fuente, A. and E. Gardner (1990), "Corporate Income Tax Harmonization and Capital Allocation in the European Community," *IMF Working Paper* 90/103, Washington.

Hines. J.R. (1996), "Tax Policy and the Activities of Multinational Corporations," *NBER Working Paper* 5589, Cambridge.

Keynes, J.M. (1936), *The General Theory of Employment, Interest, and Money,* London: Macmillan.

Shleifer, A. (1986), "Implementation Cycles," *Journal of Political Economy* 94, pp. 1163-1190.

Sinn, H.-W. (1997), "The Selection Principle and Market Failure in Systems Competition," *Journal of Public Economics* 66, pp. 247-274.

Williamson, O. (1975), *Markets and Hierarchies*, New York: Free Press.

Chapter 8

The 'New' Versus The 'Old' Economy Debate

How Old Laws Rule New Paradoxes

Arjen van Witteloostuijn[1]
Department of Economics, University of Groningen

Key words: New economy, Employee empowerment, Scale economies

Abstract: This chapter critically discusses the recent New Economy debate by identifying five paradoxes. The key argument is that, contrary to New Economy beliefs, employee control may increase, scale economies may start dominating, transaction costs may be pushed up, competitive intensity may be hampered and business cycles may become increasingly volatile. So, this chapter evaluates the forces and counterforces that may operate in the New Economy of the next decade, indicating that the only economic phenomenon that is surely here to stay is uncertainty.

1. FROM ECONOMIC ANALYSIS TO POLICY ADVICE

Simon Kuipers has, for many decades, been very active as a policy advisor through his membership of the Social-Economic Council (Sociaal-Economische Raad: SER), the key advisory body of Dutch government in the area of social-economic affairs, and his involvement with the Teldersstichting (TS), the scientific office of the, in the Dutch setting, right-wing liberal political party (the VVD). Only recently, for example, he (together with Van Dalen, Groenveld and Koning, 2000) published the latter's in-depth report about macroeconomic growth, income distribution and economic regime. The content and quality of this report are typical for

[1] Part of this chapter's argument is based upon Brakman and Van Witteloostuijn (2001), Van Wegberg and Van Witteloostuijn (2001) and Van Witteloostuijn (2000). I gratefully acknowledge Geert Duysters (Technical University Eindhoven) for providing Figure 3.

Simon Kuipers's two-legged profile as economic analyst and policy advisor. Contentwise, this report nicely reflects Simon 'the economic analyst' Kuipers's preoccupation throughout his professional career with issues of macroeconomic growth and policy intervention. Qualitywise, in both his roles of SER member and TS contributor, Simon 'the policy advisor' Kuipers emerges as an (independent) open mind who clearly favours analytical rigour over ideological prejudice.

Simon Kuipers's preference for analytical rigour is clear from his life-long emphasis on the methodology of economic modelling and the theory of the microfoundation of macroeconomics. In his teaching in the early 1980s, he wholeheartedly advocated the work of such kindred spirits as Benassy (1982) and Malinvaud (1977, 1980). So, not very surprisingly, my PhD thesis (Van Witteloostuijn, 1990), under his guidance and Hans Maks's, too, was an attempt to offer a microfoundation of macroeconomic phenomena by modelling the underlying behaviour of key economic agents. In my case, this attempt (with a strikingly unmodest title!) watered down to an odd – and not so rigorous – potpourri of (dis)equilibrium theory, evolutionary economics, game theory, industrial organisation, labour economics, strategic management and welfare economics. After this larmoyant reconnaissance, my career derailed by accepting jobs at business schools. Only recently, I returned to the my early stronghold in the Faculty of Economics of the University of Groningen. So, after such a lengthy spell in the analytical desert of business schools, this essay cannot satisfy Simon Kuipers's high standard of analytical rigour. Rather, this is just another reconnaissance of issues that are currently hotly debated in the academic and policy world of macroeconomics: what is new about the New Economy, and what might be the consequences of the emergence of the New Economy in different corners of the economic domain? By applying well-established economic reasoning, this chapter's aim is to explore what might be happening in (the microfoundation of) modern (macro)economies. In so doing, a number of exemplary paradoxes are identified that offer demanding challenges in the policy arena.

2. THREE DIFFERENT REVOLUTIONS

The impressive period of sustainable economic growth in the US in the 1990s has induced an equally impressive stream of guru-type publications that announce the birth of the New Economy (see, *e.g.*, the *Wired* journal, www.wired.com). To emphasise the revolutionary nature of what is happening, the advocates of the New Industrial Revolution promote the New Economy by introducing a lengthy list of language novelties. Apart from the habit to use capitals, this is reflected in inventing new acronyms (*e.g.* B2B), in putting a new *e* in front of well-established words (*e.g.* *e*-banking) and in revealing a preference for the new @ symbol (*e.g.* @lli@ncies). As I want to be taken seriously by those prominent in New Economy circles, this chapter fits nicely in this New Language Tradition.

The key argument of New Economy preachers is that the modern information technologies (IT) radically alter the ways in which businesses are organised, products are developed and transactions are shaped. In the context of the current chapter, I cannot discuss all the details that are so inextricably bound up with this revolution. Rather, I wish to underline what I think is essential. Basically, this involves three different revolutions (Van Witteloostuijn, 2000). In a nutshell, this argument is summarised in Figure 1.

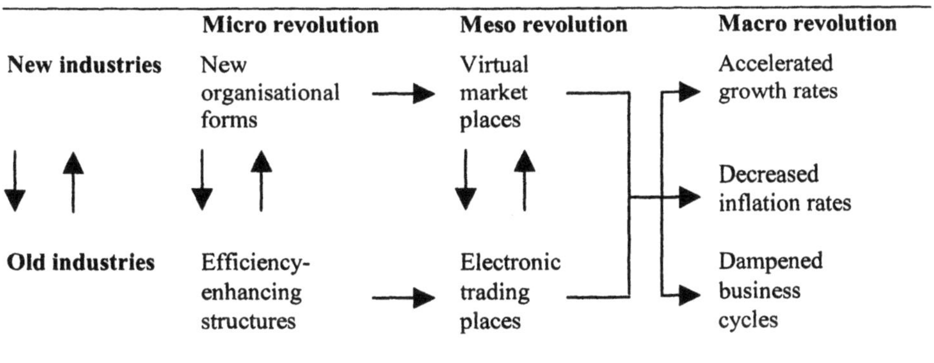

Figure 1. Three different *e*-revolutions

First, the IT revolution that attracts most attention in the popular (business) press, is related to the emergence of the many dotcom firms. This pertains to the rise (and fall?) of new industries, breeding new firms and offering new products, and their impact upon the behaviour and design of old industries. The figure heads of this micro revolution are associated with new organisational forms such as network and virtual organisations (*e.g.* Volberda, 1998), and new information products such as browsers and portals (*e.g.* Shapiro and Varian, 1999). On top of the birth of such new industries, the micro revolution is said to radically alter the way old industries are organised as modern IT offers ample opportunities to, so to say, re-animate the business process reengineering hype by introducing new efficiency-enhancing and IT-driven coordination, communication and design devices (*e.g,* Nouwens and Bouwman, 1995). Second, the meso IT revolution is argued to change the rules of the competitive game at the industry level. The key argument here is that advanced IT reduces the cost of economic transaction by providing virtual market places and electronic trading platforms in new and old industries. In such an on-line market environment, demand can match supply quickly and timely in an efficient and transparent way. The result is the entry of a large number of new 'cybermediaries' that facilitate this 'demand-matches-supply' process (*e.g.* Sarkar *et al.*, 2000). Third, the IT-driving increase of firm-level efficiency and industry-level effectiveness are the forces, according to New Macroeconomists, that underlie accelerated growth rates, decreased inflation rates and dampened (or even disappearing) business cycles. Therefore, the New *E*-conomy has brought macroeconomic Paradise to Earth (*e.g.* Cohen *et al.*, 2000). The reason for this is that IT is a break-through technology that not only produces an impressive productivity jump throughout the economy, so providing the fuel for sustainable macroeconomic prosperity (*e.g.* Gordon, 2000), but also fundamentally transforms the economic rules of production and transaction. Together, that is, the interacting micro and macro revolutions produce a really global macro revolution.

3. FIVE PARADOXES

Opposing forces

Clearly, the New Economy proponents expect much from the IT revolution(s): not only will e-organising within and between firms increase cost efficiency and reduce transaction cost, but also will e-trade reduce prices as a result of the increased intensity of competition that comes with the transparent e-market places. Ultimately, this implies that macroeconomic Nirvana will settle nicely on the globe called Earth, featuring sustainable inflation-poor and recession-proof growth. This would all be very welcome, of course. However, well-established economic reasoning must be applied in order to assess the plausibility of such beliefs. In this context, by way of illustration, I briefly develop an argument as to what (opposing) forces operate in the New Economy in five different economic domains (that move, step by step, from the micro-micro to the macro-macro level): (1) employee empowerment (micro-micro); (2) scale economies (micro-meso); (3) transaction costs (meso-meso); (4) competitive intensity (meso-macro); and (5) business cycles (macro-macro). This exercise produces five paradoxes that set an agenda for future empirical research, that offer a challenging stepping stone for further policy development, and that may well run opposite to the New Economy *communis opinio*. Clearly, the argument below can be anything but *staccato*, without any pretension of completeness. However, hopefully, this critical assessment of five New Economy debates underlines the importance of the Simon Kuipers-style preference for analytical rigour and open-mindedness.

Employee empowerment

From an intra-organisational perspective, New Economy advocates argue that the widespread introduction of IT within the organisational boundaries will shake up traditional processes and structures. Ignoring the technical ins and outs, the key story is that IT offers ample opportunities to empower employees (*cf.* Chapter 9 in Daft, 1998, and Chapter 15 in Robbins, 2001). As such, the message that the 'liberating' potential of new information technologies must be seized by adopting the human resource management (HRM) policy of empowerment is anything but new. After all, the intricate interaction of people empowerment with process reengineering was already central to many guru recipes in the late 1980s and early 1990s. However, New Economy believers emphasise that modern IT brings this 'old' potential to the full as Intranet devices relax many traditional restrictions to communication and decentralisation. After all, e-communication instruments decouple much organisational tasks from face-to-face work structures, whilst e-information devices are easily and readily accessible throughout the organisation. This implies that responsibilities can be decentralised to, so to say, the limit.

However, empowering people is one thing, but controlling employees is quite another matter. In day-to-day practice, many firms have experienced by now that modern IT software may operate as a shirking trigger. Employees can benefit from their employer's IT infrastructure to e-mail or webbrowse for private purposes. A recent German estimate is that the cost for industry of their employees' e-behaviour for private pleasure is approximately 115 billion Deutsche Mark annually. Additionally, the productivity of virtual work behaviour, at home or elsewhere, may well be harmed by the absence of face-to-face interaction and social control processes. For these and related reasons, many organisations decide to install extra control devices, such as e-mail check-ups, video camera circuits and supervisory tasks. So, this intrusion into the employees' privacy by introducing what are, essentially, old-fashioned bureaucracy-style control mechanisms produces powerful countervailing forces that run against the New Economy tendency toward increased people empowerment.

Scale economies

The growth of the New Economy stimulates a restructuring within and across industries. After all, incumbent companies may need to reassess their optimal activity scope in this New Economy, whereas new entrants may benefit from new opportunities in 'new' and 'old' industries. Basically, many organisations face a choice between, on the one hand, being a purely 'virtual' (so-called 'browse-and-click') company or purely 'physical' (so-called 'brick-and-mortar') firm and, on the other hand, becoming a combined virtual-physical (so-called 'click-and-mortar') organisation. All this produces much industry-level dynamics. Established companies re-arrange their product portfolio by adopting acquiring, allying, debundling, merging and outsourcing strategies. Additionally, new entry is all over the place, foreign companies entering through virtual portals and newly created e-companies penetrating the cyberspace. The question is what market structures will emerge after this e-dust has settled down into new equilibria.

Here, two opposing forces are at work. On the one hand, a standard New Economy argument is that the network features of new e-products stimulates a monopolising tendency: that is, the standard-setting game in many new industries is of a winner-takes-all nature (Shapiro and Varian, 1999). This implies a tendency toward increasing industry concentration. The merger between AOL and TimeWarner symbolises the current M&A wave that affects many parts of the (Old and) New Economy. On the other hand, the IT revolution is argued to shake up established industry arrangements. New value chains are designed. Manufacturers may cut out traditional distribution intermediaries, suppliers may focus on direct interaction with customers, and firms may outsource production while using fewer subcontractors. New multimarket scope strategies arise as many firms re-assess their market and product scope, merging horizontally, unbundling vertically and allying diagonally. Hagel and Singer (1999) argue in favour of, for efficiency reasons, unbundling established companies into separate firms for customer relationship management, product innovation and infrastructure management. The end result of the concentration and unbundling tendencies is, as yet, undetermined. In the case of airlines, for example, this would suggest a merger of brands (like, say, Air Italia, British Airways and KLM), while simultaneously outsourcing many operations (as already occurs in the case of ground handling and airplane maintenance).

Transaction costs

The widespread New Economy argument is that the introduction of IT within firms and markets is very likely to decrease transaction costs. Crucially, a number of key 'traditional' constraints in the market place lose their relevance (Shapiro and Varian, 1999): information products can be distributed without capacity constraints; transactions can be conducted independent of locations, across traditional country and industry boundaries;

Internet-based information transfer is timely, detailed and easy-to-access; webbrowsers are considered to be an effective and user-friendly interface for intermediating between information users and information sources; and so on and so forth. As a result, information costs fall, especially the costs of distributing and decoding information (*i.e.* the costs of gaining access to information). This is true both in the B2B (which stands for "business to business") world and in the B2C (which is the e-acronym for "business to consumer") arena. In this context, the launch of one e-trading market place after the other in many well-established industries is a case in point. Once diffusion of the Internet network exceeds a certain threshold, these falling information costs may be expected to stimulate economic growth (see Dudley, 1999, for a general model). If such transaction costs keep on falling, this will stimulate the further efficiency-enhancing division of labour, both nationally and internationally.

However, this is only half the story. For different reasons, the introduction of IT may increase rather than decrease transaction costs. Three examples may illustrate this conjecture. First, the distribution and delivery of physical goods that have been ordered electronically, is a very complicated and costly affair. Take the case of the virtual book store of Amazon.com. Although the e-ordering process benefits from all the well-known New Economy scale economies, the physical distribution is a money, people and time-consuming activity. In effect, the Old Economy scale economies of single-spot delivery, where buyers travel to a central book store, are reversed into the scale diseconomies of fragmented New Economy delivery at many individual-buyer addresses. Second, Internet browsing in search for tailor-made information may well be like jumping into a *mere à boire*. After all, this is a classic example of information overload. For sure, Internet search engines smooth the information-tracking process considerably. However, even sophisticated search engines are anything but a guarantee that the 'perfect' product – consumer match is traced easily and quickly. Third, as discussed above, the widespread introduction of IT on the work floor and in organisation offices has turned out to be an impressive stimulus of shirking behaviour. The bottom line is that, again, two opposing forces – decreasing and increasing transaction costs – together produce the multiple outcome grid that is reproduced (from Sarkar *et al.*, 2000) in Figure 2.

In combination, the transaction-cost decreasing and increasing forces generate much volatility: new transaction systems are introduced; old intermediaries may die out; new cybermediaries help to reduce the cost of e-transactions; new on-line auctions facilitate market efficiency; electronic payment services reduce the customers' barrier to engage in B2C purchasing; electronic payment may requires huge investment in security; *etcetera*.

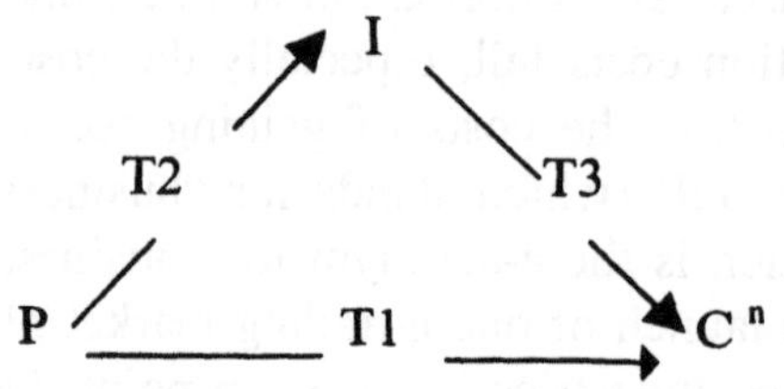

		BEFORE the IT revolution	
		T1 < T2 + T3	T1 > T2 + T3
AFTER the IT revolution	T1*<T2*+T3*	IT supplements direct markt	Threatened intermediairies
	T1*>T2*+T3*	Cybermediairies	IT supplements Intermediairies

[n] P = producer; I = intermediary, C = consumer; T*x* = cost of transaction *x* (*x* = 1, 2, 3).

Figure 2. The transaction-cost outcome grid

Competitive intensity

As is well-known from industrial organisation, an industry's competitive intensity depends crucially upon the idiosyncrasies of the prevailing rules of the game (Van Witteloostuijn, 1992). Here, the New Economy argument is that, *ceteris paribus* (setting aside the monopolising network effect tendency discussed above), the diffusion of IT devices will change the rules of the game in many – if not all – industries such that competitive intensity will increase because (a) virtual entry barriers are low and (b) e-market transparency is high. However, an opposing force may emerge as a result of the changing rules of the multicontact game (Van Wegberg and Van Witteloostuijn, 2001). After all, the New Economy is characterised by an impressive acceleration of the already impressive development of alliance networks.

Clearly, the network formation in the Internet industry is not limited to dotcom firms. Apart from the many Internet firms, with such exotic names as Comone, G-Magic and Fatbrain, a large number of well-established high-tech firms are heavily linked into the Internet knowledge @lli@ance network. Here, revealing examples are the major electronic companies (from Philips to Sony) and telecom firms (from Bell babies to Nokia). And the Internet network is even extended into other than high-tech industries (such as banking: from ABN AMRO to Citibank). So, the acceleration of @lli@nce development is not restricted to the IT industries. Figure 3 lists a number of examples of @lli@ncies in 'old' and well-established industries, so connecting the Old Economy with the New Economy.

Telecom Italia - Banca di Roma
on-line banking

Deutsche Bank - AOL - SAP
financial services in business-to-business market

KLM and partners
research and Internet travel agency

GM - Ford - Daimler/Chrysler
purchasing site

Unilever - Ariba
procurement on-line

Sears, Roebuck - Carrefour
retail consortium GlobalNetExchange for purchasing

Cargill - DuPont - Cenex
supply farmers and sell their crops via Rooster.com

Kmart - Yahoo!
marketing site

Unilever - iVillage
website for women (personal care & beauty)

Shell - CommerceOne
procurement platform

Holland Casino's - Eurocasino
on-line casino's

Ahold-Tesco-K-Mart etc.
purchasing website

KPN-Travel Unie
on-line travel agency

Fortis-Planet Internet
portal for teenagers

Figure 3. Examples of @lli@nces connecting the 'Old' with the New Economy

To give examples from B2B and B2C: the Deutsche Bank enters into B2B e-banking by teaming up with Internet provider AOL and software producer SAP; Kmart attempts to penetrate the B2C e-tail market by joining forces with the webmaster Yahoo!; an international @lli@ance of leading retailers (including Dutch Ahold, British Tesco and American Kmart) is set up to organise powerful e-procurement; *etcetera*.

Clearly, the IT revolution has further increased the contact intensity in many industries through the impressive @lli@nce network development movement. Additionally, and related to the above, IT has initiated the birth of new contact channels. That is, the electronic world of the Internet is occupied by new organisational forms that organise different channels of inter-firm contact. Here, the key example is the cybermediary (*e.g.* Sarkar *et al.*, 2000). Firms now meet in such electronic environments as e-auctions, e-malls and e-platforms, on top of and in addition to their traditional non-electronic contacts. These e-contact devices increase the number of different contact channels. Of course, the motives for innovative e-contact development and @lli@nce network formation may be anything from sharing e-customer bases and combining complementary e-capabilities to e-product development and chain e-management. However, an important additional effect of the increasing incidence of @lli@nces and other e-contacts is an increase of sustainable collusive conduct. This is standard multimarket (Bernheim and Whinston, 1990) or multichannel (Van Wegberg and Van Witteloostuijn, 2001) contact theory, relying on reputation signalling and retaliation threatening arguments. This effect is facilitated by three collusion-stimulating New Economy conditions. First, the sustainability of a collusive (multimarket) arrangement correlates positively with industry concentration (*e.g.* Bernheim and Whinston, 1990). Second, many old firms diversify into new electronic markets, as is revealed by the examples in Figure 3, whilst much empirical multimarket contact studies have produced evidence that diversification is positively associated with collusion (*e.g.* Scott, 1989). Third, by its very nature, the virtual world is global as national boundaries are meaningless in cyberspace, implying that separate national markets integrate in the global Internet world such that the number of cross-border contacts increases substantially, which facilitates the emergence of multicontact collusion (*e.g.* Van Witteloostuijn and Van Wegberg, 1991).

Business cycles

Together, the different New Economy changes at the micro (firm) and meso (industry) levels are said to produce a New E-conomy. This is, for a large part, standard Kondratieff cycle reasoning. That is, the widespread diffusion of a break-through technology, such as electricity in the early 20th century and modern IT in the 1990s and beyond, induces a new Kondratieff cycle that pushes productivity up in many different corners of the economy (Gordon, 2000). As a result, macroeconomic growth rates increase. However, New Macroeconomists argue that there is much more to the New Economy revolution. Basically, their story is that the IT-induced reduction of economy-wide transaction costs changes the structure of the E-conomy fundamentally, such that inflation-poor and recession-free growth is within reach. At the micro level, IT-based cost reduction programs, including value-chain coordination of inventory-reducing just-in-time logistics, increase firm-level efficiencies substantially. At the meso level, this cost reduction effect, in combination with the increased transparency of e-market places (B2B and B2C), triggers intensified price and quality rivalry. Together with the irrelevance of binding productive restrictions in the information product part of the New Economy (Shapiro and Varian, 1999), this changes the rules of the game toward cut-throat Bertrand rivalry in many industries. As a consequence, inflation is dampened from below (increasing cost efficiency) and above (increasing price competition).

However, this story heavily relies on the assumption that the opposing forces introduced above are relatively impotent. This may not be true, though: perhaps, the drive-to-control dominates over the empowerment tendency; maybe, the network features of many industries produce a series of monopolies; perhaps, transaction costs are increasing rather than decreasing in a majority of markets; maybe, multichannel collusion appears to be the sustainable equilibrium in many industries; *etcetera*. Then, the New Economy promise may fail to materialise. Even worse: the impressive New Economy characteristics of global market transparency and just-in-time production introduce changes in the economy's structure that can increase the world's macroeconomic volatility and vulnerability. For one, global market transparency facilitates the rapid spread of local events, both for the good and for the bad. So, herd behaviour can quickly shift an E-conomy into a higher or lower gear, depending upon the positive or negative nature of the initial shock. On top of this, the high incidence of just-in-time production throughout the E-conomy relegates the dampening buffer effect of inventories into the zone of irrelevance. As a consequence, a negative shock is very likely to trigger a knock-on effect in e-lean industries. If this countervailing force dominates, the E-conomy in the new millennium may prove to be less recession-prone than the Old Economy in the second half of the 20th century.

4. MUCH ADO ABOUT NOTHING?

Recently, the New Economy hype came to a (temporary?) end for, at least, two reasons. For one, the stock values of virtually all IT firms experience a creeping *krach* ever since the summer of 2000. In this context, Figure 4's evolution of the New York NASDAQ-index is very revealing indeed.

On top of this, the US New Economy miracle collapsed in the final quarter of the year 2000 as the American macroeconomic growth rate came to a standstill. However, all this cannot be taken as evidence for the dominance of Old Economy forces. After all, the New Economy miracle may well re-emerge after a temporary slowdown. This does suggest, though, that a well-established Old Economy law is still valid: much uncertainty rules the economic world, whether 'old' or 'new'. Precisely this endemic uncertainty asks for old-fashioned analytical rigour by those who offer advise to policy makers. Hence, Simon Kuipers could still do a good job as economic analyst and policy advisor in the New Economy.

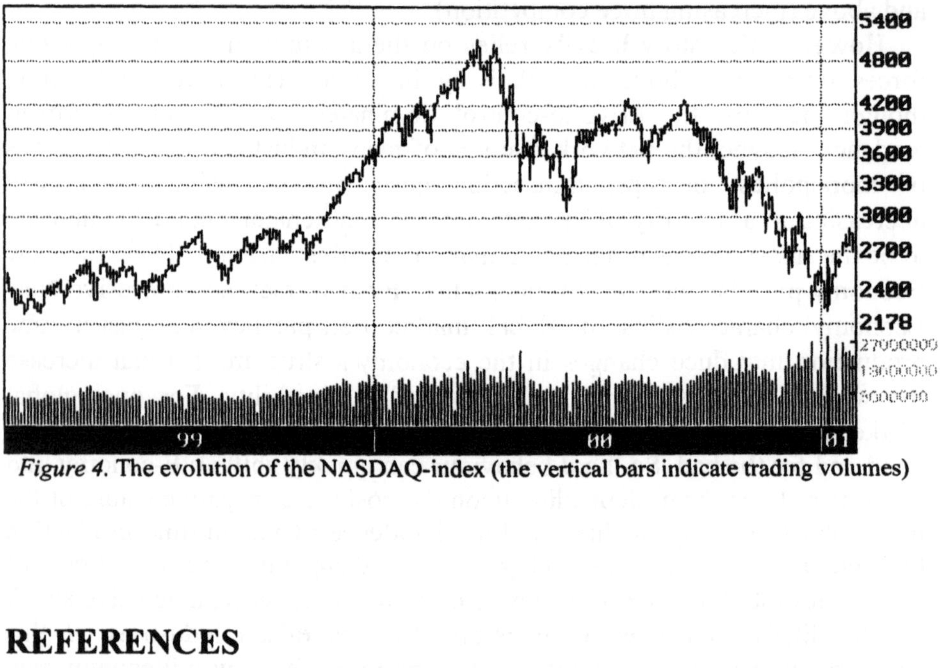

Figure 4. The evolution of the NASDAQ-index (the vertical bars indicate trading volumes)

REFERENCES

Benassy, J.P. (1982), *The Economics of Market Disequilibrium*, New York: Academic Press.

Bernheim, B.D. and M.D. Whinston (1990), "Multimarket Contact and Collusive Behavior," *Rand Journal of Economics* 21, pp.1-26.

Brakman, S. and A. van Witteloostuijn (2001), "Over wijn en zakken," in S. Brakman and. A. van Witteloostuijn (eds.), *Jonge wijn in oude zakken: op weg naar een nieuwe Nieuwe Economie?*, Amsterdam: De Arbeiderspers.

Cohen, S.S., J.B. DeLong and J. Zysman (2000), "Tools for Thought: What is New and Important About the 'E-conomy'?," *BRIE Working Paper* 138, Berkeley, University of California at Berkeley (http://econ161.berkeley.edu).

Daft, R.R. (1998), *Organization Theory and Design*, Cincinatti: South-Western College Publishing.

Dudley, L. (1999), "Communications and Economic Growth," *European Economic Review* 43, pp. 595-619.

Gordon, R.J. (2000), "Does the 'New Economy' Measure up to the Great Inventions of the Past?," *Journal of Economic Perspectives* 14, pp. 49-74.
Hagel III, J. and M. Singer (1999), "Unbundling the Corporation: What Business Are You In? Chances Are, It's Not What You Think," *Harvard Business Review,* March-April, pp. 133-141.
Kuipers, S.K., G.A.W. van Dalen, K. Groenveld and R.H. Koning (2000), *Groei, inkomensverdeling en economische orde*, Teldersstichting, Den Haag.
Malinvaud, E. (1977), *The Theory of Unemployment Reconsidered*, Oxford: Basill Blackwell.
Malinvaud, E. (1980), *Profitability and Unemployment*, Cambridge: Cambridge University Press.
Nouwens, J. and H. Bouwman (1995), "Living Apart Together in Electronic Commerce: The Use of Information and Communication Technology to Create Network Organizations," *Journal of Computer-Mediated Communication* 1 (http://www.ascusc.org/jcmc/vol1/issue3/nouwens.html).
Robbins, S.P. (2001), *Organizational Behavior*, Upper Saddle River: Prentice Hall.
Sarkar, M.B., B. Butler and C. Steinfield (2000), "Intermediaries and Cybermediaries: A Continuing Role for Mediating Players in the Electronic Marketplace," *Journal of Computer-Mediated Communication* 6 (http://www.ascusc.org/jcmc/vol6/issue3/sarkar.html).
Scott, J.T. (1989), "Purposive Diversification as a Motive for Merger," *International Journal of Industrial Organization* 7, pp. 35-47.
Shapiro, C. and H.R. Varian (1999), *Information Rules: A Strategic Guide to the Network Economy*, Boston: Harvard Business School Press.
Volberda, H. (1998), *Building the Flexible Firm: How to Remain Competitive*, Oxford: Oxford University Press.
Wegberg, M.J.A.M. van and A. van Witteloostuijn (2001), "Strategic Management in the New Economy: Modern Information Technologies and Multichannel Contact Strategies," in J.A.C. Baum and H.R. Greve (eds.), *Advances in Strategic Management: Multi-Unit – Multi-Market Strategy*, Greenwich Connecticut: JAI Press.
Witteloostuijn, A. van (1990), *Rationality, Competition and Evolution: Entry (Deterrence) in Dynamic Barrier Market Theory*, Maastricht: Datawyse.
Witteloostuijn, A. van (1992), "Theories of Competition and Market Performance: Multimarket Competition and the Source of Potential Entry," *De Economist* 140, pp. 109-139.
Witteloostuijn, A. van (2000), "Nieuwe Economie en oude wetten," *De academische boekengids* 21, pp. 12-16.
Witteloostuijn, A. van and M.J.A.M. van Wegberg (1991), "Multimarket Competition and European Integration," in A.M. Rugman and A. Verbeke (eds.), *Research in Global Strategic Management: Global Competition and the European Community*, London: JAI Press.

PART III

MONETARY ECONOMICS AND POLICY

Chapter 9

Money and Trust

Hans van Ees and Elmer Sterken
Department of Economics, University of Groningen

Key words: Monetary economics, Medium of exchange, Trust

Abstract: We analyse the role of trust in a monetary economy. First, we give a survey of the relevant literature. Next, we present an empirical model using data for 40 countries. We illustrate the relation between the income velocity of money, interest rates, and trust.

1. INTRODUCTION

Simon Kuipers always showed great interest in the working of a monetary economy. Although most of his work is of an empirical nature (*e.g.* Kuipers and Boertje, 1988, Kuipers and Sterken, 1995), occasionally a more theoretical or methodological route is followed (*e.g.* Kuipers 1991, Kuipers *et al.* 1997). While recognising the tremendous progress of economic theorising, his interest in monetary theory is firmly grounded in the recognition that we as economists do in fact know very little of the essentials of such an economy. Kuipers is well aware of the failure of modern economic theory to explain the essentials of a monetary economy. "At least we know what it is not: a monetary economy is not an economy as described by general equilibrium economics ... and although it is possible to devise constructions for including money in such a model, these constructions remain artificial in a world where individual exchange arrangements are exogeneously determined and do not take resources." (*ibid.* 1997, p. 370). As a true Keynesian Simon Kuipers is convinced by the idea that the working of an economy can only be understood by taking into account instability as a distinctive characteristic. In the end the paradox of this fundamental instability and the remarkable stability of most monetary economies can only be explained in terms of fundamental uncertainty and the fact that agents do not have complete knowledge of the economy.

In this chapter, we will attempt to deal with the working of a monetary economy by taking up the aforementioned lines of research. Hence, we will deal with the working of a monetary economy and we will do this in an empirical way. In doing this, we will recognise the most fundamental lines of thinking in monetary theory and go beyond the restrictive analysis of mainstream economics by explicitly taking into account the existence of fundamental uncertainty and incomplete knowledge.

The chapter is organised in two parts. In the first part, we shortly summarise the fundamental flaws of mainstream monetary theory in Section 2. Next, we discuss the relevance of trust in the working of an economy characterised by uncertainty and incomplete knowledge (Section 3). Here, we argue that the introduction of trust in monetary theory reveals a promising route. The second part of the chapter elaborates upon the alleged empirical relationship between money and trust. In Section 4 we describe the data we use in our empirical analysis, *i.e.* the *International Financial Statistics* for the monetary data and the *World Value Survey* (see Inglehart *et al.*, 1998) for the trust data. Additionally, we develop a simple theoretical model that provides a benchmark for our empirical analysis. In Section 5 we discuss our results. Section 6 concludes.

2. THE FUNDAMENTAL FLAWS OF MAINSTREAM MONETARY THEORY

Most modern monetary economics focuses on monetary policy issues. Inflation targeting, the independence of central banks, and the credibility of policy are only a few of the popular topics. Yet despite the tremendous progress in this research, the most important issue of monetary theory is still unresolved: what makes a monetary economy different from a barter economy? Only casual observation suffices to establish that money is an efficient medium of exchange, unit of account and store of value. Still, in the neoclassical general equilibrium world money is superfluous in all these functions. In order to explain this proposition it is most convenient to start from the fundamental distinction of the Quantity Theory of Money, *i.e.* the distinction between the quality and quantity of money (*e.g.* Samuelson, 1958). As a quality, money is the founding institution of the market economy, as a quantity, money is of no significance once the quality is established. Hence by assuming the quality of money to be known, money is neutral in the sense that is does not restrict the freedom of decision making.

Paradoxically, mainstream economics regards money both neutral and indispensable. Obviously, once money is there, it is worth accepting because of the services it renders. Money thus renders a direct utility, liquidity, and the demand for money can be derived as any other commodity. Hence by taking money's status as a collective object for granted, the demand for money can be explained from a theory grounded upon methodological individualism.

Obviously, the artificial dichotomy between the quality and quantity of money is both theoretically unsatisfactory as empirically false. From the point of view of theory it can be argued that the quantity theory of money assumes what is has to explain. In the first place the establishment of money is regarded as purely a historical matter, which disregards the fact that the sole foundation for the acceptance of money is in (contemporary) exchange. In the second place, neutrality implies that money is neither involved in interpersonal relations nor in the constitution of individual preferences, which disregards the notion of universal acceptance. From an empirical point of view it can be argued that monetary crises have presented ample evidence that quantity affects the quality of money.

Indeed, mainstream economic theory has produced a number of 'artificial' explanations for the establishment of a monetary economy. Focusing on the medium of exchange function, the first argument is that money gives utility to its holder. For instance in so-called shopping-time models this is the case. The second argument is Clower's cash-in-advance constraint, money is needed to buy goods (goods do not buy goods). Both arguments simply presume the existence of money, though. The third line of thinking is general equilibrium search models. For instance, Kiyotaki and Wright (1989) propose a simple model where each agent must trade his own produced good for a consumption good. Finally, in a recent attempt to circumvent the fact that in the former models money is imposed instead of derived from the model, a more evolutionary approach is taken by Howitt and Clower (2000). In their simulation model money is endogenous and serves as a good, commonly traded by shops. Agents can open shops that trade in two goods if they expect demand to be high enough. The Clower-Howitt model is a simulation model that endogenises one good as being money for a plausible set of parameters. As such, modern search theory surpasses the initial conclusions of the Quantity Theory. Money has no utility of its own and the choice of money is arbitrary. Money is purely of a conventional nature.

The fundamental question however, is whether the knowledge of money being a convention will affect its stability as a medium of exchange. From cooperative game theory (*e.g.* Sugden, 1995) we have learned that complete transparency of conventions (such as money) endangers the stability of conventions. To put it differently, transparency reduces the usefulness of money as a store of value. The fundamental flaw of all general equilibrium (search) models lies in the neglect of the essential characteristics of money as a pure convention.

Thus we conclude that despite the intellectual appeal of all aforementioned attempts they, apart form other flaws, all suffer from the fact the key to the relationship between the quality and quantity dimension of money is its hoarding capacity. In circularity, exchange allows the quick reproduction of initial conditions (in a monetary crises the rise in the velocity of money exemplifies this statement). However, hoarding ceases money to be neutral, it is desired as such. Hence, only in the explanation of why money is hold we have to reckon the special status of money as a social artefact. Obviously, this argument lies at the heart of macroeconomic theory. To quote Keynes "our desire to hold money as a store of wealth is a barometer of our distrust of our own calculations and conventions concerning the future ... The possession of money lulls our disquietude" (Keynes, 1937, pp. 218-219). The hoarding function of money thus exemplifies the specific nature of money in comparison to other commodities and at the same time explains the failure of mainstream economics to deal with money and monetary phenomena in a satisfactory way. In the next section we will elaborate upon this famous argument and establish the fundamental relationship between money and trust.

3. MONEY AND TRUST

Why would people hold money? The answer to this simple question goes right at the heart of a decentralised market economy. The origin of the desire for holding money to hold lies in the incomplete knowledge and thus fundamental uncertainty about the working of a market economy. In an economy with both private ownership and decentralised decision making, markets and money facilitates the coordination of numerous simultaneous economic activities. Both institutions are grounded upon the legitimacy of the belief that the opposite of a current transaction is possible in the future (Simmel, 1907). Still in view of the fundamental dispersion of knowledge, it is almost by definition that agents lack the knowledge to know this for certain. Hoarding money is the rational agent's manifestation of the doubt concerning the stability of the beliefs that govern transactions. Money in its hoarding capacity allows the agent to doubt the conventions that are a datum for individual decision making. Yet, this statement has profound implications. First, as society as whole cannot hoard more, it implies that agents in the economy can take different positions on the same set of fundamentals, a characteristic, which can only be grounded upon the notion that agents do not always perceive the economic process similarly. Second, the individual desire to hold money reveals both doubt in existing conventions as well as increased confidence in one of them, namely money. Also this paradox can only be explained if it is allowed that agents attach meaning to beliefs external to the formal economic model of a monetary economy. Only when acting upon external beliefs rather than upon economic fundamentals, agents are allowed to cut through the incompatibility between the trust in money and the mistrust in the persistence of existing institutions (Van Ees and Garretsen, 1995). The very fact that people hold money can only be explained from the fact that they do not completely understand the nature of money as well as the economy. The lack of understanding does not necessarily frustrate economic activity as agents partly ground their transactions upon their trust in external beliefs. Thus, in an economy where agents act upon their ignorance instead of their knowledge trust represents an essential element in the coordination of the economic process.

There are various reasons to believe that money as well as trust are central in coordination problems (see *e.g.* Van der Lecq, 1998). Money can be seen as an instrument in conventions. Economic agents that face large uncertainty might find it attractive to use rules of thumb or easy conventions to avoid overexposure to uncertainty. Apart from conventions, trust among agents can be used to explain the use of money. Van der Lecq discusses two levels of trust: bilateral trust and societal trust. With high societal but low bilateral trust the monetary trade would be stimulated. With low societal trust we would observe barter trade. With high bilateral and social trust economic transactions could be described by a credit economy.

To illustrate the relationship between trust and money, *e.g.* Goodhart (1989) refers to closely organised social groups in which exchanges take place without the use of money. In the groups the family tie underlies the exchange relationship, in the form of an implicit contract grounded upon bilateral trust. In more anonymous exchanges money symbolises the trust (confidence) in repayment. This trust is thus in part grounded upon symbolism, which represents a universally held social belief (societal trust). Obviously, this universally held trust is particularly pronounced in the store of value function of money. Once again, in exchange initial positions can be quickly reproduced.

4. DESCRIPTION OF THE DATA

So far, the "theory of trust" is sketchy at the most. Hence, before describing the data, let us shortly summarise the main ingredients of our approach. The first building block is a macroeconomic approach to monetary theory. Money is truly a macroeconomic phenomenon as it is the manifestation of a collective reality, *i.e.* unanimity of the members of society with respect to the medium of exchange. In the preceding section we have argued that collective realities cannot be purely grounded upon individually rational behaviour. All manifestations of general acceptance imply social belief and faith. Secondly, in view of the previous argument we regard trust as an essential characteristic of a monetary economy. In this second part of the chapter we will attempt to illustrate this proposition by an intuitive empirical illustration of the macro relationship between money holdings and trust. We use information on a cross-section of countries, *i.e.* the results of the *World Value Survey* (see Inglehart *et al.*, 1998), to proxy for trust. We find that, as predicted by economic theory there is a substitution between trust and money. Apparently, money is a hedge against mistrust, which illustrates the aforementioned paradox that individual desire to hold money reveals both doubt in existing conventions as well as increased confidence in one of them, namely money. As argued, this paradox can only be explained if it is allowed that agents attach meaning to beliefs external to the formal economic model of a monetary economy.

Before we present our data it is good to give an overview of the main determinants of trust:

1. Trust might be influenced by moral and cultural influences.
2. Trust is possibly based on past experiences. There exists a sort of reciprocity argument for trust. This idea applies both to the individual and the group level.
3. One might trust the people who are more similar to him or her self more. This applies to family, members of the same group, racial background or country.
4. People may trust more others with whom they have had a longer relationship.
5. Legal institutions may affect trust.

The first thing we need to do is to give an empirical definition of trust. For the trust data we use the data from the *World Value Survey* (see Inglehart *et al.*, 1998). In this survey a few questions are asked that relate to trust. The first question is: "Do you generally trust other people?" (Question 94). This question is used also in other papers (see La Porta *et al.*, 1997). Other questions that are interesting are: "Do you trust your family?" (question 340), and "Do you trust people of your own nationality?" (Question 341). We use the percentage of positive answers in our analysis. The data cover 40 countries (see Appendix A for a description of the list of countries). These countries include developed economies, economies in transition and developing countries. Table 1 gives some characteristics of the data. Table 1 contains various subcategories of variables, which we discuss hereafter.

We use the so-called "fixed" data as provided by the World Bank in the *Financial Structure Database* (see Beck *et al.*, 1999). This data set includes information on the geographical properties of countries (latitude, longitude, area, tropical, locked in land, oil exporting), legal origin (Common Law, French Law, Scandinavian Law, German Law, Socialist Law), and income (OECD, developing, low and middle income). The World Bank also provides data on variables that might be related with trust (possession of radio and television, life expectancy, religion, and corruption). Furthermore we use data from the *World Development Report* (see World Bank, 2000) on enrolment, unemployment, urbanisation, average inflation, real growth, income inequality (Gini-coefficient), risk rating of countries, and characteristics of the financial sector (credit to the private sector and market capitalisation). Finally we use societal indicators as proposed by Hofstede (1980). This indicators include variables that proxy for so-called power distance, individualism, masculinity and uncertainty avoidance.

Before we turn to our analysis of the role of trust we first characterise trust in our data. We use the subcategories of Table 1 for our discussion. Trust can be seen as a deep structural characteristic or societal norm of an economic system. Therefore we first try to specify the variables that go hand in hand with trust. Following the five theoretical clues above we first describe some results found by others. We discuss three results. First La Porta *et al.* (1997) find that trust is negatively correlated with hierarchical religions, especially the catholic church and the Muslim church to a lesser extent. Secondly, Zak and Knack (2001) study the relation between trust and growth. They derive a theoretical model, which shows that trust increases with formal institutions, informal institutions, wages, and decreases with population heterogeneity, and wealth. They use various proxies for trust, which will be partly use hereafter. Alesina and La Ferrara (2000) study the determinants of trust using a sample of US localities. They find that the strongest factors that reduce trust are: (1) a recent history of traumatic experiences, (2) belonging to a group that historically felt discriminated against, (3) being economically unsuccessful in terms of income and education, (4) living in a racially mixed community and/or in one with a high degree of income disparity. Opposed to La Porta *et al.* (1997) Alesina and La Ferrara (2000) do not find that religious beliefs significantly affect trust.

Given the results above we describe the factors that correlate with our main trust variable in our sample of 40 countries. We start with the economic data

Table 1. Descriptive statistics

	Mean	Correlation with trust
Trust data		
Trust in people	35.38	
Trust in countrymen	65.49	0.19
Trust in family	94.54	0.05
Keep money when found	51.00	-0.01
Economic data		
Growth of GDP per capita (%)	0.80	-0.11
GNP per capita 1998 ($)	13902	0.68
Average life expectancy (years)	69.92	0.69
Gini-coefficient	34.81	-0.62
Ethnic fractionalisation (%)	27.75	0.01
Unemployment (%)	8.01	-0.08
Legal data		
English Law	0.18	0.15
French Law	0.28	-0.36
German Law	0.13	0.07
Scandinavian Law	0.13	0.61
Socialist Law	0.30	-0.27
Corruption (index 1-10)	8.16	0.65
Religion		
Catholic	46.93	-0.62
Protestant	28.75	0.74
Muslim	0.87	-0.10
No religion	23.45	-0.02

(to be continued)

Economic variables

Trust is not so much correlated with the growth rate of per capita income. On the other hand there is a positive correlation with the level of GDP per capita for 1997 (0.68). This finding is in line with Zak and Knack (2001), who argue that an increase in wage is positively correlated with trust, but an increase in wealth is probably negatively correlated, which makes the sign of growth of output itself ambiguous. There is a negative correlation with income inequality as measured by the Gini coefficient (-0.62). Income inequality indeed affects trust negatively. This implies that population heterogeneity negatively influences trust. On the other hand we do not find support for ethnic fractionalisation being correlated with trust. Life expectancy, which is income driven, shows a strong positive correlation with trust. Overall we might conclude that economic conditions are correlated with trust.

Table 1. Descriptive statistics (continued)

	Mean	Correlation with trust
Geographic		
Latitude	38.17	0.39
Longitude	9.49	0.07
Landlocked	0.13	-0.11
Oil producer	0.03	-0.13
Transition economy	0.28	-0.36
Tropical country	0.03	-0.27
Area (square km's)	197667	-0.13
Urbanisation	69.62	0.12
Education		
Average TV/capita	0.19	0.37
Average radio/capita	0.39	0.51
Primary enrolment	104.79	-0.20
Secondary enrolment	95.42	0.55
Tertiary enrolment	39.16	0.50
Societal norms		
Power distance indicator	48.93	-0.67
Individualism	57.73	0.62
Masculinity	48.81	-0.33
Uncertainty avoidance	64.85	0.65
Financial structure (% GDP)		
Market capitalisation	50.22	0.38
Domestic credit	78.82	0.30
Credit to the private sector	63.12	0.37
Liquid liabilities	59.66	0.33
Financial rates		
Spread over LIBOR (%)	8.94	-0.50
Risk rating	65.72	0.46
Monetary development 90-97		
Money growth (%)	54.17	-0.30
Inflation (%)	22.57	-0.45

Legal data

Here we give a straightforward analysis of the influence of institutions on trust. We use legal origin as a catch all proxy. As La Porta *et al.* (1997) show legal institutions are deep structural determinants of the development of financial systems. We use the legal origin indicators as follows. We distinguish Common Law, Civil Law and Socialist Law economies. In the class of Civil Law we distinguish German, Scandinavian and French origin. There is a strong positive correlation between Scandinavian origin and trust, and a negative correlation between French (-0.35) and socialist (-0.27) origins. Trust also correlates with a high score (0.65) on the corruption index (implying low corruption).

Religion

We are able to match for 26 of the 40 countries on the fractions of religion. From that set we see that there is a very strong positive correlation between trust and the protestant church, and a negative relation with the Catholic church. This finding is consistent with La Porta *et al.* (1997) For the other indicator, the Muslim church we find no correlation.

Geography

We correlate the variable that proxies for trust in people with a number of geographical variables. We find a positive correlation between trust and latitude (and so a negative relation between trust and being a tropical country). The other correlation coefficients (for longitude, being an oil exporter, being landlocked, urbanisation, and the area in square kilometres) are not significant, except for an economy being a transition economy. In the latter case we find evidence of a negative correlation with trust. Since we have a substantial amount of transition economies in the sample we will use the transition economy classification hereafter.

Education

Here we find serious correlation between trust and especially secondary and tertiary enrolment data. We also include the per capita possession of radio and television. Trust is positively correlated with both. This might be an income effect, since Alesina and La Ferrara (2000) find a negative correlation of television and trust for the US.

Societal norms

Trust in people is strongly correlated with the Hofstede variable Power Distance. Power distance hints at inequality as observed by the subordinate. Power distance is negatively correlated with Individualism (-0.67), which we observe again in the positive correlation between trust and individualism (0.62). Trust is also negatively correlated with uncertainty avoidance (0.65). There is some negative correlation between masculinity and trust (-0.33).

Financial structure

Here we are interested in two financial characteristics. First of all, we discuss financial structure. Is it so that high societal trust leads to a relative emphasis on the stock market over the market for loans? Secondly, we are interested in the results of financial transactions. Are risk ratings lower for high trust economies? Are interest rates higher?

We find that trust is positively correlated with both credit to the private sector and market capitalisation of the stock market (0.35 for both). For the risk rating we find a positive correlation, implying that a higher trust leads to a higher risk rating (0.53). It is quite natural to find then that the spread *vis-à-vis* the London Inter Bank Offered Rate (LIBOR) is lower for high trust economies (-0.35).

We find some sound country evidence for variables that correlate with trust. Based on our sample we argue that trust is more established in economies with:

- A high income;
- Better education;
- A well-developed financial system;
- A non-French legal origin;
- Protestant religion;
- Low income inequality;
- Low power distance or high individualism;
- Larger distance from the equator;
- No recent transition.

We use this information in the next section, where we try to sketch the role of trust in a monetary economy.

5. MONEY AND TRUST

The bottom part of Table 1 gives the correlation between money growth in the 1990s and inflation with trust. We can observe that low-trust economies show higher growth rates of money and inflation. Our theoretical model predicts that high societal trust, and that is in fact what we measure, combined with low bilateral trust, which we evidently cannot observe, stimulates monetary exchange. Indirect exchange is stimulated by trust. So agents are willing to hold money if trust is established in a society. In terms of the quantity theory of money,

$$MV=PY, \qquad (1)$$

where M is the quantity of money, V is the income velocity, P is the general price level, and Y is income. In Equation (1) we expect V to be affected by trust. Rewrite (1) into:

$$1/V = M/PY, \qquad (2)$$

where we define *M/PY* as the liquidity ratio. In line with our arguments, we characterise a high-trust economy by a relatively high liquidity *ratio (cet. par.)*. So a simple monetary theory including trust would be that:

$$V = f(TRUST, R), \qquad (3)$$

where the derivative with respect to trust is negative, and the interest elasticity is positive. Model (3) is the base model of our empirical investigation. Again observe in Table 1 the line for liquid liabilities of the banking sector over nominal GDP. Trust is positively correlated with this variable.

Table 2. Determinants of trust

	(1)	(2)
Secondary enrolment	0.21	
	(2.84)	
Scandinavian legal origin	15.82	
	(3.53)	
French legal origin	-14.10	
	(3.19)	
German legal origin	-6.56	
	(1.64)	
Socialist legal origin	-10.57	
	(2.13)	
Uncertainty avoidance		-0.38
		(5.53)
Gini		-0.71
		(3.93)
Intercept	21.01	88.16
	(2.90)	(10.59)
Adjusted R^2	0.56	0.62
N	38	27

The *t*-values (within brackets) are based on White-corrected estimates of the standard errors.

We estimate Equation (3) by means of a two-step procedure. As trust is endogenous we use an Instrumental Variables estimator. In Table 1 we gave the single correlation coefficients of variables that relate to trust. Since a lot of these variables correlate we first estimate an equation for trust. After that we use the determinants of trust in our equation for the inverted income velocity.

Table 2 contains the main determinants of trust. We present two estimated equations. One for a large subset of our sample (38 countries), where we focus on legal determinants. The second uses a smaller sub-sample, where we focus on societal determinants. We find that legal origin and education (in the form of secondary enrolment) have a stable relationship with trust. English and Scandinavian legal origin countries seem to have a higher trust on average. French legal origin countries typically have lower trust. This finding is partly in line with the result of La Porta *et al.* (1997) on the negative correlation between trust and the role of the catholic church. Human capital correlates positively with trust. Column (2) presents the results for the societal norms. We only find a negative relation with uncertainty avoidance. The higher societal uncertainty avoidance, the lower trust is. In this regression we also find some evidence for the negative impact of population heterogeneity via the Gini-coefficient.

Table 3. Determinants of velocity, dependent variable: LOG(Liquid Liabilities of the Banking sector)

	(1)	(2)
LIBOR-spread	-0.02	-0.01
	(1.65)	(1.48)
LOG(Trust)	0.44	0.83
	(1.74)	(2.41)
Intercept	2.53	1.03
	(2.66)	(0.82)
Adjusted R^2	0.26	0.14
N	34	32

The *t*-values (within brackets) are based on White-corrected estimates of the standard errors.

Table 3 presents the main results of our chapter. We first estimate the log of the liquid liabilities of the banking sector on the spread of the country's interest rate versus the LIBOR and the log of the trust variable using Ordinary Least Squares. The results are in column (1). Here we observe that trust is not significantly determining the inverted income velocity. We do not find a significant impact of interest effects either. This might be due to the cross-section nature of our data. Next we estimate the same model using some of the determinants of trust: legal origin (French origin and transition economies), and secondary enrolment as instruments in an IV-regression. We observe that trust is now significant in Equation (2). The sign of trust is positive, which implies that more trust in the society leads to a larger propensity to bring cash in deposits with banks.

The results show that we can confirm the role of trust in the use of money. We show that trust has a negative impact on income velocity. We control for the impact of interest rates. What are the policy implications of this finding? First, one might argue that the government should stimulate the development of institutions that enhance trust. We can observe from Table 1 that all financial quantity indicators of financial structure are positively correlated with trust. We know from studies by Levine (1998, 2000) that financial structure matters to real development. Second, we find that apart from legal institutions, other "social" development indicators matter. Here we can think of education, healthiness, and wage structures. Thirdly, in economies with poor bilateral trust, social trust apparently stimulates the use of money.

6. CONCLUSIONS

This chapter studies societal trust and its impact on coordination of economic activity. We do not derive a theoretical model of trust (as Zak and Knack, 2001, for instance do). We use the insights of other theoretical models of trust and analyse whether trust is important in explaining money circulation. We use a set of 40 countries to illustrate the correlations between the income velocity of money, interest rates and trust. Moreover we give a statistical description of possible determinants of trust. It comes to the fore that income, education and the legal system are important for trust and money holdings.

APPENDIX A – LIST OF COUNTRIES

Argentina	Denmark	Japan	Romania
Austria	Estonia	Korea, Rep.	Russian Federation
Belarus	Finland	Latvia	Slovenia
Belgium	France	Lithuania	South Africa
Brazil	Germany	Mexico	Spain
Bulgaria	Hungary	Netherlands	Sweden
Canada	Iceland	Nigeria	Switzerland
Chile	India	Norway	Turkey
China	Ireland	Poland	United Kingdom
Czech Republic	Italy	Portugal	United States

REFERENCES

Alesina, A. and E. La Ferrara (2000), "The Determinants of Trust," *NBER Working Paper* 7621, Cambridge.

Beck, T., A. Demirgüc-Kunt and R. Levine, (1999), "A New Database on Financial Development and Structure," *mimeo*, World Bank, Washington.

Ees, H. van and J.H. Garretsen (1995), "Existence and Stability of Conventions and Institutions in a Monetary Economy," *Journal of Economic Behaviour and Organization* 28, pp. 275-288.

Fukuyama, F. (1995), *Trust*, New York: Free Press.

Goodhart, C.A.E. (1989), *Money, Information and Uncertainty*, London: MacMillan.

Hofstede, G. (1980), *Culture's Consequences: International Differences in Work-Related Values*, Beverly Hills: Sage Publications.

Howitt, P. and R. Clower (2000), "The Emergence of Economic Organization," *Journal of Economic Behavior and Organization* 41, pp. 55-84.

Inglehart, R., M. Basanez and A. Moreno (1998), *Human Values and Beliefs: A Cross-Cultural Sourcebook*, Ann Arbor: University of Michigan Press.

Keynes, J.M. (1937), *The General Theory of Employment*, in D. Moggridge (ed.), *The Collected Writings of J.M. Keynes*, vol. XIV, London: MacMillan.

Kiyotaki, N. and R. Wright (1989), "On Money as a Medium of Exchange," *Journal of Political Economy* 97, pp. 927-954.

Kuipers, S.K. (1991), "Marktwerking en werkloosheid in Nederland in de jaren dertig en tachtig," *Mededelingen van de Afdeling Letterkunde*, Koninklijke Nederlandse Akademie van Wetenschappen, nieuwe reeks, dl. 54, no. 3.

Kuipers, S.K. and B. Boertje (1988), "On the Rise of the Liquidity Ratio in the Netherlands," *De Economist* 136(1), pp. 50-90.

Kuipers, S.K., H. van Ees and S.G. van der Lecq (1997), "Money and Stability, Some Preliminary Thoughts on the Functioning of a Monetary Economy," in H. Klenner, D. Losurdo, J. Lensink and J. Bartels, (eds.), *Repræsentatio Mundi; Festschrift zum 70. Geburtstag von Hans Heinz Holz*, Köln: Springer Verlag.

Kuipers, S.K. and E. Sterken, (1995), "On the Scope for Dutch Monetary Policy," *Banca Nazionale del Lavoro Quarterly Review* 48(193), pp. 173-187.

La Porta, R., F. Lopez de Silanes, A. Shleifer and R. Vishny (1997), "Trust in Large Organizations," *The American Economic Review, Papers and Proceedings* 87, pp. 333-338.

Lecq, S.G. van der (1998), *Money, Coordination and Prices*, PhD Thesis, University of Groningen.

Levine, R. (1998), "The Legal Environment, Banks, and Long-Run Economic Growth," *Journal of Money, Credit, and Banking* 30, pp. 596-620.

Levine, R. (2000), "Bank-Based or Market-Based Financial Systems: Which is Better?," *mimeo*, World Bank, Washington.

Samuelson, P. (1958), "An Exact Consumption-Loan Model of Interest With or Without the Social Contrivance of Money," *Journal of Political Economy* 66, pp. 467-482.

Simmel, G. (1907), *The Philosophy of Money*, Reprinted in D. Frisby (ed.), 2nd enlarged edition, 1990, London: Routledge.

Sugden, R. (1995), "A Theory of Focal Points," *The Economic Journal* 105, pp. 751-785.

World Bank (2000), *World Development Report*, www.Worldbank.org.

Zak, D. and S. Knack (2001), "Trust and Growth," *The Economic Journal* 111, pp. 295-321.

Chapter 10

Overconfidence in Monetary Theory and Monetary Policy

Steven Brakman, Harry Garretsen and Lex Hoogduin
Department of Economics, University of Groningen; Department of Applied Economics, University of Nijmegen; Deputy Executive Director of the Netherlands Bank

Key words: Monetary theory, Monetary policy

Abstract: In this chapter we argue that when it comes to present-day monetary theory and policy, economists suffer from myopia and are prone to herd behaviour. As a result, too many economists give too much weight to actual economic developments which can have an excessive impact on economic theory and policy.

"Conservatively dressed central bankers may not look like fashion victims, yet they are as prone to the latest craze as anybody else. Remember when monetarism was all the rage? Then central bank independence became the 'in' thing. The latest fashion is for inflation targets."

The Economist, 25 September 1999

1. INTRODUCTION

The pecking order of economic theories is clearly not constant over time. Today's pet theories might be looked upon as very outdated in a few years time. Moreover, the history of economic thought shows that economic theorising is of a cyclical nature. New data become available, which put well-known "facts" into a different perspective, or our profession encounters some unexplained phenomenon and the resulting anomalies often lead to new theoretical models, which seem revolutionary at first. However, the traditional theories usually do not disappear forever. They temporarily move into the background, to return at a later stage in another form, but still containing their basic propositions. Similar observations can be made about economic policymaking. The Cambridge economist Dennis Robertson once famously remarked that like hunted deer, the economic discourse tends to move in circles and that if one waits long enough a particular theory or policy view will inevitably turn up again. This feature of economic reasoning can also be observed if one looks at the last thirty years, the period that more or less spans the academic career of Simon Kuipers.

Broadly speaking, the notion of whether or not the market mechanism functions well is the most important defining and dividing characteristic of economic theories (Greenwald and Stiglitz, 1987; Hoogduin, 1988). A well functioning market economy is able to absorb and correct shocks relatively easily, in other words it is stable, and on average generates full employment. On the other end of the spectrum is a more pessimistic view that tells us that the market mechanism is vulnerable to instability and that it cannot prevent long periods of below potential output and employment. The implied economic policies are naturally also different. A second important issue dividing economic theories is the assumed knowledge of private agents as well as policymakers about the (detailed) functioning of the economy. But it is especially with respect to the first issue that the leading views on economic theory and policy have changed rather strongly during the last three decades.

Although economists and policymakers do not agree on the most plausible economic theory and the implied view on how to conduct economic policy, usually with some goodwill one can distil characteristic mainstream views on economic theory and policy (the centre range of the distribution of views). Also shifts in this distribution can be identified. In particular, there appears to be a relation between the focus in economic theories and economic policy on the one hand and (the perception of) actual developments in major economies on the other hand. Causation may run in both directions (see also Van Bergeijk *et al.*, 1997). In this chapter we are primarily interested in the impact of actual economic developments on monetary theory and monetary policy. Our hypothesis is that this impact is sometimes excessive, stronger than would be in line with what can be concluded from taking into account all past information on economic developments. Or, to borrow a phrase from the modern theory of financial markets, we will argue that when it comes to present-day monetary theory and policy, economists suffer from myopia and are prone to herd behaviour. As a result, too many economists give too much weight to the recent episode of relatively favourable monetary conditions. The main reasons for the possibility that actual economic developments can have an excessive impact on economic theory and policy are discussed in more detail in Section 2.

Next we turn to the relevance of actual economic developments for present-day monetary theory and policy. To this end, Section 3 provides a very broad-brushed overview of economic developments in major industrialised economies and of developments in economic theory and economic policy. The purpose is not to give a chronological account of the last thirty years, but to suggest that actual economic developments sometimes shape (changes in) economic thinking. In doing so, both academic economists and policymakers tend to overreact. In Section 4, which contains our main case, we argue in more detail why we believe that, fuelled by notably the historically low levels of inflation, there is currently (yet again) overconfidence in monetary theory and policy. Section 5 concludes and argues in favour of methodological pluralism.

Simon Kuipers's views on economic theory and policy have definitely evolved over time, but not always in parallel with the mainstream view (Fase and Van de Klundert, 1998, reprinted in Chapter 2 of this *Festschrift*). There are at least two important constants in his thinking about economics. In combination they are not found very frequently. He has always remained a liberal in political terms, but at the same time has always taken the view that a market economy, although a powerful coordination mechanism, has some inherent deficiencies. In this respect he is and was very much a Keynesian economist. His opinion about the possibilities for policymakers to offset or soften these deficiencies has, however, developed over time. At the beginning of his career and in line with the prevailing mainstream view at that time, he believed with Modigliani that a market economy needed, could and should be stabilised (Modigliani, 1977). As a skilled macroeconometric model builder, he was relatively optimistic about the guiding role of (large-scale) econometric models for policymaking. Gradually, he has become less optimistic about our knowledge of the economy and about quantitative steering of the economy in the terminology of Tinbergen (1967). That is not so different from how the mainstream has developed on this issue. What is less in line with mainstream developments is that Simon Kuipers nowadays stresses the importance of fundamental uncertainty, in the sense of Knight, and emphasises the importance of rules, norms and institutions in the economy (Kuipers *et al.*, 1997; Kuipers *et al.*, 2000). As we will argue in the concluding Section 5, we believe that the existence of economists with "autonomous", non-mainstream views is to be viewed positively, as long as communication with the mainstream continues. It is one of the mechanisms to prevent and rapidly correct excesses in economic theory and policy. Moreover, economic theory is likely to make more progress when there is a plurality of views.

2. HERD- AND MYOPIC BEHAVIOUR ON THE "MARKET" FOR ECONOMIC THEORY AND POLICY

The choice of the most plausible economic theory and most appropriate economic policy can be analysed as a market process. The participants are academics, policymakers, journalists and the public at large. In this chapter we mainly focus on the role of academics and policymakers. The products are economic theories and policy views. The question we raise is whether the market for economic theories and economic policy views is efficient. If so, it would take into account all relevant information about past economic developments and past economic literature and use this information to assess the plausibility of economic theories and the strength and weaknesses of certain policy approaches (Van Bergeijk *et al.*, 1997).

Our hypothesis is that this market is not always fully efficient. This has two important implications. The first implication is that there is more variation in the selection of the most plausible economic theory and policy view than a complete assessment of all available information would warrant. Our approach bears an obvious similarity to the theory of behavioural finance, which argues that financial markets are inefficient and display excess volatility (Shiller, 2000). The reasoning is also similar. Economic theories and policy views cannot be simply tested. The economy is complex and in order to arrive at testable hypotheses we have to assume that many of the relevant *fundamentals* remain unchanged. In practice fundamentals are in a state of flux and it is not feasible to control for all these changes. At the same time there is only a limited role for controlled experiments in economics. Experiments can play a role in micro situations, but it is very difficult if not impossible to perform controlled macroeconomic experiments (Smith, 1998). This implies that in economics it is also very difficult to definitely refute rather general theories and views of the functioning of the economy. No clear objective criteria exist for the selection of theories and policy views. This selection is made under fundamental uncertainty, which cannot be reduced to probabilistic risk (Hoogduin, 1991; Knight, 1921).

The second implication of the (inevitably) imperfect nature of the market for economic theories and policies is that when deciding upon the most relevant theory or policy view, conventions play a significant role. One such convention is to extrapolate the present economic conditions into the future and to adapt the theory and policy views to these conditions. Human behaviour in complex decision-making situations such as those that prevail under fundamental uncertainty has been analysed extensively. Keynes (1936) was one of the first and most famous to do this. His analysis of the stock market (the well-known example of the beauty contest) is still a very effective anti-dote to the belief that financial markets are efficient. In general the analysis of decision-making under uncertainty is relevant because it explains why economic agents (and, more appropriately here, economists themselves) stick to simple conventions such as that the future will be like the present (ignoring the past) (Keynes, 1936).[1] In particular, Keynes claimed that conventions are followed in such circumstances and that people do indeed not only attach more importance to the present than is warranted but also attach great weight to the opinion of other agents when making their decisions. Herd behaviour abounds in uncertain situations where objective decision criteria do not exist. Experiments have confirmed that in complex and uncertain situations people resort to simple rules of thumb and are not able to process all available information (in line with Simon, 1976). People also make mistakes in their reasoning. Other interesting findings from psychological experiments are that people easily fall victim to wishful thinking and overconfidence (Thaler, 2000). Such overconfidence is not automatically corrected, even in a market process, when there are no clear objective standards to demonstrate that people are overconfident.[2] Overconfident people can for some time be more successful in the market than people with a more realistic assessment, if the former are in the majority. This is very well possible given the largely self-fulfilling nature of herd behaviour, and explains the existence of speculative bubbles.[3]

All these mechanisms also work in the selection of plausible theories and views. Economists, like the agents in the object of their study, are prone to herd behaviour and may attach too much attention to actual economic developments. As a consequence, economists are not so different from laymen in that they sometimes also seem inclined to believe that the present (favourable) economic conditions are here to stay forever. The recent discussion on the existence of a New Economy serves as a nice illustration.

[1] "The essence of this convention (…) lies in assuming that the existing state of affairs will continue indefinitely, except in so far as we have specific reasons to expect a change" (Keynes, 1936, p. 152)

[2] Thaler (2000, p. 133) considers overconfidence to be a crucial tenet of forecasts made by economic subjects: "ask people for 90 percent confidence limits for the estimates of various knowledge questions and the correct answers will lie within the limits less than 70 percent of the time. Overconfidence will induce (...) forecasts that are bolder than they should be".

[3] A similar reasoning, of course, applies to overpessimism but since, see Sections 3 and 4, we want to emphasise the relevance of the recent favourable economic and monetary conditions, we stress the possibility of overconfidence. Note, however, that for instance the Asian financial crisis in 1997-1998 almost immediately led to an outburst of very pessimistic publications about the near future of the Asian economies or even the world economy. Prophecies about a "Second Great Depression" at the turn of the century have however not materialised (yet?!). For examples see Krugman's *The Return of Depression Economics* (Krugman, 1999) or Garretsen *et al.* (1999).

Academics addressed the question of whether or not we see the end of inflation and the business cycle. If economic history teaches us anything, it is that inflation and business cycles are not very likely to simply disappear. The perception of what is actually occurring may therefore be overly optimistic. The line between the objective figures and the optimistic interpretation thereof is, of course, rather thin. If the economy is doing well we may come to believe that it is because of our steering skills and that ambitious targets are achievable, even though there were periods in the past when the economy fared less well. Theories, which are based on models that assume such controllability and continued bliss, are in that case more easily accepted as research tools than in less favourable times. In our view we are now in such a period as regards monetary theory and policy. Before presenting our argument with respect to monetary theory and policy, we first turn to a quick and by no means complete overview of economic developments, theories and policies in the last three decades. We shall focus on the mainstream views and do not discuss the broad spectrum of other views. The sole purpose of this overview is to show that in the (not so distant) past, economic developments have had their impact on economic theory and policy.

3. ECONOMIC DEVELOPMENTS AND THEIR IMPACT ON ECONOMIC THEORY AND POLICY: A QUICK OVERVIEW

At the end of the sixties and early seventies optimism prevailed about the possibilities to steer the economy. In our introduction we already referred to the famous remark by Modigliani in this context. It was believed that a stable short-term trade off between inflation and unemployment existed. Among other things, the existence of a stable Phillips-curve, of course, implied that the policy-mix of fiscal and monetary policy is important. The coordination of fiscal and monetary policy was therefore considered a crucial issue and macro-economic models focusing on this policy-mix, such as the Mundell-Fleming model, became prominent. The market economy was thought to be imperfect and Keynesian views had the upper hand. There was also a high degree of optimism about the degree of knowledge policymakers possessed about the workings of the economy. Large-scale econometric models were believed to provide this knowledge. Reasoning in optimal control terms was popular. Exchange rates were fixed and economies grew rapidly.

The seventies and early eighties saw this optimism coming to an end. The Bretton Woods system collapsed and the world moved to floating exchange rates, although Europe was and remains an exception. High money growth and two oil crises led to a surprising combination of accelerating inflation and lower growth (stagflation). Productivity growth slowed down for decades to come. Unemployment, notably in Europe, increased to unprecedented levels. Monetarism, with its emphasis on the benefits of flexible exchange rates and non-inflationary money-growth, became popular. Inflation fighting became the highest priority. What also became apparent in this period was that too many market rigidities had been introduced into the economy, which prevented the market to function efficiently. The belief in a stable trade-off between inflation and unemployment was abolished and replaced by the vertical long run Phillips curve according to which no trade-off at all exists in the long run. This also meant that Keynesian models with their emphasis on the merits of stabilisation policy and policy coordination came under attack. Monetary policy could thus be conducted largely independently of fiscal policy. It was also argued by some economists that political interference with monetary policy ultimately only leads to higher inflation, and not to higher output and employment. According to Lucas, the long run is not when we are dead, but when we all understand the economic situation (as cited in Krugman, 1994, p.49).

The case for central bank independence was thus given a theoretical foundation. It was also demonstrated empirically that countries with independent central banks recorded lower inflation, but not lower growth in the long run.[4] Making the central bank independent was in any event thought to lead to lower costs of disinflation and consequently many central banks were made independent (Eijffinger and De Haan, 1996, and Blinder, 1999). The optimism about the controllability of the economy disappeared. Large-scale econometric models became old fashioned. This was also triggered by the Lucas critique, showing that many of these models, in which no attention was paid to the formation of expectations, could not cope with changed expectations following changes in policy regimes (Lucas, 1976). The optimism about steering the economy turned sour. Mainstream economics now followed Milton Friedman's conviction, dated from the sixties, that it was better to follow stable policy rules. Better to be right on average than trying to be right at every moment following a discrete policy. The role of government in the economy was seen as less beneficial than before and in many countries it was seen as so large as to hamper the functioning of the market economy. The role of the government should be scaled back and

[4] More recently it is also emphasised that for countries with on average moderate inflation it is also true that an increase in inflation does not go along with lower growth (see Stiglitz, 1998). In the short run there is still a cost of bringing down inflation in terms of output and employment loss, also the empirical research found it much more difficult to establish that an increase in central bank independence went along with a lower sacrifice ratio.

markets should be allowed to function more freely. The rise of the theory of public choice in these years matched this phenomenon. Optimal control models became a scapegoat for New Classical economists like Kydland and Prescott (1977) or Barro and Gordon (1983) who by showing the time-inconsistent nature of old-style Keynesian discretionary monetary policy, provided the analytical foundations for the re-orientation of monetary policy in the direction of inflation targeting and central bank independence.

The eighties and nineties saw a gradual and uneven recovery of the world economy. The recovery was also unevenly distributed across countries. Japan for instance is still struggling today, in Europe some countries are doing very well, whereas in others unemployment is still high. In this period the focus was (almost exclusively) on the supply-side of the economy. Structural reforms to make markets function more efficiently was the key policy advise. Unemployment was thought to be of a highly structural nature. These reforms are not necessary to the same degree in all countries, nor are they implemented with the same vigour in all countries where they are necessary. The Anglo-Saxon model with its great emphasis on the working of markets was gaining ground, although this took time. Nevertheless, the last two decades of the 20th century have clearly been a period of deregulation, liberalisation of capital movements and financial innovation. This did not only lead to a number of financial and currency crises (Mexico and Latin America in general in the early eighties, Mexico again in late 1994, Asia in the summer of 1997 and Russia in 1998) and a severe stock market crash in 1987, but also to the waning of the influence of monetarism and of macroeconomics in general. The demise of monetarism was partly due to the fact that money demand became unstable in a great number of countries.[5] As a result, countries initially turned to monetary eclecticism or, contra hard-core monetarism, to exchange rate targeting. In Europe the process of European integration continued, albeit with important setbacks on the road. The pace of European integration was also influenced by that of economic growth. The Single Market programme and the introduction of the euro are the clearest manifestations of progress made in European integration. As such, this process of European integration went hand in hand with deregulation in most EU countries and as such stimulated the rise of microeconomics at the expense of macroeconomics. For macroeconomics to be taken seriously, the issue of supplying macro-economic models with micro-foundations came to the fore. Both New

[5] The label monetarism is used to group together sometimes rather different ideas (see DeLong, 2000). Here we refer to the demise of the policy influence of monetarism. Another strand of monetarism, focusing on the absence of a trade off between inflation and output in the long run, gained in importance and nowadays constitutes the backbone of almost every textbook on macroeconomics.

Classical economics and New Keynesian economics are good examples of the attempt to come up with these micro-foundations.

Even though the economic recovery of the eighties and nineties was uneven, one trend was fairly clear. Inflation was on a downward trend generally and the status of central banks was on an upward trend. In many countries inflation rates are now at the lowest level after the Second World War. The power of central banks is believed to be great and their independence is widely accepted and welcomed. The cult status of central bankers like Alan Greenspan is a nice example of the fact that we now live in the era of central banks. At the same time central banks are expected to be accountable and transparent and it is widely believed that central bank actions and their impact on actual inflation can and should be explained in detail. In academics there is a high degree of consensus that the strategy of inflation targeting is the appropriate monetary policy strategy, well rooted in the advanced knowledge in monetary economics and economic theory in general (Clarida *et al.*, 1999). New Keynesian economics (which is sometimes hard to differentiate from New Classical economics, see below) has become the leading school. The confidence is not so different from that in the sixties and early seventies, although there is perhaps somewhat more modesty now (Blanchard, 2000; Solow, 2000 and other contributions to the winter 2000 issue of the *Journal of Economic Perspectives*). We know about the disenchantment in economics after the happy sixties. Will history repeat itself as regards monetary theory and policy?

4. OVERCONFIDENCE IN MONETARY THEORY AND POLICY

So far we have argued that 1) the "market" for economic theories and policies is characterised by herd- as well as myopic behaviour and 2) in the last 30 years the prevailing mainstream views about economic theory and policy have changed considerably under the influence of actual economic developments. In this section we want to bring 1) and 2) together more in detail for the case of modern monetary theory and policy. In particular, we would like to suggest that the favourable development of inflation and economic growth in the recent past, in particular of the United States, has had an impact on monetary theory and monetary policy strategies. Outside academia this impact is clear. To use two well-known phrases, some laymen believed that *inflation is dead* and that, history repeats itself, the *business cycle is obsolete*. Not many economists and policy makers would have supported these two claims but the question remains as to whether the favourable monetary and economic conditions of the 1990s had an impact on the analytical foundation and actual conduct of monetary policy, and by implication, the same holds, *mutatis mutandis*, for the less favourable conditions we see nowadays. In our view the answer to this question must be affirmative. We first deal with this impact and then explain why we believe this has led to overconfidence in both theory and policy.

The current mainstream model of a monetary economy has strong New Keynesian features. It is a small stochastic general equilibrium model with some market imperfections imposed on it (Clarida *et al.*, 1999 and references therein). The equations are derived on the basis of the assumption that economic agents (consumers and producers) are solving an intertemporal optimisation problem. The model has micro-foundations in line with the New Keynesian rules of the game. In this case these rules, save for the imperfections, are similar to the New Classical rules. This is not a big surprise since the model we refer to is analytically very close to the class of real business cycle models.[6] In the long run changes in the stock of money only affect inflation. In the short run monetary policy has real effects owing to the existence of market imperfections such as overlapping wage contracts. Without these imperfections nominal (demand) shocks cannot have an impact on real output. The market imperfections also imply that adjustments to the stochastic shocks in the model take time and that there is a role for stabilisation policy in the short run. Unemployment is either of a temporary and cyclical nature or of a structural nature. Such structural unemployment cannot be cured by monetary policy, but only by structural reforms. Not only are monetary policy issues of countries in reasonable or good shape analysed with this kind of model, the same model has also been used to study the depressed Japanese economy and the liquidity trap (Krugman, 1998). Postulating a loss function for the central bank then enables the derivation of the appropriate monetary policy strategy in this model. Usually the arguments in this loss function are the deviation of the actual inflation rate from a certain targeted inflation rate and the deviation of actual production from potential or desired output. The central bank aims to stabilise prices and output. The degree to which output stabilisation is an objective differs across central banks. There exists however consensus among central banks that in any case price stability is a central bank objective with high priority. The given loss function is then minimised subject to the stochastic model just described. The policy instrument is a short-term interest rate, which can be fully controlled by the central bank. Optimal control techniques are employed to derive the optimal monetary policy strategy. This approach almost automatically leads to favouring inflation targeting. If one agrees that

[6] There are, of course, differences but the similarity cannot be denied and is evidence of the fact that New Keynesian and New Classical economics have converged in recent years, see Solow (2000, pp. 154-155) for a similar observation.

the stochastic general equilibrium model is an adequate representation of our knowledge about the economy, and if inflation is the most important monetary policy objective, then the best way to approach monetary policymaking is to use all available information to forecast inflation and compare this forecast with the target. In case of a difference, the message is to adjust the policy instrument accordingly. Strategies to use intermediate targets are difficult to rationalise in this framework. With such strategies not all of the available information is used or when the intermediate target has a one-to-one correspondence with inflation this would only imply that using the intermediate target would be identical to inflation targeting. Inflation targeting would always be as least as efficient as any other strategy. Monetary targeting is definitely inferior to inflation targeting in this framework. Money plays no role of its own in this model. It is completely passive and the stability of money demand is not an issue. Over the policy horizon of this model, typically around two years, inflation can be driven by a host of demand and/or supply shocks and the imperfections which determine the time path of the impact of these shocks. Shocks to money demand are often not deemed important compared with other possible shocks. Quite often money does not even appear at all in the model. We do not want to deny that this framework has attractive features and also can be and has been used to derive useful conclusions about monetary policy. Alan Blinder in his lectures on central banking in theory and practice (Blinder, 1999) implicitly uses this framework. He demonstrates a number of important insights. He shows for example very clearly that conducting monetary policy by "looking out the window" (*i.e.* basing monetary policy decisions on current variables) leads to wrong policy decisions.[7] Monetary policy must instead be forward looking in order to achieve the targets set by the monetary authorities, but at the same time be flexible enough to react to changing circumstances. In fact this is optimal control, but loosely defined! The research in this framework on the robustness of policy rules, such as the Taylor- and McCallum rule is also interesting and has for instance resulted in the conclusion that interest rates have to be increased by more than expected/forecasted inflation for monetary policy to be effective. Although this may sound trivial, in the past this rule has often been violated.

It is our contention, however, that because of the recent success and reputation of monetary policies and central bank(er)s, the weaknesses of this framework tend to be underestimated or even ignored. The framework is often taken too literally as a description of the situation central banks find themselves in, rather than as a framework (among others) which may help central banks in a rather general way to think about their strategies and

[7] Also Blinder (1999) makes clear that the approach discussed in the text is only one among many models that the central bank should use in determining its monetary policy stance.

policies. This easily leads to overconfidence in what this framework can mean for monetary policymaking and in what monetary policy can achieve. It has not only prompted the popularity of inflation targeting in policy circles and its almost unanimous acceptance as the preferred monetary policy strategy among academics. It has also contributed to the formulation of rather ambitious targets for inflation. The view of central bankers as engineers who are able to steer inflation rather precisely is becoming again an accurate picture. This was clearly not the case during the hey-days of monetarism or more eclectic monetary policy approaches in the seventies and eighties. One could call it ironic (or short-sighted) that the credibility view of monetary policy on which the model advocated by Clarida *et al.* (1999) also builds, was originally developed as a critique of the optimal control approach to economic policymaking. This approach has, however, clearly made a comeback.

The most fundamental theoretical weakness of the framework is that it is inconsistent as regards the description of a monetary economy. All behavioural equations are explicitly derived from rational optimising behaviour and it is argued that this is required in any sound economic theory. The usage of money and the role of money in this model, however, cannot be derived from rational optimising behaviour! It is small wonder then that money is often ignored in this framework or when incorporated this is done on an ad-hoc basis by simply putting money into the utility function or imposing that money has to be used in all transactions (a cash-in-advance constraint). Economists using this framework are aware of this problem and sometimes pay lip service to it. That does not prevent them from using this model without much restraint, sometimes claiming without any proof that this inconsistency is unimportant in practice. When we are honest we have to admit that in this framework we are doing monetary economics without money, or, as Kregel (1985) has put it, we are performing Hamlet without the prince.

We believe that the main problem with the stochastic general equilibrium framework, even with imperfections added to it, as a description of a monetary economy, is that in this model fundamental uncertainty does not exist. The uncertainty in this model is only of a stochastic nature. The sophisticated economic subjects who inhabit the general equilibrium model know then enough to solve their optimisation problems. There is no need for holding money, which yields less than all other assets. The fact that money is more liquid than other assets and that all prices are quoted in money has no relevance and holding money therefore logically makes no sense. This is different in a world in which not all uncertainty can be reduced to risk and in a world which is too complex to be approached by assuming that people (behave as if they) employ sophisticated optimisation techniques. In reality both the policymakers and the economic subjects know less than is assumed in the framework that is so popular to analyse a monetary economy and monetary policy. As a consequence, they cannot and do not behave as assumed in this framework. Money and liquidity in general are relevant to reduce information requirements and not to have to take all decisions at once. Money helps us to calculate and make decisions in a complex and uncertain world. A similar remark can be made with respect to the role of market imperfections in the stochastic general equilibrium framework. The economy would always be better off without these imperfections, wage contracts and the like have no function of their own, whereas in a world of fundamental uncertainty one could argue that without for example wage contracts the market economy cannot function.

As stated before, the mainstream framework has value to policymakers as a normative tool, but if they take it too literally they behave as if they know more than they do. One may argue that central bankers who perform inflation targeting emphasise that decisions are taken under uncertainty. This is true, but it only concerns risks, which can be shown in fan charts.[8] This only demonstrates that even the simple world of the stochastic general equilibrium framework is already quite complicated, even for intelligent policymakers. It does not disprove that the real world is even more complex and uncertain than conveyed by a colourful fan chart. Looking back over the last 30 years, can we really assume that the major shocks, which have hit us, can be described as drawings from a well-defined probability distribution? We are thinking of events such as the two oil crises, the unification of Germany, the end of communism, or the establishment of EMU.

It should also be kept in mind that central banks ultimately control inflation because of their monopoly in the provision of base money. That allows them to steer very short-term interest rates. The rest of the transmission process of changes in the stance of monetary policy to other economic variables with inflation at the end of the chain is far less predictable and controllable (and therefore also the topic of fierce debate in recent years, see the money versus credit view discussions). This implies that inflation cannot be steered with any great precision in the short term. It is only possible to steer inflation in the right direction over a longer time horizon. The length of this horizon cannot be precisely defined and is variable, depending, *inter alia*, on the magnitude and persistence of the shocks hitting the economy. It is fair to say that central banks are aware of this, but nevertheless there external communication is often more pretentious than warranted. The Bank of England for example has defined a single figure

[8] Wallis (1999) argues that the Bank of England in its model that underlies the (expected) inflation fan charts does not use a quadratic loss function but stronger still an "all or nothing" loss function which implies that the policy maker has to hit the inflation target.

target for inflation over a two years time horizon, rather than a target zone over a less specified horizon. Although this is applauded for being transparent, it can be doubted whether it is really credible in view of our inevitable lack of knowledge about the transmission process. But if the policy objective is stated in less precise terms, academics and international organisations criticise it. This is for example the case with the European Central Bank, which has defined price stability as a positive rate of inflation of less than 2% in the medium term.[9]

5. CONCLUSIONS

As long as inflation remains relatively low and output and employment are still at or near potential, academics and central bankers can probably get away with their overconfidence and the Greenspans of this world will maintain their high reputation. They can afford to behave as if the strategy of inflation targeting is the end of history of monetary policy strategies. It is remarkable how few critical analyses of inflation targeting are published nowadays. All this may change if and when reality will show that we know less than we now implicitly pretend and that inflation is less controllable than we now tend to think.

In the longer term developments in the information and communication technology may jeopardise the central bank's control of short-term interest rates (B. Friedman, 1999). This may happen when electronic money would substantially replace banknotes, but especially when it would be attractive for private institutions to clear and settle their payments without central bank involvement. This would at least reduce the power of central banks to influence economic developments. It is already remarkable today that there is such a high confidence in the powers of central banks. The size of central bank operations is very small compared to the size of the financial sector as a whole and central banks have only full control of the interest rates on their own limited operations.[10]

We do not see a reason to assume that we will soon return to the high inflation rates of the seventies. The insight that inflation does not solve any problem in the longer term, but only makes them worse, may have been learned forever and may not be lost anymore. At the same time risks to price stability will not disappear. Inflation remains a risk, basically because there

[9] A good example of a critique of the ECB along these lines is the bi-annual report written by a group of CEPR-economists: *Monitoring the European Central Bank.*

[10] If, as we are inclined to think, the confidence is at least partly a convention, this confidence can also be lost even without a marked increase in inflation (on the role of conventions and central banks in a monetary economy, see Van Ees and Garretsen, 1995).

is nothing that automatically guarantees a balanced development of supply and demand. The risk of deflation cannot be ruled out either, as long as the objective of price stability is defined rather ambitiously. We do not think there is reason for pessimism (warning against overconfidence does not necessarily imply that one should be pessimistic). Central banks and monetary policy are able to cope with the challenges just described. However, we should not expect more from central banks than what they can actually deliver. Central banking is different from engineering. It is less precise, not fully measurable judgement is always involved and it has even also something of an art. Although it is right to ask from central banks to be accountable and transparent, there are limits to the degree in which this can be achieved, for a larger public in particular. Our impression is that sometimes what is expected from central banks in this area is not possible without becoming dishonest. It is not simple at all to assess to what extent actual inflation was and could be influenced by central bank actions in the past. Current inflation is influenced by a number of past central bank actions, which all impacted on inflation with their own hardly measurable lags. It is even more complicated. Current inflation is also the result of past shocks, which have impacted on inflation, also with their own lags. Some of these shocks were known to the central bank when setting policy, others were not. The main risk today is that the discovery that we have been too optimistic about the power of central banks will lead the pendulum to swing too far into the other direction. A new pessimism may develop. Central banks may lose credibility leading to higher expected inflation and to higher interest rates. The loss of credibility would make the control of inflation more difficult. The independence of central banks may become a subject of debate and may even be eroded. This again may only lead to higher inflation without any benefit, as we then would have to rediscover painfully.

What can be done? The most important thing is that academics and central bankers try to avoid letting themselves carry away by actual economic circumstances and try to assess what monetary policy can and cannot achieve in a more realistic light. This should also be communicated to the press, politicians and the public at large. This is not so easy as the description of the mechanisms at play in Section 2 made clear. These very mechanisms also play an important role in the explanation of the existence of cycles in actual economic developments. Waves of optimism and pessimism, sometimes exaggerated, seem difficult to avoid. It may help to pay more explicit attention to economic history and the history of economic ideas. This may help us to anchor our views. At least academics in their research as well as in their teaching should see that as part of their job. It is for instance useful to recall the arguments of Milton Friedman for proposing the use of an intermediate target in monetary policy (Friedman, 1960; 1969).

This had more to do with what we do *not* know about the working of the economy than with what we do know. In the further development of economic theory the existence of fundamental uncertainty and complexity should be taken seriously. Again this is difficult, but more efforts are made in this direction than was the case at the beginning of Simon Kuipers's career.

What is also useful is the existence of a group of academic economists who do not take everything in the mainstream for granted. Such a group does not develop automatically. It requires the right incentives and intellectual climate. It also requires the willingness of both non-mainstream and mainstream economists to take each other's views seriously. Methodological pluralism is not very fruitful when, what is unfortunately often the case, it merely results in shouting over the fence. In that sense the retirement of Simon Kuipers from the department of economics of the University of Groningen is not well timed. He has always allowed research to take place that was not in the mainstream, also when he was himself holding more mainstream views. There is more than personal reason to be grateful for that and we hope that it will be part of the heritage of Simon to the economics faculty.

REFERENCES

Barro, R.J. and D. Gordon (1983), "A Positive Theory of Monetary Policy in a Natural Rate Model," *Journal of Political Economy* 91, pp. 589-610.

Bergeijk, P.A.G. van, A.L. Bovenberg, E.E.C. van Damme and J. van Sinderen (eds.) (1997), *Economic Science and Practice, The Roles of Academic Economists and Policy Makers,* Cheltenham: Edward Elgar.

Blanchard, O.J. (2000), "What do We know about Macroeconomics that Fisher and Wicksell did not?," *NBER Working Paper* 7550, Cambridge.

Blinder, A.S. (1999), *Central Banking in Theory and Practice,* Cambridge: MIT Press.

Clarida, R., J. Gali and M. Gertler (1999), "The Science of Monetary Policy: A New Keynesian Perspective," *Journal of Economic Literature* 37(4), pp. 1661-1707.

DeLong, J.B. (2000), "The Triumph of Monetarism?," *Journal of Economic Perspectives*, 14(1), pp. 83-94.

Ees, H. van and H. Garretsen (1995), "Existence and Stability of Conventions and Institutions in a Monetary Economy," *Journal of Economic Behavior and Organization* 28(4), pp. 275-288.

Eijffinger, S.C.W. and J. de Haan (1996), "The Political Economy of Central Bank Independence," *Princeton Special Papers,* Princeton.

Fase, M.M.G. and Th. van de Klundert (1998), "Simon Kuipers: An Economist in Search of Rigour and Relevance," *De Economist* 146(1), pp. 1-21.

Friedman, B.M. (1999), "The Future of Monetary Policy: The Central Bank as an Army with only a Signal Corps," *NBER Working Paper* 7420, Cambridge.

Friedman, M. (1960), *A Program for Monetary Stability,* New York: Fordham University Press.

Friedman, M. (1969), "The Role of Monetary Policy," in *The Optimum Quantity of Money and Other Essays,* Chicago: University of Chicago Press, pp. 95-110.

Garretsen, H., H. van Ees, H. Groeneveld and R. de Haas (1999), *Anatomie van financiële crises, over de prijs van risico (*Anatomy of Financial Crises, About the Pricing of Risk), Schoonhoven: Academic Service.

Greenwald, B. and J.E. Stiglitz (1987), "Keynesian, New Keynesian and New Classical Economics," *Oxford Economic Papers* 39, pp. 119-132.

Hoogduin, L.H. (1988), "On the Character of Macroeconomics, Macroeconomic Policy and Econometrics: The Need for Another Macroeconomic Policy Conception," *Banca Nazionale del Lavoro Quarterly Review* 164(March), pp. 105-125.

Hoogduin, L.H. (1991), *Some Aspects of Uncertainty and the Theory of a Monetary Economy,* PhD Thesis, Groningen.

Journal of Economic Perspectives, 14(1), Winter 2000.

Keynes, J.M. (1936), *The General Theory of Employment, Interest and Money,* The Collected Writings of John Maynard Keynes Vol. VIII, London: MacMillan.

Knight, F.H. (1921), *Risk, Uncertainty and Profit,* Boston.

Kregel, J.A. (1985), "Hamlet without the Prince: Cambridge Macroeconomics without Money," *The American Economic Review, Papers and Proceedings* 75(2), pp. 133-139.

Krugman, P. (1994), *Peddling Prosperity,* New York/London: Norton.

Krugman, P. (1998), "It's Baaack! Japan's Slump and the Return of the Liquidity Trap," *Brookings Papers on Economic Activity* 0(2), pp. 137-187.

Krugman, P. (1999), *The Return of Depression Economics,* New York/London: Norton.

Kuipers, S.K., H. van Ees and S.G. van der Lecq (1997), "Money and Stability, Some Preliminary Thoughts on the Functioning of a Monetary Economy," in H. Klenner *et al.* (eds.), *Repraesentatio Mundi, Festschrift zum 70. Geburtstag vor Heinz Holz,* Köln: Springer Verlag.

Kuipers, S.K., G.A.W. van Dalen, K. Groenveld and R.H. Koning (2000), *Groei, inkomensverdeling en economische orde* (Growth, Income Distribution and Economic Systems), Telderstichting, Den Haag.

Kydland, F.E. and E.C. Prescott (1977), "Rules rather than Discretion: The Inconsistency of Optimal Plans," *Journal of Political Economy* 85, pp. 473-492.

Lucas, R.E. jr. (1976), "Econometric Policy Evaluation: A Critique," in K. Brunner and A.H. Meltzer (eds.), *Volume I of the Carnegy Rochester Conferences on Public Policy,* Supplementary Series to the *Journal of Monetary Economics*, pp. 19-46.

Modigliani, F. (1977), "The Monetarist Controversy, or Should We Forsake Stabilization Policies?," *The American Economic Review* 67, pp. 1-19.

Shiller, R. (2000), *Irrational Exuberance,* Princeton: Princeton University Press.

Simon, H.A. (1976), "From Substantive to Procedural Rationality," in S. Latsis (ed.), *Method and Appraisal in Economics,* Cambridge: Cambridge University Press, pp. 129-148.

Smith, V.L. (1998), "Experimental Economics: Behavioural Lessons for Microeconomic Theory and Policy," in D.P. Jacobs, E. Kalai and M.I. Kamien (eds.), *Frontiers of Research in Economic Theory, The Nancy L. Schwartz Lectures, 1983-1997*, Cambridge: Cambridge University Press, pp. 104-122.

Solow, R.M. (2000), "Towards a Macroeconomics of the Medium Run," *Journal of Economic Perspectives* 14(1), Winter, pp. 151-158.

Stiglitz, J. (1998), "Central Banking in a Democratic Society," *De Economist* 146(2), pp. 199-226.

Thaler, R.H. (2000), " From Homo Economicus to Homo Sapiens," *Journal of Economic Perspectives* 14(1), Winter, pp. 133-141.

Tinbergen, J. (1967), *Economic Policy: Principles and Design,* revised edition, Amsterdam: North Holland.

Wallis, K.F. (1999), "Asymmetric Density Forecasts of Inflation and the Bank of England's Fan Chart," Paper presented at the seminar in honour of Ken Wallis, Honorary Doctor in Economics, University of Groningen, 9 November 1999.

Chapter 11

Monetary Policy Rules for EMU

Martin M.G. Fase
Econometric Research and Special Studies Department, De Nederlandsche Bank N.V. and University of Amsterdam

Key words: Tinbergen-Theil framework, Inflation targeting, Policy rules

Abstract: This chapter is about the feedback with a policy rule and examines the implications of a policy instrument in an areawide empirical macroeconomic model for EMU. The main policy conclusion of our exercise is that the use of policy rules for interest rate and monetary targeting enhances output and price stability.

1. INTRODUCTION

The current state of monetary analysis is remarkably different from that of 25 years ago. For example, today monetary policy rules are at the centre of monetary theory and policy in the US and EMU and thus in the member countries. This state of affairs contrasts sharply with the practice and analysis of monetary policy in the early seventies in the Netherlands, which emphasised the conceptual framework of Holtrop and the Nederlandsche Bank. Perhaps one may wish to consider this framework a particular rule for monetary policy. How this may be, Holtrop's view encompasses a theoretical model of the working of money in an economy. The first attempt to verify this model statistically initiated an interesting debate both in the Netherlands and elsewhere about the merits and shortcomings of Dutch monetarism. Kuipers (Kuipers and Wilpstra, 1973) participated in this debate. A striking feature of the Holtrop model, which several participants in the 1973 debate focused on, was the total absence of behavioural equations and the predominance of identities that were trivial in the sense that they lacked explanatory power. This coincided with an amazing bias towards conceptual emphasis rather than empirical validation. In some respect this intellectual warfare was, similar to the debate that followed the Friedman-Meiselman paper a decade earlier, an important starting point for monetary econometrics and large scale monetary models in the United States (see *e.g.* Fase, 1987, 2000). Nowadays, quantitative macroeconomic modelling of the monetary sector is *bon ton* and within this intellectual framework disagreements in policy conclusions have a common ground.

Unlike the state of the art in the seventies and early eighties, nowadays large empirical macroeconomic models are no longer *à la mode* in academia. Macroeconomic and monetary theory has been through the rational expectations revolution, the real business cycle paradigm and has arrived at a stage in which small calibrated models dominate the analytical scene in macroeconomics (see *e.g.* McCallum, 1999). Within the policy environment, however, decision makers consider macroeconomic models useful tools as illustrated *e.g.* by the European Central Bank's attempt to construct an area-wide econometric model for EMU and the existence of Euromon, *i.e.* the Netherlands Bank's multicountry model for Europe. In spite of the fact that scholarly interest in large policy models has faded away, small analytical macroeconomic models still play an important role as a new and often challenging venture of policy research. An important and newly rediscovered avenue is the analysis of policy rules, that depict the structural feedback between the working of an economy and policy shocks (see *e.g.* Poole, 1999).

This chapter is about the feedback with a policy rule defined as a systematic decision making process using economic information in a consistent and predictable way. An important motivation for this approach is the desire to increase policy transparency. This new style of research logically shifts emphasis away from target rules to instrumental rules and this chapter intends to illustrate this. Section 2 sets out the relationship between the well received reaction function in the older literature in the Tinbergen-Theil tradition and the novel and now fashionable tool of a policy rule, considered both in a static and a time consistent dynamic environment. Section 3 considers possible monetary targets and instruments to implement the Tinbergen-Theil framework postulated in Section 2. Section 4 studies this policy instrument rules for the framework of a small areawide empirically estimated model of EMU. Section 5 examines the implications of a policy instrument applied to this empirical macroeconomic model for EMU. Section 6 draws the main policy conclusions.

2. THE TINBERGEN-THEIL FRAMEWORK AND REACTION FUNCTIONS

The reaction function in a static environment

Traditionally, a central bank's policy behaviour is summarised in a policy reaction or response function, in the same way consumer market behaviour is described by demand functions for goods and services on the basis of constrained utility maximisation. Following this literature (Theil, 1964; Friedlaender, 1973; Fase *et al.*, 1977, 1980; Blinder, 1998, amongst others) we view a policy reaction function as the result of the policy maker's attempt to maximise a social welfare function (or minimise the social loss function) in targets and instruments, taking into account the relevant structural economic interdependencies. Thus, the analytical derivation of a policy reaction function has been reduced to a constrained optimisation exercise, or a problem of dynamic optimisation if a forward looking time consistent behaviour is taken into account. For simplicity, we ignore the latter for the time being and begin with the static case.

Let y_i (i = 1, 2, ..., q) denote the actual value of the ith policy target and x_j (j = 1, 2, ..., q) the actual value of the jth policy instrument. The policy maker's preferences are summarised in his welfare or loss function on targets and instruments. We assume that this function $\ell(\mathbf{x}, \mathbf{y})$, with $\mathbf{y}$ and $\mathbf{x}$ ($q\times 1$) vectors with the elements y_i and x_j respectively, can be approximated around the desired values $\mathbf{y}^*$ and $\mathbf{x}^*$ by a quadratic loss function of the form

$$\ell(\mathbf{x},\mathbf{y})=\left(\mathbf{x}-\mathbf{x}^*\right)'\mathbf{P}\left(\mathbf{x}-\mathbf{x}^*\right)+\left(\mathbf{y}-\mathbf{y}^*\right)'\mathbf{Q}\left(\mathbf{y}-\mathbf{y}^*\right), \tag{1}$$

with $\mathbf{P}$ and $\mathbf{Q}$ diagonal matrices of the appropriate order, showing the weights attached to each instrument and target in the loss function. Obviously, specification (1) implies some characteristics for the assumed loss or social welfare function, which make the problem tractable. First, the welfare function is static and the desired target values are assumed to be given for each point in time. Second, specification (1) implies the absence of interaction between instruments and target variables. This means that the policy maker is indifferent as to how targets are achieved. Third, both instruments and targets enter the loss function, to allow for the fact that there are costs involved in using the instruments for economic or monetary policy. Finally, the quadratic nature of the loss function implies that the direction of deviations from the desired values becomes irrelevant, which may be a rather restrictive assumption. This is undoubtedly a simplification, but is analytically justified to keep the algebra simple.

We assume first that the policy maker minimises (1) over a single period, subject to the constraint imposed by the structure of the economy. This is assumed to be given by a structural model

$$\mathbf{y} = F(\mathbf{y}, \mathbf{x}, \mathbf{z}), \tag{2}$$

with $\mathbf{y}$ the $(p\times 1)$ vector of endogenous variables including the $q \leq p$ policy objectives of the central bank as indicated above. Similarly, the $(q\times 1)$ vector $\mathbf{x}$ denotes the policy instruments and the $(r\times 1)$ vector $\mathbf{z}$ the non-policy exogenous variables. Imposing linearity on (2), the reduced form of this model may be written as

$$\mathbf{y} = \mathbf{Rx} + \mathbf{Sz}, \tag{3}$$

with at least one element of vector $\mathbf{y}$ a policy objective, $\mathbf{R}$ and $\mathbf{S}$ $(p\times q)$ and $(p\times s)$ matrices of reduced-form coefficients and $\mathbf{z}$ the $(p\times 1)$ vector of exogenous influences on $\mathbf{y}$. The effectiveness of instrument k in attaining target j may be measured by $\partial y_j / \partial x_k$, *i.e.* the impact multipliers at moment t. So, the elements of matrix $\mathbf{R}$ in Equation (3) contains all information about the effectiveness of the policy instruments x_k, k=1,...,q.

The optimal value of the instruments $\mathbf{x}$ are obtained by minimising Equation (1) subject to constraint (3). This results in

$$\mathbf{x} = \mathbf{x}^* + \mathbf{P}^{-1}\mathbf{R}'\mathbf{Q}(\mathbf{y} - \mathbf{y}^*), \tag{4}$$

which may be viewed as the theoretical basis for any specification of policy reaction functions or policy rules introducing feedback with actual developments. In this framework any x_j equals the corresponding desired instrument value plus a linear combination of weighted deviations of actual from desirable target values. Each weight is the product of the impact of instrument x_k with respect to the respective target and coefficients given by Equation (1).

In order to obtain the reduced-form coefficients we need to specify the relevant economic system explicitly. In the above framework the policy maker's social welfare function has been constrained by a reduced form of the economy considered. Thus, these equations should reflect the central bank's view on the working of the economy and although a stylised representation of this sort naturally ignores a lot of details which are of the outmost importance in the operations of a central bank, it does not affect it qualitatively.

So, assuming the central bank aims to achieve π^* and y^*, for inflation and output respectively, with y-y^* the output gap, the resulting policy reaction function according to Equation (4) for two single instruments χ_{it} with i=1,2, is in general:

$$\chi_{it} = \alpha_1 + \alpha_2\left(\pi_t - \pi^*\right) + \alpha_3\left(y_t - y_t^*\right),$$

with $\mathbf{y} = (\pi_t, y_t)$ and $\mathbf{y}^* = (\pi^*, y^*)$ and $\mathbf{x} = (\chi_{1t}, \chi_{2t})$. The elements of the vectors are scalars.

The reaction function in a dynamic time consistent framework

In a dynamic framework, assume that the policy maker has a discount factor $\delta \in (0,1)$, and solves

$$\min_{\{x_{t+j} \in \Omega_{t+j}\}_{j\geq 0}} E\left[\sum_{j=0}^{\infty} \delta^j \ell(\mathbf{x}_t, \mathbf{y}_t) \mid \Omega_t\right], \tag{5}$$

with the period-loss function $\ell(\mathbf{x}_t, \mathbf{y}_t)$ as in (1), subject to

$$0 = \mathbf{G}\left(\mathbf{y}_t, \mathbf{y}_{t-1}, \ldots, \mathbf{y}_{t-m_y}, \mathbf{x}_t, \mathbf{x}_{t-1}, \ldots, \mathbf{x}_{t-m_x}, \mathbf{z}_t, \mathbf{z}_{t-1}, \ldots, \mathbf{z}_{t-m_z}\right), \tag{6}$$

which summarises the structural model. In (5) and (6), E denotes the expectation operator, Ω_t the information set at time t, and m_j the longest lag for the corresponding vector of variables, $j \in \{y, x, z\}$. The lag structure in specification (6) may be thought of as the autoregressive or adaptive representation of forward-looking variables, like, for example, expected inflation. The (indirect) value function for (5) satisfies the Bellman equation

$$V_t(\Omega_t) = \min_{x_t \in \Omega_t} \{\ell(\mathbf{x}_t, \mathbf{y}_t) + \delta E[V_{t+1}(\Omega_{t+1}) \mid \Omega_t]\},$$

where $\mathbf{x}_t$ and $\mathbf{y}_t$ satisfy (5) and (6) for all $t \geq 0$.

Furthermore, imposing linearity on the structural model (6), it can be shown that the optimal policy rule is a linear feedback rule (see *e.g.* Rudebusch and Svensson, 1999). Again, as in the previous section, concentrating on the instrument x_t, say the short run interest rate, the model has a convenient state-space representation,

$$\mathbf{s}_{t+1} = \mathbf{A}\mathbf{s}_t + \mathbf{B}\chi_t + \mathbf{v}_{t+1}, \tag{7}$$

where $\mathbf{s}_t$ is the state vector, the dimension of which depends on the complexity of the structural model, and $\mathbf{v}_t$ the vector of disturbance terms. In general, the state vector may comprise lagged and current endogenous policy and exogenous non-policy variables, as well as lagged instruments.

Minimising the intertemporal loss function (5) under (7) gives an optimal linear feedback rule of the form

$$\chi_t = \mathbf{fs}_t, \tag{8}$$

where $\mathbf{f}$ is a row vector of appropriate dimension, depending on the matrices $\mathbf{A}$, $\mathbf{B}$, the parameters of the structural model and the specified weights in the period-loss function. By means of an illustration, assume that the central bank has an inflation target π^* and an output target y^*; the resulting policy reaction or response function leads to the following rule

$$\chi_t = i^* + \sum_{j=0}^{m_\pi} a_j\left(\pi_{t-j} - \pi^*\right) + \sum_{j=0}^{m_y} b_j\left(y_{t-j} - y^*\right) + \sum_{j=1}^{m_i} c_j\left(i_{t-j} - i^*\right). \tag{9}$$

Comparing rule (9) to rule (4), the optimal policy rule within a dynamic time-consistent framework is modified by the inclusion of lagged terms, which means absence of rational expectations. This time consistency is the important feature of rule (9) and the main distinction with (4), although the two have in common that the parameters are fixed. Understanding the implications of and testing this equation is the main focus of the remainder of this chapter. Recall that we need not distinguish between discretionary and commitment solutions in this case, since we have substituted out any forward-looking variables. It is interesting to point out that for $a_j = b_j = c_j = 0$, $j \geq 1$ we retrieve for χ_t the short-term interest rate a simple Taylor rule and, if an intermediate target like the money supply rather than final targets are considered, for χ_t the simple McCallum rule.

3. TARGETS AND INSTRUMENTS: A REFLECTION

The pursuit of price stability and output stabilisation

Price stability as an objective of monetary policy was first mooted around 75 years ago as the certainties of the gold standard were becoming shaky and re-emerged as a central policy focus again with the collapse of the Bretton Woods system in the early seventies. In these two episodes monetary policy lost at once both its fixed nominal anchor – the gold standard or the dollar being seen as the natural anchor at the time – and mechanical character. This created the need for a monetary policy framework.

The price stability target raises various questions. Firstly, there is the question of the justification of this target. Secondly, there is the measurement question and, thirdly, there is the question of whether price stability is a purely monetary phenomenon which can be achieved using only monetary means. Finally, there is the question of what price stability, in a European context, really means in quantitative terms and what incentives the Governing Council of the ESCB will have to pursue this goal.

A great deal has been written about the desirability of price stability. Freeman (1991) of the Bank of Canada, for example, has pointed out that a policy of price stability emanates from the conviction that an economy with stable prices is in a better shape than an economy where this is not the case. This view is strengthened by the analytical fact that it is impossible to state a specific positive rate of inflation at which the world would perform identically or better than a world with stable prices, notwithstanding the fact that, in the very short term, a certain amount of inflation can have a beneficial effect on growth. Moreover, the costs, *i.e.* the losses of welfare, associated with the transition from an inflationary world to a world of stable prices can be high and it is therefore appropriate to keep this transition as short as possible. This latter motivates considering the stabilisation of the output gap as an additional target.

Another question is what price stability means and how it is measured. The latter is mainly a technical statistical problem which as a matter of fact concerns the making of appropriate price indices. In spite of its technical nature, the measurement of purchasing power is very important for monetary policy.[1] However, for a policy aiming to create favourable conditions minute changes in the price index seem less interesting. Perhaps this holds also in a European context, playing down the question what price stability is in precise numerical terms. Reflection on this issue shifts the emphasis back to monetary disturbances in the Holtropian spirit of monetary neutrality or equilibrium. Perhaps this is the case with the Fed's current approach to monetary policy (see *e.g.* Greenspan, 2000, and Fase and Vanthoor, 2000). An incidental advantage of the Fed's approach is that it reflects the nature of the price stability goal better and avoids any fixation on newly released inflation figures, as is sometimes the case in Europe.

Monetary targeting versus interest rate targeting

Monetary policy is often taken to control of money supply according to either a broad or a narrow definition. An interest rate policy on the other

[1] It is noteworthy that the monetary economist *par excellence*, Irving Fisher, was also the author in 1922 of a monograph on index numbers, while Keynes in his monetary *magnum opus* of 1930, the *Treatise on Money* also devotes close attention to the measurement of purchasing power and the appropriateness of suitable price index numbers.

hand focuses on the nominal interest rate as an instrument and intermediate target.

A money supply policy is based on at least three assumptions. Firstly, it assumes that the money supply is relevant to the ultimate goal of monetary policy. The theoretical basis for this hypothesis is provided, for example, by the quantity theory or by the more Koopmansian view that the use of money in terms of the spontaneous hoarding or dishoarding can cause disturbances in the circular flow of goods and services. The second assumption is the possibility to define money clearly and effectively, given a stable demand for money and therefore a predictable velocity of circulation. The third assumption is that the money supply is largely determined by exogenous forces and is under control of the central bank. This too is not always a plausible assumption.

Money supply and interest rates are to a certain extent the mirrors of each other. Therefore, one may ask whether there is really a difference between a money supply and an interest rate policy. In theory, given totally deterministic economic relationships, monetary and interest rate targeting are equivalent. As soon as either uncertainty is taken into account or the relationship between money and income becomes weaker – and hence the relationship between interest rate and money – an interest rate policy becomes feasible in its own right.

It is well understood that interest rates are more easily and rapidly tracked from a statistical point of view, than money supply. This is an important point and justifies taking a closer look at interest rate policy as an alternative, although the fact that in some countries the interest rate is highly politicised should not be neglected too easily. Barro (1989) and Goodfriend (1987) have developed a theoretical basis for an interest rate policy. Their argument is that controlling real interest rates is asking too much of monetary policy but the nominal interest rate is certainly within the domain of monetary policy.

The Barro and Goodfriend argument assumes a dichotomy between the real and monetary sphere. The nominal interest rate is the sum of expected inflation and the real interest rate, which is seen as being an exogenous variable determined outside the monetary sphere. Given the exogenous nature of real interest rates, the central bank controls the nominal interest rate by influencing inflation and expectations. This implies that a rise in the nominal interest rate requires monetary expansion. However, the public sees this as a temporary expansion, not resulting in a rise of expected interest rates. Empirical evidence seems to support this theoretical view. The conclusion is – and this is the answer to the third question – that an interest rate target can be both a guide and an instrument for monetary policy and offers an appropriate alternative to monetary targeting. Interestingly enough, pleas for the abandonment of a money supply policy in favour of an interest rate policy are not entirely new. A historical example is provided by the recommendation of the erstwhile Radcliffe Committee in the United Kingdom, published in 1959.

4. ACTIVISM VERSUS POLICY RULES

The history of the debate on monetary policy rules goes back to the interwar period when it started with a series of articles by Schumpeter in 1925. He argued, mainly on ideological grounds, against the proposal to control the money supply put forward by Keynes in his *Tract on Monetary Reform* of 1923. Schumpeter put his faith in the automatic mechanism of the gold standard rather than the discretionary monetary policy of a central bank. His main argument was his fear that monetary management would systematically undermine capitalism. Schumpeter's argument was not very convincing, but sparked off an interesting academic debate in the Netherlands among J.G. Koopmans, J. Tinbergen and G.M. Verrijn Stuart. This debate became the theoretical basis of postwar monetary policy in the Netherlands until the 1970s (see Fase, 1994). The arguments put forward in this debate are partly analytical and partly ideological. The best known of them is the argument in favour of a fixed money growth rule proposed by the Chicago economist Henry E. Simons (1936) and later M. Friedman (1960). The parallel with Schumpeter's view is as unmistakable as Simons's influence on the monetary thinking of Milton Friedman. He has long argued in favour of a monetary policy according to fixed rules.

Perhaps the spirit behind the policy reaction functions derived within a Tinbergen-Theil framework reflects activism which is alien to the ancient and today's proposals of fixed or flexible policy rules The aim of any policy rule is to enhance transparency and reduce uncertainty in order to create a stable economic environment. Therefore, predictability and credibility are basic requirements which may be perfectly well served by policy rules. Two policy rules have become prominent. The oldest is the so-called McCallum rule which adjusts the monetary growth rate when nominal GDP growth deviates from a chosen target value. The McCallum rule is undoubtedly of a monetarist persuasion, but ignores perhaps the fact that central banks do not have direct control over money supply. This may perhaps explain why the other rule, which is interest rate oriented, has become more popular, with both central bankers and academics. This is the Taylor rule, which adjusts short-term nominal interest rates when expected inflation and real output deviate from their target values. The Taylor rule has the practical advantage that it pertains to the central bank's actual policy instrument and is easier to understand by the public. However, what the two rules have in common is that they are designed to keep inflation low and to stabilise fluctuations in output.

Rather than contrasting the two policy rules conceptually, we prefer to examine their comparative advantages in stabilising the euro area-wide economic output and inflation empirically. Therefore, by way of theoretical experimentation, we will in this chapter engage in a detailed empirical investigation for the two rules, which has been done by reference to an area-wide macroeconomic model for EMU. To this end, a small New Keynesian model of the euro area, given in Equations (10)-(13), is postulated. This model serves as a vehicle to explore the performance of alternative simple monetary policy rules by carrying out counterfactual historical simulations over the period 1975-1998. For the McCallum rule, given in (14), however, we employ an adjusted version taking into account that the short-term interest rate is an instrument in adjusting the intermediate target of money supply.

As to the model equations, the error correction term in (10) – in square brackets – implies that in equilibrium real GDP depends on the real short term interest rate and a time trend. Equation (11) explains price determination, with prices measured by the GDP deflator p. In equilibrium prices are determined by P-star, *i.e.* the price level, p^*, consistent with m, the actual money stock (M1), potential real GDP, y^*, and the structural level of the income velocity of money, v^* (Tödter and Reimers, 1994; Coenen, 1998; Svensson, 2000). Moreover, (11) reflects the existence of inflation inertia. The P-star approach allows for the exploration of a policy strategy in which money growth is either an intermediate target or a reference variable for the conduct of monetary policy. Equation (12) explains the demand for real balances, m, as a function of real GDP, short-term interest rates and inflation. Long rates are not included in order to keep the model's structure parsimonious. Lower case letters denote logs. The data are derived from the National Accounts figures aggregated across the 12 euro countries and are seasonally unadjusted. Volumes and values are aggregated variables measured in DM of 1990 (for further details see Fase and Winder, 1998). The equations are estimated by OLS using quarterly data for the period 1972:1-1998:4. Newey-West heteroskedasticity and autocorrelation consistent t-values are reported in parentheses. LM(4) is the Lagrange Multiplier test-statistic for residual autocorrelation up to order 4. For the sake of brevity, estimated coefficients for seasonal dummy variables are not reported. The estimated model for the sample period 1973:1-1998:4, with t-values in parentheses, is

$$\Delta y = \underset{(3.1)}{1.6813} + \underset{(1.5)}{0.1179}\,\Delta y_{-2} + \underset{(3.5)}{0.3415}\,\Delta y_{-4}$$

$$-\underset{(3.0)}{0.1192}\left[y_{-1} - \underset{(16.5)}{0.0060}\,tr + \underset{(2.2)}{0.0086}\sum_{j=2}^{3}\frac{\left(R - 100\Delta_4 p_{-1}\right)_{-j}}{2}\right], \tag{10}$$

$$\overline{R}^2 = 0.83, SE = 0.0072, LM(4) = 3.71\,(0.45),$$

$$\Delta\Delta_4 p = -\underset{(1.4)}{0.0006} - \underset{(3.1)}{0.3367}\,\Delta\Delta_4 p_{-4} + \underset{(4.8)}{0.1518}\sum_{j=1}^{8}\frac{\left(p^*_{-j} - p_{-j}\right)}{8}, \tag{11}$$

$$\overline{R}^2 = 0.18, SE = 0.0046, LM(4) = 4.58\,(0.33),$$

$$\Delta(m-p) = \underset{(4.1)}{0.0158} + \underset{(3.6)}{0.3523}\,\Delta(m-p)_{-4} - \underset{(2.7)}{0.0035}\,\Delta R - \underset{(5.6)}{0.9690}\,\Delta\Delta_4 p$$

$$-\underset{(2.4)}{0.0822}\left((m-p)_{-1} - \underset{(-)}{1.0}\,y_{-1} + \underset{(2.2)}{0.0158}\,R_{-1} + \underset{(1.6)}{0.9069}\,\Delta_4 p_{-1}\right), \tag{12}$$

$$\overline{R}^2 = 0.96, SE = 0.0097, LM(4) = 4.98\,(0.29),$$

$$p^* = m + y^* - v^*, \tag{13}$$

with y = real GDP; p = GDP deflator; m = M1 balances; R = short-term interest rate, measured in percentage points; y^* = potential real GDP, measured as HP-filter of y with smoothing parameter = 1600; v^* = structural level of M1 velocity, measured as HP-filter of *m-p-y*, again with smoothing parameter = 1600; tr = linear time trend (1970:1=1).

5. THE POLICY SIMULATIONS

The reason for considering the above representation of the way the economy works is mainly to obtain a feeling for the impact of alternative policy rules in our model.

In assessing the performance of monetary policy rules the main focus is on the operationality issue, not on robustness over different model structures. The latter issue has been extensively studied by McCallum (see *e.g.* McCallum and Nelson (1999) for further details). Two types of policies are investigated: a feedback rule for targeting money growth via interest rates and a conventional Taylor rule. The instrument of monetary policy is the policy-controlled short-term interest rate, here captured by the three-month money market rate in the euro area, *R*.

The feedback rule for targeting money growth is the adjusted McCallum rule:

$$R = R_{-1} + \lambda\left(100\left(\Delta_4 m_{-1} - \Delta_4 m_{-1}^T\right) - 100\theta\left(\Delta_4 m_{-2} - \Delta_4 m_{-2}^T\right)\right), \qquad (14)$$

$$\lambda \geq 0, 0 \leq \theta \leq 1,$$

where λ is the feedback parameter of interest rate adjustment in response to departures of money growth from target money growth $\Delta_4 m^T$. θ reflects the relative importance of feedback deviation versus feedback from cumulated disequilibria in the last quarters. Target money growth is consistent with trend growth of real output and velocity as well as an annual inflation rate of 2%. Trend growth rates of real output and velocity are exogenous and defined as the HP-filtered actual real GDP and M1 velocity.

The employed Taylor rule is of the form:

$$R = R_{-1} + \lambda\left(100\left(\gamma_y\left(y_{-1} - y_{-1}^*\right) + \gamma_p\left(\Delta_4 p_{-1} - 0.02\right)\right)\right) -$$

$$100\lambda\theta\left(\gamma_y\left(y_{-2} - y_{-2}^*\right) + \gamma_p\left(\Delta_4 p_{-2} - 0.02\right)\right), \qquad (15)$$

$$\lambda \geq 0, 0 \leq \theta \leq 1.$$

Again, λ is the general feedback parameter and θ reflects the relative importance of feedback from the last quarter's disequilibrium versus cumulated disequilibria. γ_y and γ_p are the weights for output and inflation stabilisation, respectively.

Policy rules incorporate a feedback mechanism between desirable economic performance and policy measures. This creates a situation that policy becomes pre-emptive and anticipating, with a crucial role for the parameters λ and θ in any counterfactual historical simulation exercise. The main yardstick of assessing the results is the degree of volatility in output, inflation and interest rates. This volatility is measured by the standard deviation and the root mean square error (RMSE), with those statistics for the situation without a policy rule as benchmark. In case of an effective policy rule the volatility of the simulated path should be smaller than of the historical path. The results of the counterfactual historical simulations as well as the sample statistics are reported in Tables 1 to 3. The simulation outcomes relate to dynamic simulations for the period 1975:1-1998:4 of the model consisting of Equations (10) to (13), complemented by a monetary policy rule, *i.e.* the money growth target rule (14) in case of Table 1, and the Taylor rule (15) for Tables 2 and 3.

Table 1. Performance of McCallum rule simulated over 1975:1-1998:4

	RMSE	Standard deviation for		
	price level	output	inflation	interest rate
Actual data	0.226	0.016	0.024	0.787
Simulated pattern for:				
$\lambda = 0$	0.150	0.014	0.044	0.000
$\theta = 0.95$				
$\lambda = 0.05$	0.161	0.013	0.043	0.056
$\lambda = 0.10$	0.163	0.013	0.040	0.112
$\lambda = 0.25$	0.143	0.013	0.032	0.278
$\lambda = 0.50$	0.090	0.013	0.025	0.564
$\lambda = 0.75$	0.053	0.014	0.022	0.874
$\lambda = 1.00$	0.034	0.014	0.021	1.233
$\theta = 0.80$				
$\lambda = 0.05$	0.253	0.013	0.046	0.069
$\lambda = 0.10$	0.264	0.013	0.039	0.127
$\lambda = 0.25$	0.168	0.016	0.037	0.307
$\lambda = 0.50$	0.134	0.022	0.045	0.636
$\lambda = 0.75$ *	0.127	0.025	0.057	1.035
$\theta = 0.50$				
$\lambda = 0.05$	0.304	0.014	0.039	0.108
$\lambda = 0.10$	0.220	0.017	0.048	0.231
$\lambda = 0.25$ *	0.225	0.034	0.075	0.715

Explanatory note: output is measured by $\Delta_4 y$, inflation by $\Delta_4 p$, and interest rate by ΔR; the RMSE is the root mean square deviation of the simulated price level from the target price level consistent with a constant annual inflation rate of 2%.

* marks explosive oscillatory patterns.

The first row reports the outcomes with the actual interest rate series. In the next rows, the interest rate is determined by the monetary policy rule. RMSE is the root mean square deviation of the simulated price level from the target price level consistent with a constant annual inflation rate of 2%. For the actual euro-area data this figure is 0.226 in the period under investigation. For real GDP growth, inflation and the change in the short-term interest rate, the tables show means and standard deviations, both for the actual (first row) and simulated data.

Table 2. Performance of Taylor rule simulated over 1975:1-1998:4

	RMSE	Standard deviation for		
	price level	output	inflation	interest rate
Actual data	0.226	0.016	0.024	0.787
Simulated pattern for:				
$\lambda = 0$	0.150	0.014	0.044	0.000
$\theta = 0.95$				
$\lambda = 0.05$	0.094	0.014	0.036	0.052
$\lambda = 0.10$	0.079	0.014	0.031	0.103
$\lambda = 0.25$	0.103	0.014	0.029	0.257
$\lambda = 0.50$	0.118	0.014	0.028	0.512
$\lambda = 0.75$	0.119	0.015	0.028	0.770
$\lambda = 1.00$	0.120	0.016	0.027	1.031
$\theta = 0.80$				
$\lambda = 0.05$	0.114	0.013	0.033	0.059
$\lambda = 0.10$	0.066	0.013	0.025	0.103
$\lambda = 0.25$	0.042	0.014	0.022	0.262
$\lambda = 0.50$	0.057	0.013	0.023	0.526
$\lambda = 0.75$ *	0.069	0.023	0.037	1.154
$\theta = 0.50$				
$\lambda = 0.05$	0.066	0.014	0.023	0.076
$\lambda = 0.10$	0.080	0.018	0.028	0.215
$\lambda = 0.25$ *	0.166	0.036	0.074	1.391

Explanatory note: γ_y=0.5 and: γ_p=1.0; output is measured by $\Delta_4 y$, inflation by $\Delta_4 p$, and interest rate by ΔR; the RMSE is the root mean square deviation of the simulated price level from the target price level consistent with a constant annual inflation rate of 2%.

* marks explosive oscillatory patterns.

When the money rule (14) applies (Table 1), the most favourable outcomes are achieved for high values of θ. For lower values of θ on the other hand dynamic instability problems may arise and stabilisation of average inflation comes at the cost of considerably higher inflation volatility. For $\lambda = 0.75$ or 1 and $\theta = 0.95$, inflation is close to 2% on average and output growth is only marginally weaker than in the actual data. The main drawback is some increase in interest rate volatility.

Table 3. Performance of Taylor rule simulated over 1975:1-1998:4

	RMSE	Standard deviation for		
	price level	output	inflation	interest rate
Actual data	0.226	0.016	0.024	0.787
Simulated pattern for:				
$\lambda = 0$	0.150	0.014	0.044	0.000
$\theta = 0.95$				
$\lambda = 0.05$	0.110	0.014	0.038	0.035
$\lambda = 0.10$	0.088	0.013	0.034	0.069
$\lambda = 0.25$	0.080	0.013	0.030	0.170
$\lambda = 0.50$	0.092	0.014	0.028	0.337
$\lambda = 0.75$	0.094	0.014	0.027	0.509
$\lambda = 1.00$	0.096	0.015	0.027	0.689
$\theta = 0.80$				
$\lambda = 0.05$	0.166	0.013	0.038	0.050
$\lambda = 0.10$	0.132	0.013	0.030	0.080
$\lambda = 0.25$	0.037	0.015	0.023	0.195
$\lambda = 0.50$	0.050	0.015	0.028	0.434
$\lambda = 0.75$ *	0.060	0.018	0.034	0.817
$\theta = 0.50$				
$\lambda = 0.05$	0.157	0.014	0.029	0.080
$\lambda = 0.10$	0.099	0.018	0.034	0.219
$\lambda = 0.25$ *	0.240	0.042	0.092	1.379

Explanatory note: γ_y=0.25 and: γ_p=1.0; output is measured by $\Delta_4 y$, inflation by $\Delta_4 p$, and interest rate by ΔR; the RMSE is the root mean square deviation of the simulated price level from the target price level consistent with a constant annual inflation rate of 2%.

* marks explosive oscillatory patterns.

The performance under the Taylor rules depends on the weights the policy maker attaches to output and inflation stabilisation. The results reported in Table 2 are based on an output weight of 0.5 and an inflation weight of 1. Performance, in terms of inflation volatility, is relatively unfavourable for high values of θ. At high θ, inflation volatility and output growth may be improved upon by raising λ, but at the cost of higher average inflation. For lower values of θ the results for average output growth, average inflation and inflation volatility improve. However, the lower θ, the sooner dynamic instability problems arise. If policy makers care relatively less about output stabilisation, average inflation tends to be somewhat lower *ceteris paribus*. This follows from a comparison of Tables 3 and 2. On the other hand, inflation volatility is slightly higher in Table 3 compared to Table 2.

All in all the counterfactual simulation results show that adhering strictly to a monetary policy rule pays off in terms of lower average inflation rates for a wide range of parameter constellations, bringing average inflation down from 5.2% to a rate between 2% and 3.5%. However, for most parameter constellations this would come at some cost in terms of higher inflation volatility and slightly lower output growth. Of course these conclusions draw on the implicit assumption that the structure of the model and the behaviour of economic agents would not have been changed by the introduction of a monetary policy consistent with simple feedback rules as used in the present exercise.

The findings are surprising. For the postulated model, application of the monetary policy rule either *à la* McCallum or *à la* Taylor reduces instability compared to the situation without such a rule. Moreover, according to our experiments interest rate targeting seems to be superior to monetary targeting. If we take the situation without policy rules to be a regime of active or discretionary monetary policy then a policy according to rules is preferable from the point of view of stability of inflation or of the business cycle stabilisation. This result, supports the hypothesis that policy rules, either of monetarist or other persuasion, enhance transparency and stability for EMU as a whole.

6. CONCLUSIONS

The first conclusion of our analysis is that the reaction function derived within the conventional Tinbergen-Theil framework is logically equivalent to a particular policy rule. However, in spirit the two are completely different because policy rules like that of Taylor or McCallum are designed to generate transparency and reduce uncertainty around decision making of monetary authorities in a similar way as budgetary rules attempt to do with respect to government behaviour. Thus, the Taylor or McCallum policy rules do not reflect the monetary policy activism which is embodied in the Tinbergen-Theil framework. The second conclusion of our analysis is that for the macroeconomic modelling attempted here, monetary policy rules matter in creating stability and therefore transparency.

REFERENCES

Barro, R.J. (1989), "Interest Rate Targeting," *Journal of Monetary Economics* 23, pp. 3-30.
Blinder, A.S. (1998), *Central Banking in Theory and Practice*, Cambridge: MIT Press.
Coenen, G. (1998), "Inflation Versus Monetary Targeting in a P-Star Model with Rational Expectations," in *Topics in monetary policy modeling*, BIS Conference Papers 6, pp. 215-234.
Fase, M.M.G. (1987), "Geld en inkomen," in H.J. Bosman and J.C. Brezet (eds.), *Sparen en investeren: Geld en banken*, Leiden/Antwerpen: Stenfert Kroese, pp. 187-214.
Fase, M.M.G. (1994), "Rise and Demise of Dutch Monetarism: The Schumpeter-Koopmans-Holtrop Connection," *History of Political Economy* 26 (1), Spring 1994, pp. 21-38.
Fase, M.M.G. (2000), *Tussen behoud en vernieuwing: de geschiedenis van de Nederlandsche Bank 1948-1973*, 's-Gravenhage: Sdu.
Fase, M.M.G. and F.A.G. den Butter (1977), "The Endogeneity of Monetary Policy in the Netherlands: Two Reaction Functions of the Central Bank," *Cahiers Économiques et Monetaires* 6, pp. 177-204.
Fase, M.M.G. and A.P. Huijser (1980), "A Reaction Function for Foreign Exchange Intervention in the Netherlands," *Kredit und Kapital* 13, pp. 290-319.
Fase, M.M.G. and W.F.V. Vanthoor (2000), *Het Federal Reserve stelsel belicht: proeve van een vergelijkende analyse*, Financiële en Monetaire Studies 18(4), Groningen: Wolters-Noordhoff.
Fase, M.M.G. and C.C.A. Winder (1998), "Wealth and the Demand for Money in the European Union," *Empirical Economics* 23, pp. 568-589.
Freeman, C. (1991), "The Goal of Price Stability: The Debate in Canada," *Journal of Money, Credit, and Banking* 23, pp. 613-618.
Friedlaender, A.F. (1973), "Macro Policy Goals in the Postwar Period: A Study in Revealed Preference," *Quarterly Journal of Economics* 87, pp. 25-54.
Friedman, M. (1960), *A Program for Monetary Stability*, New York: Fordham University Press.
Goodfriend, M.M. (1987), "Interest Smoothing and Price Level Trend-Stationarity," *Journal of Monetary Economics* 19, pp. 335-348.
Greenspan, A. (2000), *Technology and the Economy*, Speech in New York, January 13, 2000.
Kuipers, S.K. and B.S. Wilpstra (1973), "Over Holtrops monetaire theorie," *Maandschrift Economie* 37, pp. 489-511.
McCallum, B.T. (1999), "Recent Developments in Monetary Policy Analysis: The Roles of Theory and Evidence," *Review Federal Reserve Bank of St. Louis* 81, pp. 3-11.
McCallum, B.T. and E. Nelson (1999), "Performance of Operational Policy Rules in an Estimated Semiclassical Structural Model," in J.P. Taylor (ed.), *Monetary Policy Rules*, Chicago: Chicago University Press, pp. 15-56.

Poole, W. (1999), *Monetary Policy Rules*, Lecture given at Michigan State University, March 16 (mimeo).

Rudebusch, G.D. and L.E.O. Svensson (1999), "Policy Rules for Inflation Targeting," in J. B. Taylor (ed.), *Monetary Policy Rules*, Chicago: University of Chicago Press, pp. 203-246.

Simons, H. (1936), "Rules versus Authorities in Monetary Policy," *The American Economic Review* 26, pp. 530-552.

Svensson, L.E.O. (2000), "Does the P* model provide any Rationale for Monetary Targeting?," *German Economic Review* 1, pp. 69-82.

Theil, H. (1964), *Optimal Decision Rules for Government and Industry*, Amsterdam: North-Holland.

Tödter, K.H. and H.E. Reimers (1994), "P-Star as a Link between Money and Prices in Germany," *Weltwirtschaftliches Archiv* 130, pp. 273-289.

Chapter 12

Credit Demand Asymmetry in the Netherlands 1983-1997

Jan Jacobs and Jan Kakes
CCSO and Department of Economics, University of Groningen; Monetary and Economic Policy Department, De Nederlandsche Bank

Key words: Credit demand asymmetry, Monetary policy, Business cycles

Abstract: We employ a threshold regression model to investigate asymmetry in the Dutch credit demand equation. Our results show that in periods of expansionary monetary policy, the impact of interest changes is larger than in periods of monetary tightening. We do not find different effects over the business cycle, i.e. between booms and recessions. Both findings are in line with previous studies. Our results imply that non-linearity in de credit demand equation should be taken into account in assessments of monetary policy stance.

1. INTRODUCTION

In the past few years, there has been increasing attention for various kinds of asymmetries in the monetary transmission mechanism. Is the impact of monetary policy asymmetric over the business cycle? Does a monetary contraction have a stronger impact than a monetary expansion? Is the transmission of large interest rate changes different from that of small steps? Obviously, these issues are important to take into account in the formulation of monetary policy. In this chapter, we investigate asymmetries in the credit demand equation. We do this by giving an overview of previous studies as well as presenting new results based on Dutch data. In line with most empirical work in this field (*e.g.* Fase, 1995; Kakes, 2000) we focus on the demand side of the credit market. This choice can be further motivated by empirical evidence that, at least in the short run, the Dutch credit market is demand determined (see *e.g.* Kakes, 2000) and can be characterised as a customer market (Swank, 1994).

Prior to the start of the Economic and Monetary Union (EMU), the Dutch credit market was a relevant factor for monetary policy, despite the fact that monetary autonomy was significantly reduced because of the fixed exchange rate *vis-à-vis* the Dmark and the high degree of capital mobility. Due to the imperfect integration of the credit market with international capital markets there was even scope for a domestic money supply target (see Kuipers and Sterken, 1995), which was actually pursued in some way or another until 1991. Is it still interesting to focus on the Dutch credit market after the start of EMU? After all, monetary policy is first and foremost based on euro-wide aggregated data now.

However, credit markets of individual member states are still likely to exhibit specific national characteristics (see *e.g.* De Bondt, 2000). Hence, as cross-national differences in monetary transmission may complicate the implementation of a common monetary policy, it is still useful to consider individual EMU economies. Furthermore, credit growth is also interesting from a financial stability point of view, which has clearly a national dimension.

We investigate two sources of non-linearity in the credit demand equation: monetary policy asymmetry and business cycle asymmetry. Our results show that in periods of expansionary monetary policy, interest rate changes have more impact on aggregate credit than during monetary contractions. This result corroborates the findings of Van Ees *et al.* (1999) and Kakes (2000). Rather than making an *a priori* distinction between positive and negative monetary policy shocks, as these two studies do, we employ a threshold regression model and explicitly test whether nonlinearities are present. Interestingly, our conclusion is different from the standard 'credit view' literature. In particular, studies emphasizing the importance of a 'financial accelerator' (*e.g.* Bernanke *et al.*, 1994) imply an asymmetry in the opposite direction. In line with Kakes (2000), we do not find evidence for business cycle asymmetry in the credit demand equation in the Netherlands.

This chapter is organised as follows. In Section 2, we present an overview of previous literature on asymmetric effects of monetary policy. In Section 3, we briefly discuss the methodology we applied, and in Section 4 we present our results. Section 5 concludes.

2. NONLINEARITIES IN THE MONETARY TRANSMISSION MECHANISM

Is the monetary transmission mechanism characterised by asymmetric effects? This rather old theme in monetary economics goes back to pre-war theories. An early example of monetary transmission being dependent on the state of the economy is the liquidity trap, first described by Keynes (1936) and recently restated by Krugman (1998). Another example is that the impact of monetary policy may be different over the business cycle. Credit market imperfections and downward price rigidities may cause monetary policy to have more of an impact in a recession than during a boom (see Walsh, 1998 or Kakes, 2000, for a discussion of underlying theories). Furthermore, interest rate changes themselves may have asymmetric effects. It is often stated that especially monetary contractions have a real impact, whereas monetary expansions are ineffective (like 'pushing on a string'). Hence, monetary policy cannot be used to stimulate the economy or, as it was formulated in the 1930s, 'one can lead a horse to the water but one cannot make him drink' (Edie, 1931).

In recent years, many empirical studies have investigated whether these asymmetries can be observed in practice. Asymmetry over the business cycle was found for the United States by Thoma (1994), Gertler and Gilchrist (1994), Kashyap *et al.* (1994), Garcia and Schaller (1995) and Weise (1999). Kakes (2000) finds asymmetric effects of monetary policy over the business cycle for the United States, Germany, the UK and Belgium, but not for the Netherlands. Asymmetric effects on real activity between monetary contractions and expansions have been established by Cover (1992) for the United States and by Karras (1996a, 1996b) and Kakes (2000) for various European countries and the United States.

Several studies have found that credit market imperfections play an important role in the monetary transmission process. These include analyses based on aggregate data (*e.g.* Bernanke and Blinder, 1992 and, for the Netherlands, Garretsen and Swank, 1998a, 1998b, and Kakes, 2000) as well as micro-data (*e.g.* Fazzari *et al.*, 1988; Whited, 1992; Kashyap and Stein, 2000 and, for the Netherlands, Van Ees *et al.*, 1998). Most of these studies do not explicitly consider asymmetric effects on credit aggregates, though, but focus on one or more of the underlying conditions (*e.g.* heterogeneity among borrowers). Only a few studies analyse credit market asymmetries in relation to the business cycle or monetary policy directly. Asea and Blomberg (1998) investigate how banks' loan standards change over the business cycle. They find that during the expansionary regime lending conditions are relaxed while during recessions they are tightened, which causes a pro-cyclical effect of credit supply. Interestingly, their results also imply that the impact of banks' lending policy on the economy is particularly great during booms, which is in contrast with the general view that credit market imperfections have a stronger impact in recessions (as follows from *e.g.* the 'financial accelerator' literature). Asea and Blomberg stress that their results imply the opposite of Akerlof's 'lemon' problem, according to which bad projects drive out the good ones. Rather, asymmetric information in credit markets may cause good projects to draw in bad projects during a boom. Azariadis and Smith (1998) develop a general equilibrium model which provides a theoretical foundation of Asea and Blomberg's results.

Van Ees *et al.* (1999) and Kakes (2000) find that expansionary monetary policy measures have more of an impact on credit growth than monetary contractions in the Netherlands. Van Ees *et al.* analyse the instalment and withdrawal of direct credit constraints, a policy instrument that was used by the Dutch central bank until 1991, and conclude that only the latter had a significant effect. Kakes (2000) finds the same result for a group of European countries (including the Netherlands) but not for the United States, using several monetary policy indicators. After a description of our methodology, we provide new evidence in the spirit of these two studies in Section 4. An important extension of our approach is that we do not make an *a priori* distinction between monetary expansions and contractions. Rather, we employ a threshold model in which the border between the expansionary and contractionary regime does not necessarily coincide with a distinction between interest rate increases and interest rate decreases, but may also be at a point slightly different from zero (*e.g.* increases higher than x% versus decreases and increases below x%).

3. THRESHOLD REGRESSION MODELS

Threshold regression models are a popular vehicle in non-linear modelling. They can be applied in models with multiple equilibria, or in situations where the sample must be split on the basis of a (continuously-distributed) variable. Recently, Hansen developed the statistical theory of threshold models further and made it accessible to a more general audience in a series of articles (Hansen, 1997, 1999a, 1999b and 2000). The exposition of threshold regression models in this section draws heavily on the Hansen papers.

Suppose we have n observations of the endogenous variable y_t, the m-vector of predetermined variables x_t and the threshold variable q_t. A threshold regression (TR) model takes the following form:

$$y_t = \theta_1' x_t + e_t, \qquad q_t \le \gamma, \tag{1a}$$

$$y_t = \theta_2' x_t + e_t, \qquad q_t > \gamma, \tag{1b}$$

where e_t is the regression error. The threshold variable q_t splits the sample in two regimes: the parameters may differ depending on the regime, which are determined by the threshold value γ.

The threshold regression model of Equations (1a)-(1b) can be expressed in a single equation

$$y_t = \theta_1' x_t I(q_t \le \gamma) + \theta_2' x_t I(q_t > \gamma) + e_t, \tag{2}$$

where $I(.)$ denotes the indicator function, which has the value one if the argument is true and zero if the argument is false. Defining

$$x_t(\gamma) = (x_t I(q_t \le \gamma) \quad x_t I(q_t > \gamma))' .$$

Equation (2) becomes

$$y_t = x_t(\gamma)' \theta + e_t, \tag{3}$$

where $\theta = (\theta_1' \quad \theta_2')'$. The regression parameters in this equation, θ and γ, can be estimated by least squares (LS). Note that the LS estimator is equivalent to the maximum likelihood estimator (MLE) when the regression error e_t is iid $N(0, \sigma^2)$. The easiest method to obtain the LS estimates is to use sequential conditional LS: compute the sum of squared residuals for all values of the threshold variable to find the minimum. More formally, for a given value of γ the LS estimate of θ is

$$\hat{\theta}(\gamma) = \left(\sum_{t=1}^{n} x_t(\gamma) x_t(\gamma)' \right)^{-1} \left(\sum_{t=1}^{n} x_t(\gamma) y_t \right), \tag{4}$$

with residuals $\hat{e}_t = y_t - x_t(\gamma)' \hat{\theta}(\gamma)$ and variance

$$\hat{\sigma}_n^2(\gamma) = \frac{1}{n} \sum_{t=1}^{n} \hat{e}_t(\gamma)^2 . \tag{5}$$

The LS estimate of γ is the value that minimises the sum of squared errors of Equation (6):

$$\hat{\gamma} = \arg\min_{\gamma \in \Gamma} \hat{\sigma}_n^2(\gamma), \text{ for } \gamma \in \Gamma = [\underline{\gamma}, \bar{\gamma}], \tag{6}$$

where $\underline{\gamma}$ and $\bar{\gamma}$ are the lower and upper value of the threshold variable. If the number of observations, *n*, is very large, Γ can be approximated by a grid. The LS estimate of θ is computed as $\hat{\theta} = \hat{\theta}(\hat{\gamma})$.

An important question is whether the threshold regression model of Equations (1a-1b) is statistically significant to the linear alternative, which has the null hypothesis H_0: $\theta_1 = \theta_2$. In this situation the threshold parameter is not identified under the null hypothesis, which makes the testing problem complex. Hansen (1996) proposes a (heteroskedasticity-consistent) Lagrange Multiplier test. The *p*-values are computed by a bootstrap analogue, fixing the regressors from the right-hand side of the equation that is estimated and generating the bootstrap dependent variable from the distribution $N(0, \hat{e}_t^2)$, where $\hat{e}_t$ is the OLS residual from the estimated threshold regression model. Hansen (1996) shows that this bootstrap analogue produces asymptotically correct *p*-values.

Confidence intervals

Valid confidence intervals for the threshold parameter can be based on the likelihood ratio (or *F*) statistic

$$LR_n(\gamma) = n\frac{\hat{\sigma}_n^2(\gamma) - \hat{\sigma}_n^2(\hat{\gamma})}{\hat{\sigma}_n^2(\hat{\gamma})}, \tag{7}$$

which tests the null hypotheses $H_0 : \gamma = \hat{\gamma}$. The null hypothesis is rejected for large values of $LR_n(\gamma_0)$. Note that the likelihood ratio statistic is equal to zero at $\gamma = \hat{\gamma}$. Confidence intervals for the threshold parameter are constructed by inverting the likelihood ratio statistic $LR_n(\gamma)$. The asymptotic critical values for this statistic are listed in Hansen (1997, Table 1) and Hansen (2000, Table 1). A graphical method to find the confidence interval for the threshold parameter is to plot the likelihood ratio statistic $LR_n(\gamma)$ for all values of γ and to check for which values of γ the statistic crosses the horizon line that belongs to the confidence level of the test. The confidence region is constructed under the assumption that the error terms are homoskedastic. If the conditional homoskedasticy condition $E(e_t^2 \mid q_t) = \sigma^2$ does not hold, the same analysis can be done with an appropriately scaled likelihood ratio statistic to which an amended confidence region belongs.

The distribution of the parameters $\hat{\theta} = \hat{\theta}(\hat{\gamma})$ can be approximated by the conventional normal approximation if the threshold value γ is known with certainty. However, the uncertainty regarding the estimation of γ needs to be taken into account, especially in small samples like ours. Hansen proposes to do this as follows. Construct a β-level confidence interval for γ, calculate the confidence interval for θ for all γ's in this interval, and take these intervals together.

4. RESULTS

We construct a threshold regression equation for credit in the Netherlands, which we interpret as representing the demand side of the credit market. This is consistent with the signs we find for the interest rate coefficients (insofar as these are significant), but also with studies that conclude that the credit market is – at least in the short run – demand determined (Kakes, 2000) and shows the characteristics of a customer market (Swank, 1994). We use quarterly observations from the first quarter of 1983 up to and including the final quarter of 1997. This is a homogeneous period for monetary policy, given the fact that the Dutch guilder was pegged to the Dmark at a constant parity. Furthermore, it is important to note that we do not include the late 1990s, which has been a period of very high credit growth in combination with decreasing interest rates. Hence, our results cannot be attributed to this specific period. Typically, credit demand (*CR*) depends on output (*GDP*), a long-term interest rate (r_l) and a short-term interest rate (r_s).[1]

Two general remarks can be made about the role of interest rates in our analysis. First, because the short-term interest rate is largely controlled by the central bank, being its main operational target, this variable is often considered an accurate measure of monetary policy stance. Note, however, that the short-term interest rate also reflects endogenous responses of the central bank to developments in the economy. One way to circumvent this endogeneity problem would be to use VAR-based measures to isolate the

[1] We use the following data and sources. Credit is domestic credit, published in the IMF's International Financial Statistics (IFS), which includes credit by banks and institutional investors. Output is GDP published by Statistics Netherlands. The long-term interest rate is the government bond yield and the short-term interest rate is the overnight interest rate, both taken from the IFS. Real credit and real GDP are obtained using the GDP deflator, also published by Statistics Netherlands. All variables, except interest rates, are taken in natural logarithms.

unanticipated part of monetary policy.[2] This would be difficult to implement in our single-equation setting, though. Furthermore, Kakes (2000) shows that, for the Netherlands, monetary policy measured by the short-term interest level or by VAR-based interest rate shocks have a similar impact on credit and other variables. Our second remark is that the interest rates we include are only indirectly related to the lending rates that actually play a role in the credit market. Lending rates are not directly observable and are not the same for each client due to differences in creditworthiness and other customer idiosyncracies.

The estimated equation looks as follows

$$y_t = \theta_1' x_t I(q_t \leq \gamma) + \theta_2' x_t I(q_t > \gamma) + e_t,$$

where the endogenous variable is credit and the set of regressors consists of a constant, lags of credit, (lags of) output and (lags of) the interest rate(s). Because we allow all parameters in the credit demand equation to be regime-dependent, while we believe it is unrealistic to assume that credit can be explained by either output or interest rates alone, the number of parameters to be estimated is large. As a consequence, we cannot include many lags. To keep the analysis tractable in terms of degrees of freedom, we set the maximum lag of the right-hand-side variables at two quarters.

We consider two threshold variables: (i) changes in the short-term interest rate, which can be interpreted as monetary policy, and (ii) business cycle changes. For these threshold variables we investigated several specifications distinguishing: (i) nominal or real credit and GDP; (ii) variables in levels, first differences and annual differences; and (iii) the threshold variable in first differences or in annual differences. The threshold variable was allowed to have a lag between 0 and 6 periods. For all specifications we carried out the linearity test described in Section 3, using 1000 replications to compute the bootstrap-calculated *p*-values. In the computations the top and bottom 25% of the sample of observations on the threshold variable were trimmed. There was no evidence of residual heteroskedasticity in any of the models we estimated, so we did not make a correction for this.

For all specifications where linearity is rejected, we computed the estimates of the parameters of the linear model and the threshold value and the parameters in both regimes. A general observation is that interest rates are hardly significant in the linear versions of the credit demand equation, in

2 Further refinements of this approach are structural VARs, which are more explicitly based on an *a priori* economic structure and take into account (changes in) the central bank's operating procedures over time (see *e.g.* Walsh, 1998, for a discussion). For instance, Bernanke and Mihov (1998) develop a structural VAR in which they model the federal funds market.

which credit is typically explained by the constant term, lagged credit and economic activity. Previous studies on the Dutch credit market have also found very low or insignificant interest rate elasticities, particularly for short-term credit (see Fase, 1990, for an overview).[3] However, interest rates enter the scene when we split the sample and estimate a threshold regression.

Table 1. Threshold regression for real credit (*cr*): threshold variable $q_t = \Delta_4 r_{s,t-3}$

	Linear model		Threshold regression			
			Regime I: $q_t \leq -.30$		Regime II: $q_t > -.30$	
Variable	Estimate	St. error	Estimate	95% interval	Estimate	95% interval
Constant	-.593	.293	-1.233	[-2.126; -.358]	-2.908	[-5.264; .017]
cr_{t-1}	.795	.164	.296	[-.078; .671]	.622	[-.084; 1.491]
cr_{t-2}	-.032	.165	-.029	[-.430; .400]	-.268	[-.898; .330]
gdp_t	.805	.405	-.444	[-.541; 1.428]	1.187	[.030; 2.188]
gdp_{t-1}	-.458	.541	.597	[-.598; 1.890]	-.460	[-1.991; .873]
gdp_{t-2}	.037	.412	.038	[-.924; .919]	.611	[-.829; 1.757]
$r_{l,t}$	-.010	.007	-.00001	[-.027; .024]	-.005	[-.029; .145]
$r_{l,t-1}$	.002	.012	-.041	[-.037; -.005]	.013	[-.014; .046]
$r_{l,t-2}$	.004	.008	.015	[-.007; .036]	-.009	[-.037; .013]
$r_{s,t}$	-.001	.006	-.013	[-.027; .004]	-.006	[-.028; .020]
$r_{s,t-1}$	.006	.010	.022	[-.003; .046]	-.003	[-.033; .022]
$r_{s,t-2}$	-.009	.006	-.027	[-.042; -.012]	-.013	[-.035; .016]
# of obs.	50		26		24	
SSE	.008		.0004		.0012	
R^2	.993		.999		.996	

Table 1 presents the outcomes of the best threshold regression with the short-term interest rate as threshold variable.[4] Here, credit and GDP are in real terms, all variables are in levels except the threshold variable for which the annual difference is taken (with a three-quarter lag). The linearity null hypothesis is rejected with a *p*-value of 0.025. The LS estimate of the threshold value equals -0.30, with a 95% confidence interval of [-0.48;-0.08] as can be verified in Figure 1. Looking at the results for the two regimes, both interest coefficients are significant in regime 1 (annual interest short-term rate changes below the threshold value of -0.30%) and substantially higher in absolute terms than in the linear equation. By contrast, interest

[3] Fase (1995) finds significant interest rate elasticities in a linear framework, but his approach differs from ours in several respects. He focuses on short-term credit whereas we consider aggregate credit; he estimates over a different sample (1970-1990) and his elasticity refers to the lending rate, whereas we include the short-term interbank rate and the government bond yield.

[4] This 'best' regression is the result of several criteria. First, the *p*-value is required to be lower than 0.05. Second, the threshold value must be plausible. Third, there should be sufficient observations in both regimes.

rates are insignificant in regime 2 (interest changes higher than -0.30%). Hence, the impact of both short-term and long-term interest rate changes on credit is substantial in a regime of declining short-term interest rates, whereas it is insignificant in a regime of only modestly declining or increasing short-term rates.

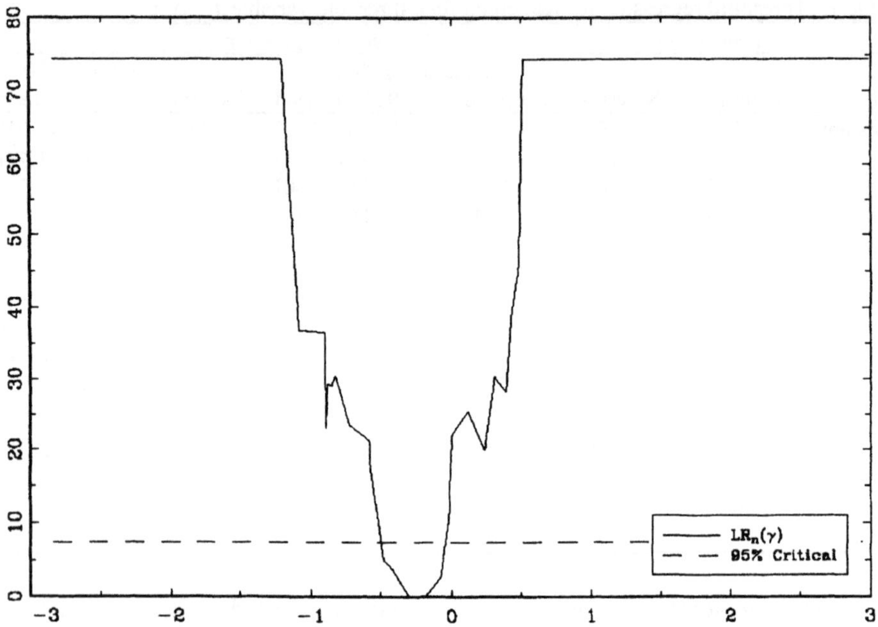

Figure 1. Confidence interval for threshold variable $\Delta_4 r_{s,t-3}$

This is confirmed by Figures 2 and 3, in which the impact of 1%-point increases in the short-term and the long-term interest rates is simulated over ten quarters, using the estimated threshold regressions of both regimes in Table 2.[5] Presented are both the effect of a one-period increase, denoted as a 'temporary shock', and a permanent increase of the interest rates, denoted as a 'permanent shock'. Since these simulations also take into account the lag structure of the other variables, they give a more complete picture of the impact of interest rate changes than just the estimated interest rate coefficients.

[5] Note that in all cases we simulate interest rate increases. Given the fact that the individual equations of each regime are linear, the effect of an interest rate decrease mirrors the simulation results that are presented here. In addition, it should be noted that each simulation is based on only one equation, and thus does not take into account the possibility of regime switches during the simulation period.

Our result corroborates the conclusion of Van Ees *et al.* (1999) and Kakes (2000) that monetary policy has more impact on credit aggregates if monetary conditions are expansionary. This is also in line with the experience in the past few years, when credit growth increased markedly while interest rates decreased. It is hard to explain this acceleration in credit growth with a linear model.[6]

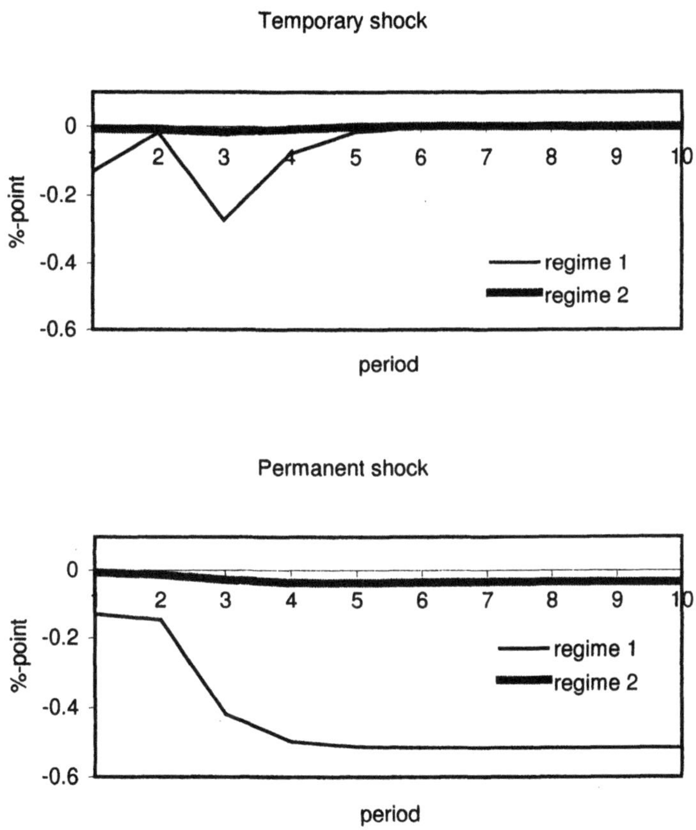

Figure 2. Simulated impact short-term interest rate shock on credit

How can this asymmetry be explained? Our findings are inconsistent with the standard credit view literature which implies the existence of asymmetric effects in the other direction, namely that a monetary contraction has more impact on credit than a monetary expansion. However, an

[6] For example, the Dutch central bank's macroeconometric model MORKMON can only explain 60% of the increase in bank lending to the corporate sector in 1998 (see De Nederlandsche Bank, 1999).

explanation based on credit market imperfections along the lines of Asea and Blomberg (1998) may be useful to explain our results, by taking into account heterogeneity among borrowers. Following a monetary contraction, there may be a shift from lending to low-quality borrowers towards high-quality borrowers: the first are rationed, while the latter try to create a buffer of external funds, possibly anticipating a further contraction. At the aggregate level, these two effects may cancel out, which implies that total credit is not significantly affected by a monetary tightening.

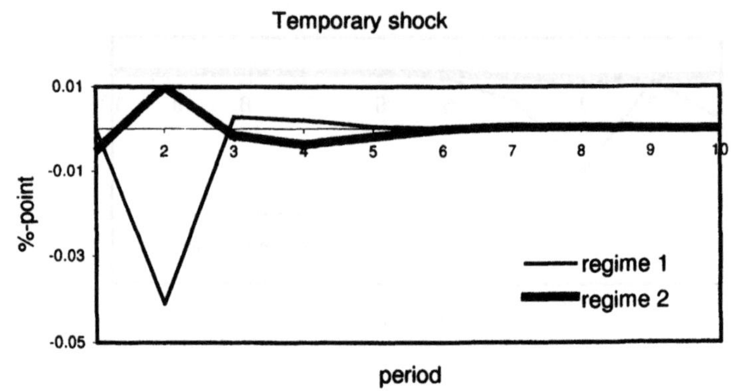

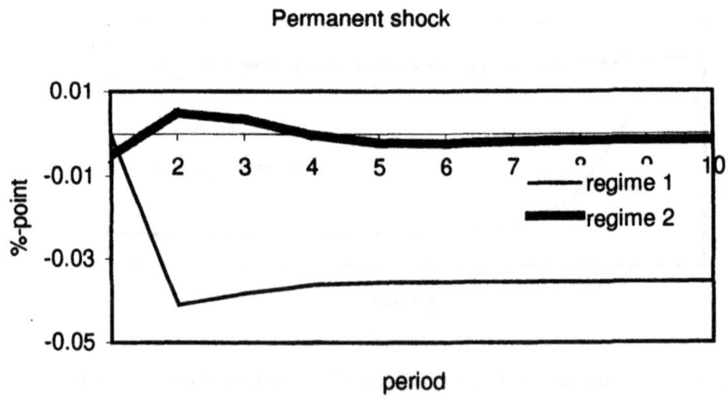

Figure 3. Simulated impact long-term interest rate shock on credit

By contrast, following a monetary expansion loans are given more easily to both low-quality and high-quality borrowers (in the terminology of Asea and Blomberg, 'good projects draw in bad projects'), so in this case there will be a significant impact on aggregate credit. Unfortunately, it is difficult to test whether this explanation is relevant for the Netherlands, as disaggregated time series for several types of borrowers are not available.[7]

Another possible explanation for the observed asymmetry is that the Dutch credit market may be regarded as a 'customer market', rather than an auction market (Okun, 1981). An important characteristic of customer markets is that banks attach value to long-term client relationships, which implies that they shield their loans portfolio after a monetary contraction. An interview study among banks by Swank (1994) provides empirical support for the concept of a customer market in the Netherlands.

Detailed analysis of the regression outcomes with the business cycle as threshold variable showed that here the evidence of threshold effects is weak. In most of the cases the grid search produced corner solutions, which implies that the number of observations in one regime becomes so low that unrealistic parameter estimates are obtained.

Table 2. Threshold regression for nominal credit (*cr*): threshold variable $q_t = \Delta gdp_{t-5}$

	Linear model		Threshold regression			
			Regime I: $q_t \leq .002$		Regime II: $q_t > .002$	
Variable	Estimate	St. error	Estimate	95% interval	Estimate	95% interval
Constant	-.244	.162	-.776	[-1.815; .262]	-.274	[-.558; .009]
cr_{t-1}	.699	.159	.086	[-.665; .836]	1.004	[.679; 1.329]
cr_{t-2}	.230	.159	.656	[-.149; 1.461]	-.117	[-.449; .215]
gdp_t	-.076	.255	-.681	[-2.178; .816]	.224	[-.238; .686]
gdp_{t-1}	.119	.403	1.351	[-1.338; 4.041]	-.113	[-.787; .561]
gdp_{t-2}	.076	.261	-.269	[-1.800; 1.261]	.056	[-.411; .522]
$r_{l,t}$	-.002	.006	.035	[-.037; .107]	-.018	[-.029; -.007]
$r_{l,t-1}$	-.005	.009	-.054	[-.143; .034]	.020	[.003; .038]
$r_{l,t-2}$	.006	.006	.018	[-.012; .048]	-.010	[-.021; .001]
$r_{s,t}$	-.0002	.005	.002	[-.023; .027]	.006	[-.004; .016]
$r_{s,t-1}$	.004	.008	.012	[-.041; .065]	-.002	[-.018; .014]
$r_{s,t-2}$	-.007	.005	-.025	[-.060; .010]	-.003	[-.012; .006]
# of obs.	53		14		39	
SSE	.0056		.0004		.0019	
R^2	.998		.999		.999	

7 The only distinction that can be made is between households and firms (see *e.g.* Garretsen and Swank, 1998b; Kakes, 2000). However, the interpretation of this distinction is not straightforward. On the one hand, the information asymmetry is larger for household credit than for corporate credit. Firms are generally better screened, particularly regarding expected cash flows. On the other hand, the bulk of loans to households consist of mortgages, which significantly reduces their risk. This would imply that households are for that part to be considered the 'high quality' borrowers.

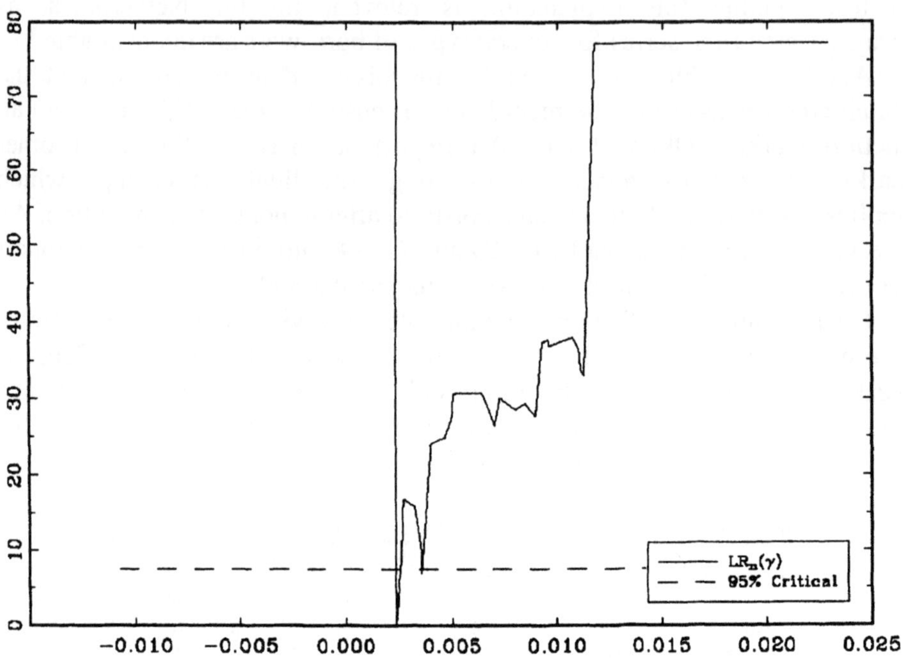

Figure 4. Confidence interval for threshold variable Δgdp_{t-5}

Table 2 lists the outcome with the lowest *p*-value: the combination of nominal credit and GDP, variables in levels and the first difference Δgdp_{t-5} as threshold variable. The LS estimate of the threshold value is 0.002 with 95% confidence interval [0.002; 0.003]. Figure 4 illustrates that this is a corner solution. Hence, we cannot conclude that there are asymmetries over the business cycle. This corresponds to the conclusion of Kakes (2000) who finds that business cycle asymmetry can be established for the United States, Germany, Belgium and the United Kingdom, but not for the Netherlands, using a Markov switching model to separate recessions and expansions.

5. CONCLUDING REMARKS

In this chapter we investigated whether a non-linear relationship between credit, output and interest rates in the Netherlands can be established for the 1983-1997 period. We found evidence of asymmetric effects of monetary policy on aggregate credit: if the monetary stance is expansionary, the impact of interest rate changes on credit is larger than in periods when the monetary stance is tightening. This finding is in line with previous studies based on different methodologies and different sample periods, and with the credit boom in the second half of the 1990s which coincided with decreasing interest rates. We could not establish asymmetry over the business cycle in the Netherlands for the 1983-1997 period. This finding is also consistent with previous research.

Two further remarks can be made. First, we have focused on the first stage of the monetary transmission process. We did not analyse the consequences for inflation or real activity. Nevertheless, credit growth is generally considered an important information variable for monetary policy. Our results thus imply that non-linearity in credit demand should be taken into account for the assessment of the monetary policy stance. Perhaps this would explain the finding of Garretsen and Swank (1998a), based on a linear model, that credit does not perform very well as a leading indicator for inflation and real activity in the Netherlands. Second, we did not explicitly investigate the underlying cause of the observed asymmetry. This would probably require an analysis with disaggregated data, in order to investigate the behaviour of different types of borrowers and lenders. The fact that our result differs from the standard 'credit view' is consistent with recent studies (Garretsen and Swank, 1998a, 1998b; Kakes, 1998b) which conclude that a bank lending channel is not important for the Netherlands.

In this chapter we looked for asymmetries in credit demand in the Netherlands using a single-equation threshold regression model. The research can be extended in several directions. A next step may be to investigate asymmetries in credit demand using aggregated euro area data. In addition, other methods can be applied. Candidates are the smooth transition regression models advocated by Teräsvirta (1994, 1998), which assume a gradual transition from one regime into the other, or a multivariate threshold regression model (Tsay, 1998; Choi, 1999; Shen and Chiang, 1999; Weise, 1999).

REFERENCES

Asea, P.K. and B. Blomberg (1998), "Lending Cycles," *Journal of Econometrics* 83, pp. 89-128.

Azariadis, C. and B. Smith (1998), "Financial Intermediation and Regime Switching in Business Cycles," *The American Economic Review* 88(3), pp. 516-536.

Bernanke, B. and A.S. Blinder (1992), "The Federal Funds Rate and the Transmission of Monetary Policy," *The American Economic Review* 82(4), pp. 901-921.

Bernanke, B., M. Gertler and S. Gilchrist (1994), "The Financial Accelerator and the Flight to Quality," *NBER Working Paper* 4789, Cambridge.

Bernanke, B. and I. Mihov (1998), "Measuring Monetary Policy," *Quarterly Journal of Economics* 113, pp. 869-902.

Choi, W.G. (1999), "Asymmetric Effects on Interest Rates across Monetary Policy Stances," *Journal of Money, Credit, and Banking* 31(3), pp. 386-416.

Cover, J.P. (1992), "Asymmetric Effects of Positive and Negative Money-Supply Shocks," *Quarterly Journal of Economics* 107(4), pp. 1261-1282.

De Bondt, G. (2000), *Financial Structure and Monetary Transmission in Europe*, Cheltenham: Edward Elgar.

De Nederlandsche Bank (1999), "The Dutch Economy in 1999-2001: A Forecast based on MORKMON," *Quarterly Bulletin*, June, pp. 39-49

Edie, L.D. (1931), *The Banks and Prosperity*, New York: Harper & Row.

Ees, H. van, H. Garretsen, L. de Haan and E. Sterken (1998), "Investment and Debt Constraints: Evidence from Dutch Panel Data," in S. Brakman, H. van Ees and S.K. Kuipers (eds.), *Market Behaviour and Macroeconomic Modelling*, London: MacMillan, pp. 159-179.

Ees, H. van, H. Garretsen and E. Sterken (1999), "Some Evidence on the Relevance of Bank Behaviour for the Lending Channel in the Netherlands," *De Economist* 147(1), pp. 19-37.

Fase, M.M.G. (1990), "Over bankkrediet en rentegevoeligheid," in M.M.G. Fase (ed.), *Aspecten van financiële intermediatie*, NIBE, Amsterdam.

Fase, M.M.G. (1995), "The Demand for Commercial Bank Loans and the Lending Rate," *European Economic Review* 39(1), pp. 99-115.

Fazzari, S.M., R.G. Hubbard and B.C. Petersen (1988), "Financing Constraints and Corporate Investment," *Brookings Papers on Economic Activity* 0(1), pp. 141-195.

Garcia, R. and H. Schaller (1995), "Are the Effects of Monetary Policy Asymmetric?," Paper presented at the EEA Congress, Prague.

Garretsen, H. and J. Swank (1998a), "The Transmission of Interest Rate Changes and the Role of Bank Balance Sheets: A VAR Analysis for the Netherlands," *Journal of Macroeconomics* 20(2), pp. 325-339.

Garretsen, H. and J. Swank (1998b), "The Bank Lending Channel in the Netherlands: The Impact of Monetary Policy on Households and Firms," *mimeo*, University of Nijmegen

Gertler, M. and S. Gilchrist (1994), "Monetary Policy, Business Cycles, and the Behavior of Small Manufacturing Firms," *Quarterly Journal of Economics* 109(2), pp. 309-340.

Hansen, B.E. (1996), "Inference when a Nuisance Parameter is Not Identified under the Null Hypothesis," *Econometrica* 64(2), pp. 413-430.

Hansen, B.E. (1997), "Inference in TAR models," *Studies in Nonlinear Dynamics and Econometrics* 2(1), pp. 1-14.

Hansen, B.E. (1999a), "Testing for Linearity," *Journal of Economic Surveys* 13(5), pp. 551-576.

Hansen, B.E. (1999b), "Threshold Effects in Non-Dynamic Panels: Estimation, Testing and Inference," *Journal of Econometrics* 93(2), pp. 345-368.

Hansen, B.E. (2000), "Sample Splitting and Threshold Estimation," *Econometrica* 68(3), pp. 575-603.

Kakes, J. (2000), *Monetary Transmission in Europe: The Role of Financial Markets and Credit*, Cheltenham: Edward Elgar.

Karras, G. (1996a), "Are the Output Effects of Monetary Policy Asymmetric? Evidence from a Sample of European Countries," *Oxford Bulletin of Economics and Statistics* 58(2), pp. 267-278.

Karras, G. (1996b), "Why Are the Effects of Money-Supply Shocks Asymmetric? Convex Aggregate Supply or 'Pushing on a String'?," *Journal of Macroeconomics* 18(4), pp. 605-619.

Kashyap, A.K., O.A. Lamont and J.C. Stein (1994), "Credit Conditions and the Cyclical Behavior of Inventories," *Quarterly Journal of Economics* 109(3), pp. 565-592.

Kashyap, A.K. and J.C. Stein (2000), "What do a Million Observations on Banks Say about the Transmission of Monetary Policy?," *The American Economic Review* 90(3), pp. 407-428.

Keynes, J.M. (1936), *The General Theory of Employment, Interest and Money*, London: MacMillan.

Krugman, P. (1998), "It's Baaack! Japan's Slump and the Return of the Liquidity Trap," *Brookings Papers on Economic Activity* 0(2), pp. 137-187.

Kuipers, S.K. and E. Sterken (1995), "On the Scope for Dutch Monetary Policy," *Banca Nazionale del Lavorno Quarterly Review* 48(193), pp. 173-187

Okun, A.M. (1981), *Prices and Quantities*, Oxford: Basil Blackwell.

Shen, C.H. and T.C.-N. Chiang (1999), "Retrieving the Vanishing Liquidity Effect: A Threshold Vector Autoregressive Model," *Journal of Economics and Business* 51(3), pp. 259-277.

Swank, J. (1994), "An Interview Survey of Bank Behaviour in the Netherlands," *Banca Nazionale del Lavoro Quarterly Review* 47(189), pp. 199-235.

Teräsvirta, T. (1994), "Specification, Estimation, and Evaluation of Smooth Transition Autoregressive Models," *Journal of the American Statistical Association* 89(425), pp. 208-218.

Teräsvirta, T. (1998), "Modelling Economic Relationships with Smooth Transition Regressions," in A. Ullah and D.G.A. Giles (eds.), *Handbook of Applied Economic Statistics*, New York/Basel/Hong Kong: Marcel Dekker Inc., pp. 507-552.

Thoma, M.A. (1994), "Subsample Instability and Asymmetries in Money-Income Causality," *Journal of Econometrics* 64(1/2), pp. 279-306.

Tsay, R.S. (1998), "Testing and Modeling Multivariate Threshold Models," *Journal of the American Statistical Association* 93(443), pp. 1188-1202.

Walsh, C.E. (1998), *Monetary Theory and Policy*, Cambridge: MIT Press.

Weise, C.L. (1999), "The Asymmetric Effects of Monetary Policy: A Nonlinear Vector Autoregression Approach," *Journal of Money, Credit, and Banking* 31(1), pp. 85-108.

Whited, T.M. (1992), "Debt, Liquidity Constraints and Corporate Investment: Evidence from Panel Data," *Journal of Finance* 47(4), pp. 1425-1460.

PART IV

ECONOMIC GROWTH

Chapter 13

Limits-to-Growth Theory

Reyer Gerlagh and Michiel A. Keyzer
IVM, Institute for Environmental Studies, Vrije Universiteit, Amsterdam; SOW-VU, Centre for World Food Studies, Vrije Universiteit, Amsterdam

Key words: Growth models, Development economics, Limits to growth

Abstract: The paper studies the implications for growth theory of the limits-to-growth debate, discussing three issues that have occupied a prominent place since the seventies. (1) Maintaining growth: can growth be sustained in the rich and still growing countries despite the limited supply of production factors such as land and labour? (2) Initiating growth: will per capita growth also be possible for those who are currently poor? (3) Avoiding decline: how to manage the exhaustibility of natural resources and the possible irreversible degradation of reproductive systems?

1. INTRODUCTION

Economic growth belongs to the phenomena that are easy to grasp intuitively but very difficult to pinpoint in the real world. Statistical publications present time series for hosts of variables but as some fall while others rise, the answer to the question whether the economy has been growing or contracting remains ambiguous, even though the message conveyed by growth figures on the sales of gasoline or beer is often most compelling. The common practice for measuring economic performance is to summarise the underlying information about individual people and commodities by a few aggregate numbers. It is commonplace to note that any such aggregation introduces a great deal of subjectivity. The yardstick of gross domestic product also suffers from this limitation, even though the problem becomes less severe when the time period is relatively short, say, a few years, as the change in commodity composition will then be minor. Despite these difficulties in measuring aggregate growth empirically, economic theory spent much effort in designing aggregate models with one, two or three commodities, and analysing their properties in the long run, when the interpretation of the aggregates is especially problematic.

In 1971, professor Kuipers asked the second author to prepare, jointly with Jan Willem Gunning, an update of the syllabus on growth theory to account for such concerns. At the time, the capital controversy was raging (Robinson, 1970, 1971) and Marxist criticism had become very loud. This called for incorporation into the syllabus of various more disaggregated models. On the one hand the multisectoral versions of the Solow model had to be included so as to distinguish capital by vintage and sector. On the other hand, models with intermediate deliveries should figure more prominently, along the lines of the theories of reproduction *à la* Von Neumann (1945) and Morishima (1964). In addition, the ongoing transition from formulations with savings functions to intertemporal optimisation in the Ramsey tradition had to be reported on (Hahn and Matthews, 1964). Finally, growth accounting had become an active field of empirical research, attempting to explain the empirical fact that in developed countries growth of income exceeded growth of labour and capital by far (Denison, 1962).

Unfortunately, the assignment was never completed. It may have been too difficult for Kuipers's inexperienced assistants. But the lack of progress was also to some extent attributable to the serious doubts raised after the publication of the first report to the Club of Rome, entitled *World Dynamics* (Forrester, 1971), soon to be followed by *Limits to Growth in a Finite World* (Meadows *et al.*, 1972). Both reports questioned the usefulness of mainstream growth theory. They attracted much attention in Groningen, also at the department of economics (Kuipers and Nentjes, 1973), but primarily in the physical sciences. In an early attempt at interdisciplinary research professors Smith (physics), Commandeur (chemistry) and Nauta (philosophy), started the Club of Groningen to investigate these matters in more depth and quite a few of the students enlisted at the time have remained active in the environmental field until the present day.[1]

At the time, Simon Kuipers could have insisted that, Club of Rome or not, the syllabus should be completed but, with his usual magnanimity, he did not complain. A contribution to the present volume seems to offer a good

[1] Leo Meijer became director at the Ministry of the Environment, Aart de Zeeuw who joined later, professor of environmental economics in Tilburg. Jan Willem Gunning worked for the Club of Groningen before leaving to the World Bank, eventually to become professor of development and international economics at the Free University and at Oxford University. Michiel Keyzer left to join the Club of Rome project headed by Hans Linnemann in Amsterdam.

occasion to requite a small part of the original debt. Thus, we inquire in this chapter about growth perspectives, and more specifically, on the long-term effects of the Limits-to-Growth debate on growth theory. In the sections that follow we discuss three issues that have occupied a prominent place since the seventies: (1) *maintaining growth*: can growth be sustained in the long run despite the limited supply of production factors such as land and labour; this is mainly a concern of countries that are relatively rich and growing; (2) *initiating growth*: will per capita growth, under appropriate government policies, eventually be possible everywhere; this obviously is the relevant question for the poor; and finally the typical Club of Rome question of (3) *avoiding decline*: how to manage the exhaustibility of natural resources and reproductive systems.

2. MAINTAINING GROWTH

The early reports of the Club of Rome successfully convinced the public at large that it is physically impossible for demand of any commodity to grow at a fixed exponential rate for an indefinite time as it would soon have to fill the atmosphere. They also conveyed the message that the depletion of mineral resources and the degradation of natural resource systems would make themselves felt in the immediate future, and in a dramatic way. The ensuing oil crises of 1973 and 1978 did much to emphasise these points, and the concept of zero-growth gained popularity. The basic idea was as simple as attractive, and required moving the world economy to a steady state that would provide every person with sufficient food, shelter, medical care, education, and discretionary luxuries, without causing lasting environmental damage. But the limits to growth concept immediately faced vehement opposition from all circles. Mainstream economists (Nordhaus, 1973) dispelled the message as a doomsday scenario that was counting without human inventiveness and foresight, and even neglected economic theory altogether. Others pointed out that although moving to a state of zero growth might be possible technically, the coordination requirements for the transition were unimaginably demanding. They would involve immense transfers from the rich to the poor, and it would take centuries until all the poor would have the educational skills to earn their own income, whereas their numbers would rise dramatically in the meantime. And if all consumers were to accept their commodity bundles as being ideal, this would cause demand to become satiated, with consumer prices falling to zero, resulting in a full collapse of the market system.

Obviously, less radical versions of zero-growth have been proposed since, that only restrict demand for the rich but the dim experiences of centrally planned economies that endured almost zero per capita growth in consumption did little to promote this kind of interventionism. Moreover, in OECD countries, the rise in unemployment and the recession experienced after the oil crises also limited the enthusiasm. Thus, until the present-day the dominant view among economists remains that the world economy must grow, and that technological innovation will create the efficiency gains and the qualitative changes that enable it to do so indefinitely. However, growth theory itself was never as confident that this is possible, and it is not a major simplification to claim that ever since Ricardo and Marx maintaining growth has been the main concern of growth theory.

Until the late sixties growth models were formulated in the spirit of Newtonian mechanics, as ordinary differential (or difference) equations describing the recursive cycle from production to income and savings, and from savings to investment and capital accumulation. The emphasis was placed on the convergence of these forward dynamics to a balanced growth path where per capita consumption would remain fixed, and population was growing at a fixed rate. For a long time disaggregation was the major concern. In response to the Capital Controversy, and building on the Von Neumann model, theories of reproduction with heterogeneous capital enjoyed renewed attention (Bliss, 1975; Burmeister, 1980). Elegant turnpike properties could be established (Morishima, 1964) but only for special cases whereas cycles could persist in general.

As growth analysis left the confines of the balanced path, the need became more pressing to restore the intertemporal efficiency and formulations shifted in favour of the Ramsey model with perfect foresight. Along the balanced growth path savings functions can always be reconciled with optimal intertemporal consumption planning, but off this path, forward dynamics and the Ramsey approaches have little in common.[2] Gradually, perfect foresight became the standard, and it has the virtue of clarity and preserves the link to welfare analysis. It also avoids the Lucas critique towards specifications whereby the modeller claims to have deeper insights into the functioning of the economy than the agents in the model, being able to anticipate their reactions unilaterally.

Despite the emphasis on dynamically efficient paths, growth theory soon turned to the more practical comparative static analysis, comparing the steady state of particular models to a given initial situation and concluding that growth can be maintained if the steady state yields higher welfare. Obviously, this comparative static analysis presupposes that the dynamic path will eventually converge to this steady state, and for the Ramsey model with a single capital stock this holds true. However, from a fundamental

[2] Though the Ramsey model also defines a savings function, it is not in closed form. See Cooley (1995) and Böhm and Schenk-Hoppé (1998) for discussions.

paper by Boldrin and Montrucchio (1986), it follows that when the Ramsey model is extended to allow for heterogeneous capital, the dynamic path loses almost all its properties and may in particular cycle, converge, diverge, or even be chaotic.

To allow for disaggregate multiple consumers with heterogeneous preferences, the Ramsey model was embedded within the general equilibrium framework, both in a dynastic context with a finite number of infinitely lived dynasties, and in overlapping generations (OLG) context with an infinite sequence of finitely lived consumers. The dynastic formulation essentially inherits the dynamic properties of Ramsey model, since a social welfare function can be constructed from the weighted sum of separate utilities, with weights set so as to meet the intertemporal budget constraint of every dynasty (Negishi, 1960; Kehoe, 1991; Ginsburgh and Keyzer, 1997). In contrast, for OLG models the dynamic efficiency and the convergence to a steady state can only be established for special formulations.

However, even if the path does not converge to a steady state growth dampening is inescapable in these models whenever the supply of a production factor such as labour or land is kept fixed. Specifically, under the common Inada assumptions – whereby returns to capital drop to zero when capital rises to infinity – per capita consumption stops rising eventually. It still is possible to fuel growth via exogenous technological progress, but such "manna from heaven" hardly offers a solid basis for economic policy. In response, the concept of endogenous growth gained popularity (Romer, 1986, 1990; Lucas 1988). Through it, the decreasing returns can be offset by productivity gains from economies of scale, scope, and experience. Part of this endogenous growth theory has developed in Schumpeterian direction. Large firms can mobilise more savings from monopoly rents and will presumably spend more resources on strategic planning for their own growth. If innovations are the engine, innovations they will finance. But for those insisting on Pareto optimality, the price paid is high, since it amounts to accepting external effects and monopolies, and hence distortions as the engine of growth.

Yet this literature assumes that firms actually know their production technology and thus move along their production possibility frontier, rather than groping in inefficiency somewhere in the interior of a production set. This assumption is especially questionable for sectors with fast technical progress. Current speculations about fantastic potential profits for some of the internet companies would seem to suggest that in these branches firms and investors are simply experimenting. When the concept of the production function becomes questionable, growth theory loses a keystone of its foundation and the Inada condition much of its relevance. The traditional concept of technology defined as a given set of input output vectors might indeed have become less compelling at a time that machines become ever smaller and smarter and production management is largely guided by logistics and marketing considerations. In such a situation, economic growth originates largely from improved organisation and restructuring of firms (Freeman and Soete, 1997).

This changing understanding of growth has stimulated the expansion of a less macro-oriented line of research that concentrates on describing the cycle of innovation and diffusion by small, anonymous producers who are driven by evolutionary pressure. Those who make profits can expand; the others must shrink. Success is rewarded but it eventually attracts followers. All moves are small and randomness is the major driver. Clearly, it is not difficult to generate growth in this setting, provided the shocks cause the technology parameters to improve, *i.e.* to require less inputs for the same output or for a, possibly newly designed, close substitute. So far, the main applications in this evolutionary branch are partial. They describe the technological innovations (Arthur *et al.*, 1987; Dosi *et al.*, 1994; Nelson, 1995) or the development of institutions (Van der Laan, 1998), and aim to highlight basic mechanisms rather than to reproduce historical patterns of growth. There is a long way to go until economy-wide models can accommodate evolutionary ideas even though the calibration of real business cycle literature (Cooley, 1995) already seeks to account for random shocks that occurred in the past. In the evolutionary framework, the perfect foresight of the Ramsey framework can no longer serve as reference. Instead, a short-term price adjustment mechanism has to be specified. Ermoliev *et al.* (2000) propose a stochastic version of the Walrasian *tâtonnement* that incorporates evolutionary principles of adaptive learning within the price adjustment process itself and converges to a competitive equilibrium. While the evolutionary line of research is still far from being able to explain or predict economic growth, through its emphasis on path-dependency it points to the danger of getting locked-in and calls for ample funding of scientific research and social experiments.

3. INITIATING GROWTH

Whereas the main body of growth literature has predominantly dealt with the problem of maintaining per capita growth, since the fifties development economists have been concerned with the question how to initiate it in countries whose per capita incomes have not been rising in any appreciable way for decades.

Priority was soon given to channelling capital flows in the direction of developing countries, while the alternative option of allowing the poor to migrate freely out of their country was not considered realistic (Tinbergen and Bos, 1972). In many newly independent states, a Planning Commission was entrusted with the task of effectuating investment projects in physical infrastructure (irrigation, land reclamation, roads, dams, electricity). The limitations of growth-by-investment are well known. Some of the projects never materialise or undergo fast decay because spare parts are lacking or power supply is interrupted too often, and more generally, because capacity expansion takes longer and is more costly than anticipated while the technical efficiency can only build up slowly through learning-by-doing. Moreover, by tying foreign aid to specific projects, the planner is effectively subsidising these projects and channels resources to the direction of his choice.

Like in growth theory itself, when capital accumulation was no longer seen as the major bottleneck, restructuring became the central topic. The free market provided a perspective of reaching a presumably superior steady state and the move towards it would expectedly be sufficient to get the engine running. As the national planning commissions lost their clout, finance ministries gained influence and successfully argued for replacing project aid by the less specific program aid and balance of payment support, preferably via multilateral agencies. Next, aid itself became exposed as part of the problem rather than as a solution, since it created new distortions and reduced the pressure on government to maintain budgetary discipline and foster efficiency (Dollar and Pritchett, 1998).

Once a developing country has reached a growth track, it will like any other country have to focus on innovation and accumulation of experience. But it faces a special dilemma in this respect because on the one hand its infant industry calls for some protection, whereas on the other hand its lack of research capacities makes it dependent on imports and foreign investments for innovations. The increased R&D intensity of virtually every branch of industry makes it very difficult to develop in isolation from international networks and, consequently, the infant industry argument has become less convincing. Few are those who still believe that developing countries can design "appropriate technologies" that would be commensurate with their specific factor proportions. Cellular phones and the internet are clear illustrations of the benefits developing countries can derive from importing general purpose products at a price many times lower than that of any specially designed product.

Yet, the mere fact that technological progress is now a global process is not to imply that outsiders should dictate reforms. The understanding that successful development strategies are usually domestically controlled resulted in the recognition of the need for "local ownership" of development initiatives. This concept originates from the sociological literature on emancipation, where it relates to the willingness and capacity of agents to assume responsibility. It has enhanced the support to non-governmental organisations that engage in capacity building at community level so as to promote private initiative. Unfortunately, this led in some cases to a weakening rather than a strengthening in governance because local governments were being bypassed. Nonetheless, the ownership concept has been effective in highlighting that when government reduces its interventions, the void is not automatically filled by the private sector in a manner that respects the principles of democracy and free markets (Ellerman, 2000). For research, the implication has been that development studies have gradually evolved away from dynamic growth models to become more interdisciplinary and empirical, with special attention for aspects of accountability.

Finally, the conclusion that sustained accumulation of physical and human capital is not a sufficient prerequisite for growth may need qualification. While the Soviet experience after World War II would seem to corroborate this viewpoint, there is ample evidence to show that the capital stock constitutes a critical element for re-initiating growth after crises and recessions. Europe's reconstruction through Marshall aid is a classical example, but recently Lebanon's return to the group of medium income countries illustrates that even fifteen years of a devastating civil war cannot destroy the potential for growth when human capital is preserved. The East Asian recovery also confirms this. It would seem that as economies build up their human and physical capital stock, they eventually cross some threshold of resilience. The problem with this observation is, however, that current levels of foreign assistance are by far insufficient to move all poor countries across that level.

4. AVOIDING DECLINE

Debates on growth and the environment show a divergence of opinions. The mainstream expects that the Limits-to-Growth will not be reached in any foreseeable time because technological progress will make it possible to find substitutes for scarce natural resources (Schelling, 1992). Models with endogenous technological innovation strengthen the view that sustained growth is possible, even with limited supply of labour, land, and other environmental resources (Aghion and Howitt, 1998, Chapter 5). Since environmental constraints are not a problem, the studies focus their attention on the effect of environmental policies on economic growth (Bovenberg and Smulders, 1995; Stokey, 1998).

At this point, it is worth mentioning that the practice of limiting the analysis to steady states – and for endogenous growth models to path with positive growth – strongly reflects on the optimism of the conclusions. The steady state is taken to be unique, viable and independent of the initial resource stock. As environmental damage decays, by construction, postponement of effective resource management policies causes no harm in the longer term. Moreover, most analyses assume that there is no bound to the substitution of an increased consumption of man-made goods for decreasing environmental resources. The possibility to restore all damages and to substitute for scarce resources justifies a focus on efficient resource use, a concept known as the weak sustainability paradigm (Solow, 1974; Hartwick, 1977).

The more ecologically oriented economists are not so sure. They agree on the central role of R&D in reducing the material requirements of consumption, but fear that this will not help very much. In their view the major problem is due to the exhaustibility and degradation of environmental resources, rather than the depletion of particular minerals for which international markets exist and substitutes might be found (Clark, 1997). Their concerns include a loss of biodiversity and global climate change caused by antropogenic emissions of greenhouse gases (Daly, 1996) and they propose to insert safeguards in the form of quantitative restrictions on emission and extraction or equivalent price mechanisms. They concur that markets for environmental resources are currently missing and that all measures should be taken to fill this void, by Pigouvian taxes to begin with, to be followed by the installation of private property rights and competitive markets for resource use (Dales, 1968). However, focusing on efficiency and property rights through grandfathering resources is insufficient, since it often amounts to distributing all natural resources to the present generation, and it thereby cannot prevent a persistent decline in well-being from one generation to the next (Mourmouras, 1993). As an alternative, Gerlagh (1998) and Gerlagh and Keyzer (2001) propose to give the natural resource in property of a trust fund that evenly distributes its value over generations in the form of consumption entitlements. A different distribution of environmental property rights could also have far-reaching implications for income distribution and development. An equitable distribution of natural resources over individuals would provide a basic income to all; the poor who would use less than their entitlements could lease their surplus and finance part of their expenditures on food and other basic needs from this source. Furthermore, considering persistent resource degradation also requires a different look at steady state analyses. The steady state that is reached in the long term depends on the resource extraction in initial periods. And when resource regeneration is possible but taking centuries at the least – the common situation for complex ecological systems – the qualitative dynamics will be very similar in the near centuries, notwithstanding the fact stock levels can eventually return to a steady state at a higher level (Gerlagh and Keyzer, 1999).

What matters most in this context is not so much what the present generation feels in this respect but how much it is willing to account for the needs of future generations. Even if substitution is possible with respect to the production of man-made goods, it eventually reaches its limits on the demand side where consumers become satiated in man-made goods and want to enjoy nature itself. For example, consider a situation where natural resources provide an amenity service (the landscape) and where production of man-made goods uses labour, man-made capital, and irreversible extraction of this resource while future generations are expected to become satiated in man-made goods but appreciate the unspoiled landscape. Since they cannot be compensated for a resource loss, it follows that strict conservationism is dynamically efficient, despite the fact that a cost-benefit analysis at competitive prices may show that resource extraction is warranted (Chichilnisky, 1997).

Be this as it may, it would appear that the divisions are much wider in applied policy than within economic theory. The choice whether quantitative restrictions are to be accepted until Pigouvian taxes are implemented would seem a matter of expediency rather than of principle. In practical policy terms, the real issue is that none of the proposed measures are being taken in a substantive matter. Moreover, environmental economics itself needs to enhance its capabilities to represent the environmental impact of economic activity, as it is hard to imagine how hydrological or carbon-dioxide cycles could ever fit within a framework that only admits perfect divisibility, possibility of inaction and free disposal as representation of biophysical "technology".

5. CONCLUSION

After two oil crises and the demise of communism, the Limits-to-Growth debate lost much of its vehemence. It is no longer common to read that satiation in demand, impoverishment of the masses and environmental degradation will cause the capitalist system to collapse. Except in the countries that were previously under Soviet control and in major parts of sub-Saharan Africa, the growth record has generally been by far superior to what was anticipated in the seventies. Rightly or wrongly, the internet boom and its new economy implications have created a mood of optimism and innovation in which the group of around 800 million malnourished people find it hard to make their voice heard, and where environmentalists appear like pessimists. While it is only fair to admit that it did not take growth economists to invent the internet, economists may claim that their advice has exercised decisive influence with respect to policy reforms. One might even argue that these reforms have opened markets allowing firms to grow and to invest in R&D.

However, growth theory itself still offers no clear-cut policy advice, basically because it is so hard to measure economic efficiency in a comprehensive manner, and no unambiguous link can be established between aggregate growth and individual welfare. This uncertainty leaves room for a division to emerge between optimists and pessimists. The optimists argue that technological progress will make it possible to generate sustained growth everywhere in the world and that markets are efficient and have sufficient foresight to initiate timely substitution before resource scarcities make themselves felt. This justifies non-interventionism, but also creates a paradox. While growth becomes fully dependent on technological innovation, fast technological change makes efficient production less likely, since producers and social institutions cannot adapt sufficiently fast to move to the production possibility frontier. The pessimists for their part call for intervention and since there is so much wrong, it becomes easier to promote growth by enhancing efficiency through re-structuring firms and government. Whereas growth theory cannot resolve these paradoxes, through its embedding within the dynamic general equilibrium framework it still is the best-developed tool for analysing the major issues. Yet, since the opportunities for maintaining growth, initiating it, and avoiding decline appear to depend mostly on the ingenuity of engineers and marketeers, and on the abilities of individuals to organise themselves and to adapt, growth studies will increasingly have to venture outside economics.

REFERENCES

Aghion, P. and P. Howitt (1998), *Endogenous Growth Theory*, Cambridge: MIT Press.

Arthur, W.B., Y.M. Ermoliev and Y.M. Kaniovski (1987), "Path-Dependent Processes and the Emergence of Macro-Structure," *European Journal of Operational Research* 30, pp. 294-303.

Bliss, C.J. (1975), *Capital Theory and the Distribution of Income*, Amsterdam: North-Holland.

Böhm, V. and K.R. Schenk-Hoppé (1998), *Macrodyn, a User's Guide*, Department of Economics, University of Bielefeld, Discussion paper 400.

Boldrin, M. and L. Montrucchio (1986), "On the Indeterminacy of Capital Accumulation Paths," *Journal of Economic Theory* 40, pp. 26-39.

Bovenberg, A.L. and S.A. Smulders (1995), "Environmental Quality and Pollution-Augmenting Technological Change in a Two-Sector Endogenous Growth Model," *Journal of Public Economics* 57, pp. 369-391.
Burmeister, E. (1980), *Capital Theory and Dynamics*, Cambridge: Cambridge University Press.
Chichilnisky, G. (1997) "What is Sustainable Development," *Land Economics* 73, pp. 467-491.
Clark, C.W. (1997), "Renewable Resources and Economic Growth," *Ecological Economics* 22, pp. 275-276.
Cooley, T.F. (ed.) (1995), *Frontiers of Business Cycles Research*, Princeton: Princeton University Press.
Dales, J.H. (1968), "Land, Water, and Ownership," *Canadian Journal of Economics* 1, pp. 791-804.
Daly, H.E. (1996), *Steady-State Economics*, 2nd edition, London: Earthscan.
Denison, E.F. (1962), "Education, Economic Growth, and Gaps in Information," *Journal of Political Economy* 70, pp. 124-128.
Dollar, D. and L. Pritchett (1998), *Assessing Aid: What Works, What Doesn't, and Why*, New York: Oxford University Press.
Dosi, G., Y.M. Ermoliev and Y.M. Kaniovski (1994), "Generalized Urn Schemes and Technological Dynamics," *Journal of Mathematical Economics* 23, pp. 1-19.
Ellerman, D. (2000), *Helping People Help Themselves: The Challenge of Autonomy-Compatible Assistance*, World Bank, New York.
Ermoliev, Y.M., M.A. Keyzer and V. Norkin (2000), "Global Convergence of the Stochastic Tâtonnement Process," *Journal of Mathematical Economics* 34, pp. 173-190.
Forrester, J.W. (1971), *World Dynamics*, Cambridge: Wright-Allen Press.
Freeman, C. and L.G. Soete (1997), *The Economics of Industrial Innovation,* London: Pinter.
Gerlagh, R. (1998), *The Efficient and Sustainable Use of Environmental Resource Systems*, Amsterdam: Thela Thesis.
Gerlagh, R. and M.A. Keyzer (1999), *Postponing Efficiency: Effect on Equilibrium Selection in Economies with Exhaustible Resources and Amenity Values*, WP-99-09, SOW-VU, Centre for World Food Studies, Amsterdam.
Gerlagh, R. and M.A. Keyzer (2001), "Sustainability and the Intergenerational Distribution of Natural Resource Entitlements," *Journal of Public Economics* 79(2), pp. 315-341.
Ginsburgh, V. and M.A. Keyzer (1997), *The Structure of Applied General Equilibrium Models*, Cambridge: MIT Press.
Hahn, F.H. and R.C.O. Matthews (1964), "The Theory of Economic Growth: A Survey," *The Economic Journal* 74, pp. 779-891.
Hartwick, J.M. (1977), "Intergenerational Equity and the Investing of Rents from Exhaustible Resources," *The American Economic Review* 67, pp. 972-974.
Kehoe, T.J. (1991), "Computation and Multiplicity of Equilibria," in W. Hildenbrand and H. Sonnenschein (eds.), *Handbook of Mathematical Economics,* Part IV, Amsterdam: North-Holland, Chapter 38.
Kuipers, S.K. and A. Nentjes (1973), "Pollution in a Neo-Classical World: The Classics Rehabilitated?" *De Economist* 121, pp. 52-67.
Laan, G. van der (1998), *Evolutionary Game Theory and the Modeling of Economic Behavior*, Dordrecht: Kluwer.
Lucas, R.E., jr. (1988), "On the Mechanics of Economic Development," *Journal of Monetary Economics* 22, pp. 3-42.
Meadows, D.H., D.L. Meadows, J. Randers and W.W. Behrens (eds.) (1972), *The Limits to Growth*, London: Earth Island Limited.

Morishima, M. (1964), *Equilibrium, Stability and Growth*, Oxford: Oxford University Press.
Mourmouras, A. (1993), "Conservationist Government Policies and Intergenerational Equity in an Overlapping Generations Model with Renewable Resources," *Journal of Public Economics* 51, pp. 249-268.
Negishi, T. (1960), "Welfare Economics and Existence of Equilibrium for a Competitive Economy," *Metroeconomica* 12, pp. 92-97.
Nelson, R.R. (1995), "Recent Evolutionary Theorizing about Economic Change," *Journal of Economic Literature* 33, pp. 48-90.
Neumann, J. von (1945), "A Model of General Economic Equilibrium," *Review of Economic Studies* 13, pp. 1-9.
Nordhaus, W.D. (1973), "World Dynamics: Measurement without Data," *The Economic Journal* 83, pp. 1156-1183.
Robinson, J. (1970), "Harrod after Twenty-One Years: A Reply," *The Economic Journal* 80, pp. 741.
Robinson, J. (1971), "The Existence of Aggregate Production Functions: Comment," *Econometrica* 39, pp. 405
Romer, P.M. (1986), "Increasing Returns and Long-Run Growth," *Journal of Political Economy* 94(5) , pp. 1002-1037.
Romer, P.M. (1990) ,"Endogenous Technological Change," *Journal of Political Economy* 98(5), pp. S71-S102
Schelling, T.C. (1992), "Some Economics of Global Warming," *American Economic Review* 82, pp. 1-14.
Solow, R.M. (1974), "Intergenerational Equity and Exhaustible Resources," *Review of Economic Studies* 41, pp. 29-45.
Stokey, N.L. (1998), "Are there Limits to Growth?," *International Economic Review* 39(1), pp. 1-31.
Tinbergen, J. and H.C. Bos (1962), *Mathematical Models of Economic Growth,* New York: McGraw-Hill.

Chapter 14

Skill Biases in Employment Opportunities and Income Perspectives

Should We Try to Shake the Invisible Hand?

Adriaan van Zon and Joan Muysken[1]
Department of Economics and Maastricht Economic Research Institute on Innovation and Technology, Maastricht University

Key words: Endogenous growth, Skill asymmetries, Wage subsidies

Abstract: The rigidities inherent in the stable wage development in Europe hamper the Schumpeterian process of creative destruction and therefore are a barrier to productivity growth. This notion, amongst others, motivated the deregulation programme in Europe. However, in the discussion on this programme and in its far-reaching policy implications, a crucial public good aspect of technological change has been ignored. Recognition of this aspect and the market failures it invokes, together with concern about the income inequality implied by forceful deregulation of the labour market, inspired us to the current analysis. We show that well-targeted wage subsidies are welfare improving.

1. INTRODUCTION

The (continental) European economy is often compared to the US economy in order to analyse and emphasise the impact of economic institutions on economic performance. Although both economies have been exposed to similar shocks in the seventies of the last century, their performance in the eighties and nineties was quite different. A typical example, which has been widely discussed in the literature, is the strong increase in unemployment in

[1] We thank Mark Sanders for his very useful critical comments on a draft version of this paper.

Europe as opposed to the situation of near full employment in the US. This coincided with an increasing wage inequality in the US, while the relative wage structure in Europe remained remarkably stable. Krugman (1995) dubbed this phenomenon as two sides of the same coin, suggesting a trade-off between wage flexibility and unemployment.[2]

An element that has attracted less attention in the literature, is that the rigidities inherent in the stable wage development – for instance due to minimum wages – might also be a barrier to productivity growth and hence may serve as an additional explanation of the poor performance of Europe relative to the US in the eighties and nineties. The reason is that these rigidities hamper the Schumpeterian process of creative destruction.[3] This notion is also one of the arguments that inspired the deregulation programme in Europe.

We think that in the discussion on this programme and in its far-reaching policy implications, a crucial public good aspect of technological change has been ignored. Recognition of this aspect and the market failures it invokes, together with concern about the income inequality implied by forceful deregulation of the labour market, inspired us to the current analysis.

In our view the two-sides-of-the-same-coin debate is part of the discussion on the trade-off between equity and efficiency. Actually, this discussion is almost as old as the science of economics itself – if not older. Simon Kuipers contributed to this discussion for a large part of his professional life. He particularly emphasised the importance of macro-economic stability to reduce uncertainty and therefore pointed at market failures as a result of uncertainty – both implicitly and explicitly.[4] Such an interference with the free markets process is something we phrase tongue in cheek as 'shaking the invisible hand'. However, Kuipers also recognises a complicated trade-off with efficiency, since he is in favour of a medium-term oriented stabilisation policy in "an institutional structure which makes it possible to prevent the allocational distortions to a considerable extent" – in particular preventing the use of these policies for distributional aims.[5]

[2] Krugman (1995). *Cf.* also Freeman (1995), Nickell (1997) and Siebert (1997).

[3] This notion is reminiscent of Kleinknecht's (1998) critique on wage moderation (not minimum wages) in the Netherlands. However, Kleinknecht also opposes wage flexibility, because he thinks it would allow badly performing firms to lower their wages instead of innovating. In our view this is not correct because Kleinknecht then ignores the fact that better performing firms that do apply technological change would also be able to pay higher wages, thus outcompeting the non-innovating firms by taking over their labour force. That is the true nature of the Schumpeterian creative destruction.

[4] See Kuipers (1990) for a discussion in a macroeconomic setting and Kuipers (1995) in a somewhat more microeconomic setting.

[5] Kuipers (1990, p. 254). He considers the guided wage policy in the Netherlands in the Fifties as a good example of such an institution.

In this contribution, we intend to provide an additional argument to show that the popular belief of a trade-off between efficiency and equity is not quite as simple as is often perceived. However, we look at market failures created by the public good nature of technological change, also from a macroeconomic perspective.[6]

Romer (1990) argues that technological knowledge is not a totally excludable good. He exemplifies this by distinguishing between a variety of new products. The designs of these products can be protected by copyrights. These designs are excludable since their use can be limited to the owners of the products. However, the knowledge embodied in these designs is widely observable and will inspire further designs – this aspect of new designs is not excludable and serves therefore as a public good. Thus creation of new designs has spill-over effects, which are not accounted for when these designs are traded on the market.

Inspired by this notion, Van Zon and Sanders (2000) developed a model in which they distinguish between two varieties of goods: a high-tech variety produced by skilled workers and a low-tech variety produced by unskilled workers. The research sector, which employs skilled workers only, generates both product and process innovations. Product innovations lead to new varieties – which in the initial stages of their life cycle are high-tech by assumption. Process innovations enable unskilled workers to produce varieties that initially were of a high-tech nature – these then become low-tech. The process innovations also induce a 'business stealing' effect: by buying designs for these innovations firms can employ unskilled labour, hence freeing skilled labour that can be employed elsewhere. Producers of established products can thus outcompete the early adopters of new products. The spill-over effects of new designs mentioned by Romer, are present in the production of both product and process innovations.

We use this model to analyse the impact of a rise in consumer preferences for high-tech goods, while consumers love variety of goods in general too. It is obvious that in the free market this leads to a higher rate of product innovation, *i.e.* more new varieties, and to a stronger divergence in wages between skilled and unskilled workers. The introduction of a binding minimum wage would then typically hamper this form of technological change and cause unemployment. This is in line with the popular notions underlying the deregulation policy. However, if we correct for the market failure on the research market by subsidising R&D, financed in an otherwise neutral way, we find that a minimum wage could in principle be sustained and a higher welfare can be obtained than in the free-market solution: it may therefore help to 'shake the invisible hand'.

6 Kuipers (1996) also points at market failures due to spill-over effects.

The structure of the chapter is as follows. We present the model in Section 2. In Section 3 we analyse the results of some simulation experiments. Some concluding remarks follow in Section 4.

2. THE MODEL

General features

There are intrinsic asymmetries between the employment opportunities of unskilled and skilled workers. As in Hirsch's (1965) life-cycle theory, unskilled workers produce goods and services using established production techniques, while skilled workers are used in the initial stages of a products life cycle. For reasons of simplicity, we assume that established products are generated using unskilled labour only, whereas new products are produced using skilled labour only: we disregard other production factors. As in Krugman (1979), production technologies are linear, while the demand for goods is described using a CES utility function with love of variety. All new products enter the utility function in a symmetric way. This also holds for established products. However, the direct contribution to utility of a new product may differ from that of an established product.

Technical change is the result of R&D efforts driven by profit seeking motives – *cf.* Romer (1990) and Aghion and Howitt (1992, 1998). We distinguish two types of research: basic R&D that leads to new products that can only be produced (initially at least) by skilled workers, and process R&D by firms that 'borrow/steal' the ideas embodied in the products coming from the basic R&D sector. The firms use these ideas to devise a production process that is suitable for unskilled workers to use – the products in question then become 'established' instead of 'new'. The right to use this production process is then sold to the final output sector, as are the designs for new products.

Price-setting and equilibrium on the goods market

For reasons of simplicity, we use a homothetic CES utility function with degree of homogeneity equal to α, and an elasticity of substitution equal to $\sigma = 1/(1-\alpha)$ to describe the demand for each good. Each established good is weighted with intensity β^e and each new good with intensity β^n in the utility function. Moreover, due to love of variety consumers positively value an increase in the total number of goods n for a given real budget.

Utility maximisation, after normalising prices such that the price of an util equals unity, then results in:

$$c_i = (p_i / \beta^i)^{-\sigma}, \tag{1}$$

where c_i is the level of demand for good i, p_i is its corresponding price and $\beta^i = \beta^e$ or β^n is the associated distribution parameter of the CES utility function. We assume $0 \le \alpha < 1$, so that the elasticity of substitution $\sigma \ge 1$.

Every good is produced by a single producer. That producer must first buy the right to produce the good in question from the R&D sector that generates blueprints for new products – in case of a new good – or the right to use a new production process – in case of established products. The demand schedule given by (1) serves as a constraint for the monopolist to set his profit maximising price. This price is given by the Amoroso-Robinson condition, that in turn summarises the first order condition for a profit maximum:

$$p_i = m_i / \alpha, \tag{2}$$

where m_i is the marginal production cost of good i. In that case (and for constant marginal cost), profits at time t from producing good c_i are given by:

$$\Pi_i = (1-\alpha)p_i c_i = (1-\alpha)p_i^{1-\sigma}(\beta^i)^{\sigma} = (1-\alpha)(m_i/\alpha)^{1-\sigma}(\beta^i)^{\sigma}. \tag{3}$$

Wage formation and equilibrium in the labour market

Let μ_e and μ_n be parameters that describe the productivity of labour in new and established product industries. Then we can obtain aggregate demand for unskilled and skilled production workers – l and s, respectively – directly from (1) and (2) and the within product group demand and supply symmetries:

$$l = n_e (w_e /(\beta^e \alpha))^{-\sigma} \mu_e^{1-\sigma}, \tag{4a}$$

$$s = n_n (w_n /(\beta^n \alpha))^{-\sigma} \mu_n^{1-\sigma}, \tag{4b}$$

where w_e and w_n are the wage rates of unskilled workers in the established industries and of skilled workers in the new product industries, respectively. The number of established and new products is n_e and n_n, respectively.

The total supply of unskilled and skilled workers is given, and equals $\bar{l}$ and $\bar{h}$, respectively.[7] Equilibrium wages by skill can then be obtained by equating labour supply to labour demand by skill.

Substituting the exogenous supply of labour used for the production of established and new products into Equation (4a), we can obtain the equilibrium wage rates by skill by solving (4a-b) for wages:

$$w_e = \beta^e (\bar{l} / n_e)^{-1/\sigma} \alpha \, \mu_e^{\;1-1/\sigma}, \tag{5a}$$

$$w_n = \beta^n (s / n_n)^{-1/\sigma} \alpha \, \mu_n^{\;1-1/\sigma}, \tag{5b}$$

where $s = \bar{h} - r$ is the number of skilled production workers and r is the total number of skilled research workers, employed in the research sector.

Profit erosion

For a typical industry we may combine Equations (3) and (5) to obtain:

$$\Pi_i^x = (1-\alpha)(w_x / \mu_x / \alpha)^{1-\sigma} \mu_x^{\;\sigma-1} \left(\beta^x\right)^\sigma, \tag{6}$$

for x=n,e. Equation (6) shows that profits will be eroded over time by increases in wage rates, since $\sigma \geq 1$. Wages in the established industries and the new industries rise with the number of goods produced by those industries – *cf.* Equation (5). Hence, the rate of profit erosion depends on the absolute amount of R&D and also on its distribution over basic R&D and process R&D. The latter depends on the relative profitability of both activities as compared to final output production.

The R&D sectors

Substitution of Equation (5) into (6) provides the value of both types of blueprints to a producer, which is the price that a producer would be willing to pay to the R&D sector. Combining Aghion and Howitt (1998) and Van Zon, Sanders and Muysken (1998), we assume that this willingness to pay

[7] This obviously implies that a wage tax or subsidy will change only the sectoral distribution of labour, and not total labour supply.

provides the incentive to a competitive research sector to hire skilled labour and to try and invent a new product or a new process. In a competitive R&D sector arbitrage ensures that the value of the marginal blueprint is equated to the marginal cost of producing that new blueprint. These marginal costs consist of skilled wages only.

In the research sector that generates new products an intertemporal externality exists – *cf.* Romer (1990). With respect to research into new processes we assume a positive external spillover from the introduction of new goods that can be turned into established ones. However, this type of research is subject to diminishing returns in the sense that once all products are established, none are left to transform. Defining $z=n_e/n_n$, the above can be summarised by:

$$\frac{dn}{dt}=\kappa_n n r_n \qquad \Rightarrow \hat{n}=\kappa_n r_n \ , \tag{7a}$$

$$\frac{dn_e}{dt}=\kappa_e n_n r_e \qquad \Rightarrow \hat{n}_e=\kappa_e r_e / z \ , \tag{7b}$$

$$\frac{dn_n}{dt}=\frac{dn}{dt}-\frac{dn_e}{dt} \qquad \Rightarrow \hat{n}_n=(1+z)\hat{n}-z\hat{n}_e \ , \tag{7c}$$

where r_n and r_e refer to the number of research workers engaged in generating new or established products, respectively, and where $\hat{x}=(dx/dt)/x$.

Assuming that the probability of any new product becoming established is independent of the product under consideration, it follows that each new product has a certain probability per unit of time of becoming an established product. This probability is given by the ratio of the number of newly established products (*i.e.* dn_e/dt) relative to the number of not yet established products (*i.e.* n_n). As in Aghion and Howitt (1998), the probability of a new product being replaced by an established one can be accounted for in the present value of the corresponding expected profit stream in the effective rate of discount:

$$V^x=\Pi^x/(\rho+\delta_x), \tag{8}$$

where $x=n,e$. In Equation (8), ρ is the nominal rate of discount, while δ_x is the additional discount on the expected present value of a blueprint due to 'business stealing' and wage induced profit erosion. The wage changes are in turn induced by the growth of the number of new and established products, as is apparent from Equation (5).

From Equation (5) it is easily seen that for a constant size and skill-composition of the labour force, as well as a constant allocation of skilled and unskilled workers (which would be the case in the steady state) we have:

$$\hat{w}_x = \hat{n}_x / \sigma, \tag{9}$$

for x=n,e. From Equations (6) and (9) it follows that the growth of profits due to technical change induced changes in wages would be equal to $1-\sigma$ times the growth in wages as given by Equation (9). Obviously, for $\sigma \geq 1$, the growth in profits would be non-positive for a positive growth in wages. In addition to this, the profits in the new products final output sector are also eroded due to new products becoming established. The proportional rate at which this happens is given by $(dn_e / dt) / n_n = z\hat{n}_e$, as was mentioned earlier. Using this information and Equations (7a-c) and (9) we find for the additional discount factors in Equation (8):

$$\delta^n = \alpha(1+z)\kappa_n r_n + (1-\alpha)\kappa_e r_e, \tag{10a}$$

$$\delta^e = \alpha\kappa_e r_e / z. \tag{10b}$$

Equation (10a) shows that the rate of profit erosion in the new products final output sector depends positively on the number of research workers in the other research sector. However, it also depends positively on the number of research workers employed in the research sector that generates new products. The latter is due to the fact that more new products make skilled workers scarce, which tends to increase wage costs in the R&D sectors. The former effect is our version of business-stealing effect – *cf.* also Aghion and Howitt (1992, 1998).

The steady state solution

The steady state requires the constancy of the ratio z=n_e/n_n. This ratio would remain constant only if the rates of growth of the number of new and established products are equal to the growth rate of total products. Let the steady state value of z be denoted by $\bar{z}$. Then it follows directly from Equations (7a-c) that:

$$\hat{n} = \hat{n}_e = \hat{n}_n \quad \Rightarrow \quad \bar{z} = \frac{r_e}{r_n}\frac{\kappa_e}{\kappa_n}. \tag{11}$$

It follows from Equation (11) that for a given allocation of research workers, the ratio of established products to new products will be larger, the higher is the ratio of the R&D productivity parameters κ_e / κ_n.

Following Romer (1990) and Aghion and Howitt (1998), labour market arbitrage for skilled workers now implies:

$$\frac{dn}{dt}\frac{\Pi^n}{\rho+\delta_n} / r_n = \frac{dn^e}{dt}\frac{\Pi^e}{\rho+\delta_e} / r_e = w_n = \beta^n((\bar{h}-r)/n_n)^{-1/\sigma}\alpha\,\mu_n^{\;1-1/\sigma}. \tag{12}$$

The right-hand side of (12) is the skilled wage rate in the new product final output industries. The left most part of (12) is the present value of total expected profits per researcher associated with the marginal blueprints in the basic R&D sector. The middle part of (12) refers to the present value of total expected profits per researcher associated with the marginal blueprint in the other research sector.

The model cannot be solved analytically, but both a graphical and a numerical solution are provided in Van Zon and Sanders (2000).

3. POLICY INTERFERENCE WITH MARKET OUTCOMES: SOME SUBSIDY EXPERIMENTS

Since the model presented above cannot be solved analytically, in particular its out of steady state dynamics, we illustrate its most interesting properties by means of a number of simulation experiments. Of course, there are some parameter constraints that have to be satisfied in order to obtain generally meaningful results, but these are easily met in practice.[8] Nonetheless, it should be kept in mind that other (relatively unlikely) parameter sets can be envisaged that would change the analysis in a qualitative way. For our present illustrative purposes, we don't need generality, however: likely qualitative results will suffice.

We used the base-run of the model presented in Van Zon and Sanders (2000, Section 4) as a starting point for some simulation experiments in

[8] See Van Zon and Sanders (2000) for more details. For their simulations, Van Zon and Sanders have chosen a parameter set consistent with these restrictions.

order to analyse the impact of minimum wages and subsidies on technical change, economic growth and the distribution of income.[9] The aim is to show that the market failures implied by the public good character of technological change can be partly remedied by subsidies paid out of taxes on wage income, and that minimum wages are not necessarily harmful in that context.[10] The latter implies that equity considerations do not have to hamper the restoration of efficiency.

In order to induce a change in the rate of process and product innovations, we investigated the impact of a preference shift towards high-tech goods on the economy. As might be expected, this leads to a higher production of new designs, because of the increase in profits to be earned on new products. This results in a reallocation of skilled labour from the production of both high-tech goods and in particular of process innovations to the production of new designs. As a consequence, skilled wages increase while unskilled wages fall. Thus we find an increase in technological change accompanied by a strong wage divergence as the outcome of the free-market process. It is obvious that in this context a minimum wage will cause unemployment and will hamper technological change.[11] However, things are different when we introduce wage-costs subsidies, as we did in four separate simulation experiments, where we subsidised wage costs in each of the four sectors.[12]

The outcomes of the simulation experiments are summarised in Table 1, where a "+" indicates an increase relative to the free-market solution, a "–"

[9] In this base-run, about one third of the skilled labour available is allocated towards R&D and the relative wage for unskilled workers is roughly half that of skilled workers. As one would expect, the profits in the new goods sector are discounted at a much higher rate than those in the established goods sector due to the business stealing effect. Finally the economy grows at about 3.6 % in steady state.

[10] The model has been constructed in such a way that all income earned is eventually (and completely) paid as wages in either the final output sector or the R&D sectors. Thus, income taxes boil down to wage taxes. We furthermore assume that labour itself is inelastically supplied, hence neutral taxation simply implies the same tax rate for all workers, regardless of their sector of employment. Because of the assumed neutrality, we do not formally specify the taxation side of our illustrative simulation experiments later on.

[11] Van Zon and Sanders (2000) did an experiment (nr. 7) in which they introduce a minimum wage. They find unemployment and an initial increase in technical change. However, they ignore the costs of unemployment that have to be borne somehow. Moreover, they do not consider the impact on utility, which certainly is negative in the longer run, because then technological change grows at its initial rate, while unemployment persists.

[12] As we have indicated above, these subsidies are financed by taxing wage income. An important simplifying assumption in this context is that this does not affect labour supply – which is true by construction, since labour supply is price-inelastic.

indicates a decrease and a "0" means no change.[13] "+/–" signals a positive deviation from the reference run at first, followed by a negative one later on.

Table 1. Effects of subsidising wage costs in the four sectors, relative to the 'free-market' solution

	Technological change				Skilled labour			Utility		
	Old (n_e)	New (n_n)	Tot (n)	W_L/W_H	Old (r_e)	New (r_n)	Prod (s)	Un-skilled	Skilled	Tot
Low-tech	0	0	0	++	0	0	0	+	–	0
High-tech	+/–	–	+/–	–	–	–	+	–	+/–	– –
Process innovation	+/0	–/0	–/0	+	++	–	–	+	–	–
New designs	–/+	+	+	–	–/+	+	–	–/+	+	–/+

The first experiment shows that subsidising wage costs in the established goods sector will increase competition for unskilled workers, while profits will not increase. The outcome is that all subsidies will be passed on to unskilled workers and, since profits are not affected, relative demand for high-skilled workers will not change. Total utility will not change either, but it is redistributed in favour of unskilled workers. Therefore, a minimum wage at a level higher than the free-market outcome together with subsidising unskilled wage costs can be imposed without lowering total utility in the process. Market failures do not grow worse, because of the effective isolation of the unskilled labour market from the rest of the economy through the lack of a real impact of the unskilled wage cost subsidy on profits. The latter leaves the incentives that influence the allocation of skilled workers, and therefore R&D efforts, unchanged.

Subsidising wage costs in the high-tech-goods producing sector will generate adverse results, since skilled workers will be lured away from the R&D sector and both the generation of process and product innovations will be lower in comparison to the free-market outcome. Utility of skilled workers will be higher initially, because of the upward pressure on skilled wages, but in a later stage it will decrease relative to the free-market outcome because of the relative decrease in innovations. The latter is self-reinforcing due to negative external effects. Total utility will be lower over the whole period.

[13] The experiment for each sector is a permanent subsidy of 10 percent on the wage costs of that sector, financed by a tax on wage income in all sectors. Because labour is supplied inelastically, this has no real effects on the supply of labour. Moreover, full employment is always maintained.

Subsidising wage costs in the process innovation part of the R&D-sector will affect unskilled wages positively, since the unskilled workers will be involved in the production of more low-tech goods, relative to the free-market solution. The downside of this subsidy is that business stealing will be stimulated. Moreover, more skilled workers will be employed in the process-innovation part of the R&D-sector at the detriment of the design of new products – again with self-reinforcing negative external effects. This will be the cause of a lower total utility, although the utility of the unskilled will increase.

As one might expect, the market failure due to the public good character of new designs will lead to too low a production of those designs. Subsidising wage costs in this part of the R&D sector therefore might be expected to improve both total utility and the utility of the unskilled. One can see that this is indeed the case. Initially, however, the utility of the unskilled will be lower in comparison to the free-market solution, because skilled workers will be involved in the design of new varieties instead of process innovations. But the external effect of new designs will soon increase the productivity of the R&D-sector in process innovations, and from then on utility of unskilled workers increases too, despite the decrease in relative unskilled wages. Moreover, the utility will increase persistently at a faster rate, when compared to the free-market solution, due to these external effects.

This last experiment shows that subsidies can indeed be used to correct for the market failure in technological change. Moreover, a combination with the first experiment – *i.e.* temporarily subsidising unskilled wage costs in the low-tech sector – seems to be an attractive policy option if one would want to avoid, or at least limit, the initial decrease in per capita utility of the unskilled.

4. THE ART OF SHAKING THE INVISIBLE HAND

In Van Zon, Muysken and Meijers (1998) we argue that in a situation of excess supply of skilled workers, the creation of skilled jobs may promote unskilled employment more than the creation of unskilled jobs does. The reason is that these skilled jobs will reduce the bumping down of unskilled workers by skilled workers who occupy unskilled jobs. This is the so-called chimney effect. In Van Zon *et al.* (2001), we provide some empirical results for the Netherlands and Germany, after having extended the model above with asymmetries in learning costs by skill. We show that policies aimed at furthering the employment prospects of the unskilled may take different forms, ranging from subsidising the creation/use of unskilled jobs to subsidising the creation of skilled jobs. Not surprisingly, the effectiveness of each policy measure depends very much on the existence of binding supply constraints in the various skill-segments of the labour market. Moreover, technological change does not play an explicit role in these models.

The perspective taken in the previous models is short term rather than the long-term perspective taken in this chapter. In the long run the binding character of a supply constraint at a certain moment invokes counteracting technology responses through the reallocation of R&D activities. This is recognised in Muysken *et al.* (2001), although technological change is exogenous.[14] There we point out that the activation of the chimney effect by stimulating product innovation may have serious equity implications, because of the negative impact on both wage inequality and asymmetries in unemployment. Therefore we argue in favour of stimulating process innovations, that is to make the production of new goods accessible to unskilled workers as an alternative to educating these workers and raising their skill levels. In that paper, however, we have focused on the influence of employment asymmetries in a given technology environment. Thus we neglect again the endogenous technology reactions that dominate economic developments in the long run, as we have highlighted in our wage cost subsidy experiments in Section 3 of this chapter. This change of perspective also makes for differences in the corresponding policy considerations, as will become more clear below.

Since we treated the process of technological change as exogenous in our earlier papers, we have also ignored the spill-over effects inherent in this process. It is obvious that these spill-over effects, that are at the heart of the public good aspects of technological change, may lead to a serious underestimation of the full impact of technological change on economic activity. The market imperfections implied by these public good aspects might lead to underinvestment in R&D and new technologies.

Underinvestment has been a central theme in the work of Simon Kuipers.[15] However, as we already mentioned in the introduction, his focus was on market failures due to uncertainty rather than spill-over effects. In the analysis above, we have ignored the aspect of uncertainty, although one could argue that a long-term perspective should include uncertainty from the outset, in particular when the effects of technological change in the long run are analysed. Clearly, our long-term analysis applies to a steady state situation where all adjustments in wages, prices and the (re-)allocation of (skilled) labour are both certain, flexible and complete.

[14] In that paper the focus is more on the response under different labour market institutions (in Europe and the US) to technological change.

[15] The most recent contribution is Kuipers (1999).

Pending these uncertainties, our long-term analysis leads to the conclusion that product innovations should be stimulated in order to improve the position of unskilled workers, while the stimulation of process innovations will have an adverse effect on the economy. On the other hand our short-term analyses typically favour subsidising process innovations and indicate a negative impact of product innovations.

The apparent policy dilemmas do underline the notion that economic policymaking is an art as much as a science. However, they are also a warning of the danger of taking too narrow a policy stance too early. Shaking the invisible hand may help, but it is a very delicate process. With this in mind, the main conclusion that we draw from our experiments is that it is of crucial importance to have a keen eye for the intertemporal distribution of the effects of policy measures – repairing in the short run what is clearly undesirable, without however endangering long term growth and employment perspectives, through the forceful and coordinated application of technology policy, structural policy as well as employment policy. Guess who already said that early in our careers, in 1979 ... [16]

REFERENCES

Aghion, P. and P. Howitt (1992), "A Model of Growth through Creative Destruction," *Econometrica* 60, pp. 323-351.

Aghion, P. and P. Howitt (1998), *Endogenous Growth Theory,* Cambridge: MIT Press.

Freeman, R. (1995), "The Limits of Wage Flexibility to Curing Unemployment," *Oxford Review of Economic Policy* 11(1), pp. 63-72.

Hirsch, S. (1965), "The United States Electronics Industry in International Trade," *National Institute of Economics Review* 34, pp. 92-107.

Kleinknecht, A. (1998), "Is Labour Flexibility Harmful to Innovation?," *Cambridge Journal of Economics* 22(3), pp. 387-396.

Krugman, P. (1979), "A Model of Innovation, Technology Transfer and the World Distribution of Income," *Journal of Political Economy* 87(2), pp. 253-265.

Krugman, P. (1995), "Growing World Trade: Causes and Consequence," *Brookings Papers on Economic Activity* 0(1), 1995, pp. 327-362.

Kuipers, S.K., J. Muysken, D.J. van den Berg and A.H. van Zon (1980), *Sectorstructuur en economische groei*, Den Haag (WRR).

Kuipers, S.K. (1990), "Stabilization Policy: A Non-market Clearing View," in K. Groenveld, J.A.H. Maks and J. Muysken (eds.), *Economic Policy and the Market Process: Austrian and Mainstream Economics*, Amsterdam.

Kuipers, S.K. (1995), "Wanneer de veilingmeester faalt," *Economisch Statistische Berichten* 80(4028), pp. 900-903.

Kuipers, S.K. (1996), "Coördinatie, concurrentie en doelmatigheid," in A. Nentjes (ed.), *Marktwerking versus coördinatie*, Preadviezen van de Koninklijke Vereniging voor de Staathuishoudkunde, Utrecht: Lemma, pp. 37-51.

[16] Well, Simon Kuipers, of course – *cf.* Kuipers, *et al.* (1980, pp.100-101).

Kuipers, S.K. (1999), "The Natural Rate of Unemployment: An Alternative Perspective," *CPB Report* 99/4, pp. 59-61.

Muysken, J., M. Sanders and A.H. van Zon (2001), "Wage Divergence and Asymmetries in Unemployment in a Model with Biased Technical Change," *De Economist* 149(1), pp. 1-19.

Nickell, S. (1997), "Unemployment and Labor Market Rigidities: Europe versus North America," *Journal of Economic Perspectives* 11(3), pp. 55-74.

OECD (1996), *Employment Outlook*, Paris, July.

Romer, P.M. (1986), "Increasing Returns and Long Run Growth," *Journal of Political Economy* 94(5), pp. 1002-1037.

Romer, P.M. (1990), "Endogenous Technological Change," *Journal of Political Economy* 98(5), pp. S71-S102.

Siebert, H. (1997), "Labor Market Rigidities: At the Root of Unemployment in Europe," *Journal of Economic Perspectives* 11(3), pp. 37-54.

Zon, A. H. van, M. Sanders and J. Muysken (1998), "Modelling the Link between Skill-Biases in Technical Change and Wage Divergence through Labour Market Extensions of Krugman's North-South Model," *MERIT Research Memorandum* 2/98-027 and in L. Soete and P. Petit (eds.) (2001), *Technology and the future of European Employment*, Cheltenham: Edward Elgar.

Zon, A. H. van, J. Muysken and H. Meijers (1998), "Asymmetric Skill Substitution, Labour Market Flexibility, and the Allocation of Qualifications," in H. Heijke and L. Borghans (eds.), *Towards a Transparent Labour Market for Educational Decisions*, London: Avebury Publishers, pp. 151-195.

Zon, A. H. van, H. Meijers and J. Muysken (2001), "On Trickling Chimneys and Other Unemployment Misery, " in H. Heijke and J. Muysken (eds.), *Education and Training in a Knowledge based Economy*, London: MacMillan, pp.117-158.

Zon, A. H. van and M. Sanders (2000), "Endogenous Technical Change and Skill Biases in Employment Opportunities," *MERIT Research Memorandum* 2/20-004.

Chapter 15

Some Observations on Recent Growth Theory

Arnold Heertje
Department of Economics, University of Amsterdam

Key words: Growth, Non-reproducible goods, Non-scale models

Abstract: This chapter deals with an important aspect of recent growth theory. On the basis of a study by Eicher and Turnovsky on non-scale models of economic growth, some critical observations are presented. Growth theory is still restricted to welfare in the material sense and to reproducible goods. These drawbacks have to remedied in the future.

1. INTRODUCTION

On a macro-economic level, growth theory is in a certain sense the core of economic theory, it being concerned with the development over time of the economic process as a whole. On a micro-economic level, general equilibrium theory may be seen as the essence of economics. The integration of growth theory and general equilibrium theory under the assumption of strategic behaviour of consumers, entrepreneurs and owners of factors of production may be viewed as the long-run aim of economic theory.

This rather general statement is in order of several qualifications. First of all, it assumes an institutional set-up of the economy, in which individuals have enough freedom of behaviour to act independently with respect to their consumption and production. In fact, some kind of capitalism is involved. Secondly, only reproducible goods are taken into account. The distinction between reproducible goods and non-reproducible goods has been made long ago by David Ricardo in his *Principles* of 1817 (Ricardo, 1817, p. 2). Non-reproducible goods like paintings and antiquarian books are not part of the production set, considered in growth theory. Only the production of reproducible goods is taken into account, mostly by means of a more or less sophisticated production function. Technical change does influence both the number of goods and the methods of their production. Non-reproducible goods, however, also are relevant for the level of satisfaction of wants of the consumers in society and even of individuals who are not living yet. This brings us to a third restriction of modern growth theory. Growth theory restricts the welfare of consumers to the production of goods and services, leaving out other components like the preservation of nature and culture and the environmental issues that are considered by the consumers as relevant for their level of satisfaction of wants, in other words welfare in the broad sense. Of course, Paretian welfare theory is a building block of general equilibrium theory, so that the future development of growth theory can no longer neglect the broad concept of welfare as a more appropriate description of the growth of an economy than is implied in the present yardstick of the rate of growth of an economy in terms of material production.

Against this general background, I would like to discuss a recent analysis by Eicher and Turnovsky on non-scale models of economic growth (Eicher and Turnovsky, 1999).

2. NON-SCALE MODELS OF ECONOMIC GROWTH

Growth theory of the sixties concentrated on the relationship between the long-run growth rate and the exogenous rates of population growth and technical change, often assuming Harrod-neutral technical change. In that case technical change is purely labour-augmenting. Growth theory of the eighties concentrates on endogenous factors such as the productivity of capital, the accumulation of knowledge and public investment in education. Eicher and Turnovsky divide the new growth models into two classes. R&D-based growth refers to models in which growth is due to innovation (Romer, 1990). Investment-based growth refers to models in which growth is due to private investment in physical and human capital, like in AK models (Barro, 1990; Aghion and Howitt, 1998). Both types of growth models may show scale effects in the case of non-rivalry and externalities. Changes in the scale of the economy do alter the long-run equilibrium growth rate. However, empirical evidence does not support the existence of scale effects. A recent illustration in this respect is a study by Vanhoudt on the question whether European unification did induce economic growth. He did not find support for any scale effect (Vanhoudt, 1999). A theoretical restriction of endogenous growth models is that to generate an equilibrium of ongoing growth – a steady state – all production functions must reflect constant returns to scale in the accumulated factors of production. Both the empirical and theoretical considerations raise for Eicher and Turnovsky the question under which conditions non-scale balanced growth models can be developed. To this end they study a general two-sector growth model. Let c denote per capita consumption and assume constant intertemporal elasticity of substitution, so that the intertemporal utility of the representative agent reads:

$$U(c)=\frac{1}{1-\gamma}\int_0^{\infty} c^{1-\gamma}e^{-\rho t}\,dt \quad \rho>0 \text{ and } \gamma>0.$$

The inter-temporal elasticity of substitution equals $1/\gamma$. The coefficient ρ reflects the unique rate of time preference of the representative consumer. The central planner wants to maximise utility over time. The economy produces two goods, final output and technical change. Production of the final good takes place through three factors, the social stock of technology, labour and capital. The production function reads:

$$Y=F_I(A,\Theta N,\varphi K), \quad 0\le\Theta\le1, \quad 0\le\varphi\le1.$$

In the production function Y denotes final output, A denotes the stock of technical knowledge, K denotes the social stock of physical capital and N denotes the social labour force. The constant growth rate of the labour force is n. The coefficients Θ and φ reflect the fraction of labour and capital devoted to the production of the final good. The stocks are social in the sense of including social spillovers. The returns to scale are characterised in terms of the social production function. It is assumed that physical capital does not depreciate and that the capital stock accumulates according to $K=Y-C$, where C equals cN. Technology is produced in the other sector of the economy according to the production function:

$$\dot{A}=F_{II}\left(A,(1-\Theta)N,(1-\varphi)K\right).$$

In other words capital and labour are divided over the two sectors I and II and technology is not only a public good but is also produced. The problem of the central planner now is to maximise the intertemporal utility function, in view of the two production functions, the rate of accumulation of capital and the initial conditions. The decision variables are c, Θ, φ, K and A. The scale of the economy is reflected by the population size N. A balanced growth path is defined as one along which all real quantities grow at a constant, but not identical, rate. The authors require that the output/capital ratio remains constant in the case of balanced growth. Under these conditions the balanced growth rates can be obtained, as well as further economic restrictions along the path in view of the optimality conditions. Several propositions can be derived. First of all, the necessary and sufficient conditions for positive growth and output, capital, consumption and technology in the two-sector non-scale growth model. Secondly, sufficient conditions can be derived for balanced growth in non-scale growth models. These conditions are specific properties of the production functions in both sectors. Further, positive sustained balanced growth rates are consistent with increasing, constant or decreasing returns to scale in one or both sectors. In other words, the authors do succeed in showing that balanced growth rates are determined in general by production conditions and not by the scale of the economy. For economic policy this implies that the long-run rate of economic growth can be influenced through the underlying production structure and not by influencing the size of the economy, as measured by the size of population.

3. CRITICAL OBSERVATIONS

I would like to raise the question how sensitive the outcome of the very profound and carefully worked out analysis is for the assumptions made. Let us concentrate on two aspects of the model, the intertemporal utility function and the assumption on the capital/output ratio.

Many years ago Phelps pointed out already, in a discussion of the Ramsey problem and the golden rule of accumulation, that a utility function which makes the rate of social utility an increasing, concave and unbounded function only of per capita consumption, is said to involve no discounting of future utilities (Phelps, 1966, pp. 83-85). He indicated that while such a function may treat generations alike, it does not treat individuals alike. In a certain sense this issue is concealed in the approach of Eicher and Turnovsky by using the concept of a representative agent, with a constant rate of time preference. In fact, the structure the authors choose for their utility function does not contradict the possibility treating all consumers alike in all generations, so that there is a uniform way of discounting of individual utility rates. Under these circumstances the size of the population N does not matter. However, if we assume heterogeneous consumers in each generation and from generation to generation, from the point of view of discounting the future, the distribution of the consumers as well as their total number, I suspect does have an influence on the balanced growth rate. This brings us to a second consideration. Although the model does not restrict the form of technical knowledge *A*, along the balanced growth path technical change is neutral in the sense of Harrod, *viz.* it is purely labour augmenting. The definition of the steady state is determined by this crucial assumption. If we drop the assumption of a constant capital/output ratio and allow for different types of technical change, the picture changes. My guess is that with capital augmenting technical change à la Solow, where capital is embodied in new vintages of capital, the scale of the economy will appear to influence the equilibrium rates of growth of the economy. In a broader normative perspective this conclusion might be relevant for economic policy (Buchanan and Yoon, 1994, p. 11).

Let me end up with the observation that our discussion remains within the realm of what is called by Day "simple dynamics" (Day, 1994, p. 1). We are outside the sphere of types of change over time that are not periodic and not balanced and that do not produce a balanced pattern. Complex economic or non-linear dynamics includes nonperiodic fluctuations, overlapping waves and switches in regime or structural change. Against that background the issue of non-scale models of economic growth seems to be less relevant.

REFERENCES

Aghion, P. and P. Howitt (1998), *Endogenous Growth Theory,* Cambridge: MIT Press.

Barro, R.J. (1990), "Government Spending in a Simple Model of Endogenous Growth," *Journal of Political Economy* 98, pp. 103-126.

Buchanan, J. and Y.J. Yoon (1994), *The Return to Increasing Returns*, Ann Arbor: University of Michigan Press.

Day, R.H. (1994), *Complex Economic Dynamics* Volume I, Cambridge: MIT Press.

Eicher, T. and S.J. Turnovsky (1999), "Non-Scale Models of Economic Growth," *The Economic Journal* 109, pp. 394-415.

Phelps, E.S. (1966), *Golden Rules of Economic Growth*, Amsterdam: North-Holland.

Ricardo, D. (1817), *On the Principles of Economics, and Taxation*, London: John Murray.

Romer, P.M. (1990), "Endogenous Technological Change," *Journal of Political Economy* 98(5), pp. S71-S102.

Vanhoudt, P. (1999), "Did the European Unification Induce Economic Growth? In Search of the Scale Effects and Persistent Changes," *Weltwirtschaftliches Archiv* 135, pp. 193-221.

Chapter 16

Identifying Regimes for the Netherlands in the 19th Century

Nanne Brunia and Gerard H. Kuper
Department of Economics, University of Groningen

Key words: Capital shortage, Labour shortage, Investment

Abstract: We develop a microeconomic model of entry and exit starting with some typical Post Keynesian assumptions. When capital or labour is expected to be scarce the optimal price firms charge is higher than in the case in which both inputs are abundant. Therefore, in a macroeconomic context low shares of labour income are associated with expected shortages of the inputs. We use this result to identify regimes of expected shortages in the Dutch economy in the 19th century. We also use the unemployment rate and utilisation rate of capital to identify regimes of realised shortages. Roughly 50% of the realised shortages were expected.

1. INTRODUCTION

The most favourable thing mainstream economists write about the Harrod-Domar models from the 1940s and 1950s these days is that these models stimulated the development of neoclassical growth theory. In the *Handbook of Macroeconomics*, which was published in 1999, Harrod, Domar and the models named after them, are mentioned only once: notably, in the chapter on neoclassical growth theory written by Solow (Solow, 1999). Why is it that Harrod-Domar models seem to be laid aside? Is it that these models do not fit the data (anymore)? Do mainstream economists dislike the pessimistic predictions of these models? Are entrepreneural investment decisions more rational than Harrod thought they were? Simon Kuipers is not one of those mainstream economists. He has always had a profound interest for non-mainstream research (*cf.* Brakman *et al.*, 2001).

Before turning to the aim of our contribution to this *Festschrift* we discuss briefly the essence of Post Keynesian growth models. Post Keynesian growth models in their purest forms lead to rather pessimistic conclusions about the stability of economies. Equilibrium requires the savings rate, the capital-output ratio, the rate of population growth and the rate of labour-augmenting technical progress to satisfy a particular relation. Since none of these parameters are endogenous, this *fundamental equation* is met only by coincidence. Hence, a typical Harrod-Domar economy alternates between long and prolonged periods of capital shortage with increasing unemployment and labour shortage. According to Solow: "... this is an unsatisfactory picture of 20th century capitalism ..." (Solow, 1999, p. 641). In the Harrod-Domar models, adjustment towards some sort of steady state, in a neoclassical sense, is non-existent. For instance, capital shortage leads to ever increasing unemployment rates, simply because entrepreneurs fail to increase the stock of capital. This increase in the stock of capital is required to increase employment in order to avoid instability. This outcome, obviously, results from the assumptions of fixed prices and wages and lack of substitution between the various inputs in the production process. In other words, there is no coordination mechanism as in Solovian growth models. In most of his academic work, Kuipers emphasises the importance of coordination failures which do not allow markets to function frictionless. Most recently, he explains adverse trends in productivity by discriminating between periods of capital shortage and capital abundance (see Kuipers and Kuper, 2001). The underlying assumption in that paper is the lack of substitutability between capital and labour. This paper undoubtedly has been one of the sources of inspiration for our contribution. Here, we develop a small theoretical model that starts from typical Post Keynesian assumptions. The basic assumption here is that the existence of monopoly profits induces new firms to enter the market even in a situation of capital shortage. The reason may be an autonomous increase in demand (*cf.* Campbell (1998) who argues that entry is procyclical) or a drop in the cost of capital. We assume that capital goods are identified by the number of firms or plants. Since new plants embody the latest technology with higher productivity it would be interesting to introduce vintage effects in this framework (see Campbell, 1998, p. 3). However, to keep the model as simple as possible we refrain from this interesting extension.

In this chapter we present a microeconomic model of entry and exit. We will derive conditions for entry and exit in regimes of shortage and abundance of inputs. Based on these conditions we try to identify the different regimes for the Netherlands in the 19th century. The novelty in this chapter is that we do not only classify the data using *ex post* information about rates of labour and capital utilisation. We also employ the information derived from the microeconomic model to classify the data *ex ante*, *i.e.* the model provides a tool to make an expected classification of the data. The information from the microeconomic model is summarised by the share of labour in total income. This share, or rather one minus the share of labour in income, measures profitability and hence influences future investment. Using this criterion we identify periods with expected shortages of labour or capital and confront these periods with realised (*ex post*) periods of shortages.

2. A SIMPLE MODEL OF ENTRY AND EXIT

There are N firms producing a differentiated product. The demand for the product of an individual firm q is given by

$$q = Q\left\{\frac{1}{N} - b\left(P - \widetilde{P}\right)\right\}, \tag{1}$$

where Q denotes total demand, N the number of firms, P the price the firm charges and $\widetilde{P}$ the average price competitors charge. Note that b is the price elasticity of demand. Output in each firm is produced according to a Leontief production function with fixed technical coefficients α_K and α_L:

$$q \leq \min\left\{\alpha_K \bar{k}, \alpha_L \bar{l}\right\}, \tag{2}$$

where $\bar{k}$ is the capital stock of the firm and $\bar{l}$ is the maximum quantity of labour the firm can hire. The capital stock that is used for actual production is

$$k = \frac{q}{\alpha_K}, \tag{3}$$

and employment is

$$l = \frac{q}{\alpha_L}. \tag{4}$$

The utilisation rate of capital is defined as

$$v = \frac{k}{\bar{k}}. \tag{5}$$

We introduce the notion of *going concern*, that is firms reinvest their depreciation in order to remain in operation. Thus at the end of each year the firm has to reinvest $\delta P\bar{k}$ in order to maintain production capacity. If in any year the firm does not reinvest this amount the production capacity is assumed to be lost forever. Firms are assumed to maximise the market value given their expectations about the prices competitors charge, costs and total demand. We assume that firms have perfect knowledge with respect to the current economic situation and have static expectations with respect to future developments. Since all firms are identical, in equilibrium firms charge the same price and have equal market shares. If the net present value of continuing operations is negative, a number of firms does not reinvest and exits the market. On the other hand if the net present value of operations exceeds the investment outlays new firms enter the market.

The specification of the production structure implies that we can identify four regimes:

1. capital and labour abundance,
2. capital shortage and labour abundance,
3. capital abundance and labour shortage, and
4. capital and labour shortage.

The optimal pricing policies of firms and the conditions for entry and for exit in each regime are discussed below.

Capital and labour abundance

Given our assumptions with respect to the formation of expectations maximising the market value of the firm is equivalent to maximising current profits. Profits π are equal to

$$\pi = q\left(P - \frac{W}{\alpha_L}\right) - \delta P\bar{k}, \tag{6}$$

where W denotes the nominal wage rate. Maximising Equation (6) subject to Equation (1), we can derive the first-order condition for profit maximisation:

$$\frac{\partial \pi}{\partial P} = -Qb\left(P - \frac{W}{\alpha_L}\right) + q - \delta\bar{k} = 0, \tag{7}$$

and we can derive the following expression for the optimal price the firm charges:

$$\hat{P} = \frac{W}{\alpha_L} + \frac{1}{bN} - \frac{\delta \bar{k}}{bQ}. \tag{8}$$

The optimal price is a mark-up over marginal costs. Below we show that the mark-up is always positive. The mark-up depends on the sensitivity of the firm's demand for price changes, b, and the size of the market, q and N. An increase in total demand given the number of firms increases the optimal price, an increase in the number of firms given total demand reduces the optimal price. Note that if the number of firms goes to infinity, the optimal price equals marginal costs (given the level of demand).

Firms do not reinvest and therefore exit the market if the market value of the firm becomes negative, that is if

$$\frac{q(P - W/\alpha_L) - \delta P \bar{k}}{r} < 0, \tag{9}$$

where r denotes the weighted average cost of capital. The weighted average cost of capital is a weighted average of the required return of bonds and equity. Both required rates of return are equal to the risk free interest rate and a risk premium for the systematic risks they bear. The weights depend on the debt structure of the firm. The break-even exit price is therefore:

$$\underline{P} = \frac{W/\alpha_L}{1 - \delta \bar{k} N/Q}. \tag{10}$$

The break-even exit price increases as wages go up or the number of firms increases and falls if total demand increases. Firms enter the market if the market value of entering is positive, that is if

$$\frac{q(P - W/\alpha_L) - \delta P \bar{k}}{r} > P\bar{k}. \tag{11}$$

This condition resembles Tobin's Q. For a survey we refer to Abel (1990). The break-even entry price equals

$$\overline{P} = \frac{W/\alpha_L}{1 - (r + \delta)\bar{k} N/Q}. \tag{12}$$

The break-even entry price increases as wages go up or the number of firms increases and falls if total demand increases. If exit and entry takes place immediately the actual price is larger than or equal to the break-even exit price and lower than or equal to the break-even entry price. Equation (10) can be rewritten as

$$\frac{W}{\alpha_L P} = \frac{WL}{PQ} = 1 - \delta \bar{k} N / Q . \tag{13}$$

The left-hand side of Equation (13) equals the income share of labour in total income. Since this share is always smaller than unity, the mark-up is always positive.

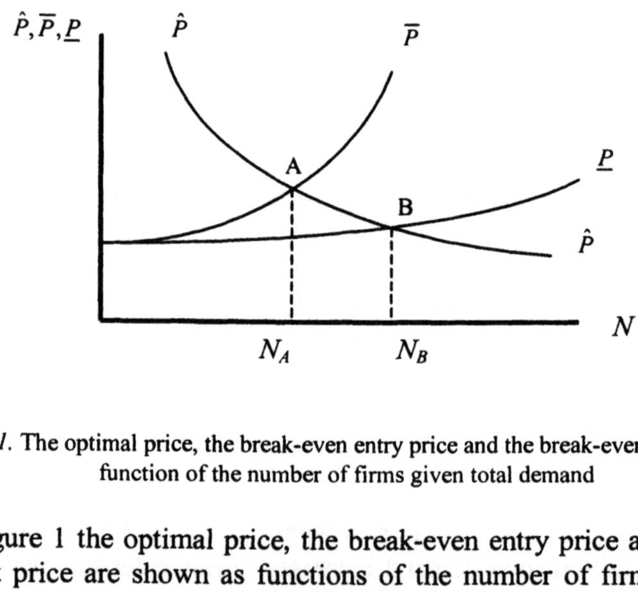

Figure 1. The optimal price, the break-even entry price and the break-even exit price as function of the number of firms given total demand

In Figure 1 the optimal price, the break-even entry price and the break-even exit price are shown as functions of the number of firms. Given the level of total demand, the optimal price falls and both break-even prices rise if the number of firms increase. If exit and entry takes place immediately the number of firms is larger or equal to N_A and smaller or equal to N_B. In equilibrium, capital is not necessarily fully utilised. Suppose that the number of firms is somewhere between N_A and N_B. An increase of total demand shifts $\hat{P}$ up and $\overline{P}$ and $\underline{P}$ down. With a small increase, the optimal price remains smaller than the break-even entry price, there will be no new entrants. Additional demand is produced by the existing capacity, hence the utilisation rate of capital increases. With a large increase of total demand, that is the optimal price exceeds the break-even entry price, new firms enter the market. Hence, new capacity is added despite the fact that existing production capacity might have been sufficient to produce the additional demand. In order to determine the effect on the utilisation rate of capital rewrite Equation (8) as

$$\hat{P} = \frac{W}{\alpha_L} + \frac{1}{bN}\left(1 - \frac{\delta}{v\alpha_K}\right), \tag{14}$$

and Equation (12) as

$$\overline{P} = \frac{W/\alpha_L}{1-(r+\delta)/v\alpha_K}. \tag{15}$$

In Figure 2 the optimal price and the break-even entry price are shown as functions of the number of firms. Given the utilisation rate of capital an increase in the number of firms lowers the optimal price and has no effect on the break-even entry price. The difference between Figure 1 and Figure 2 in this respect is that in Figure 1 total demand is kept constant and in Figure 2 the utilisation rate of capital is kept constant.

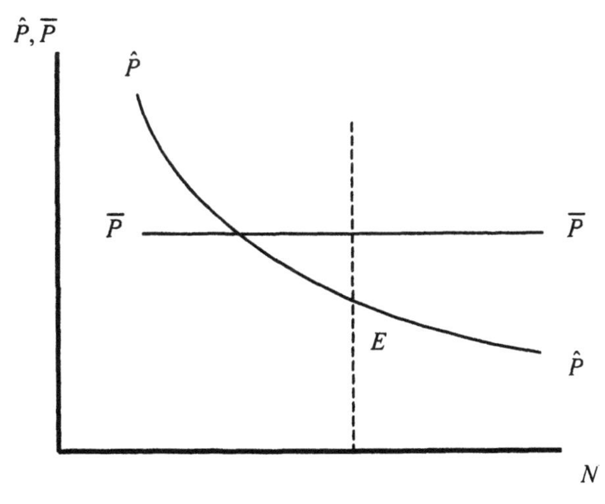

Figure 2. The optimal price and the break-even entry price as function of the number of firms given the capital utilisation rate

The point of departure is point E. Suppose that due to an increase in total demand the number of firms increases and the utilisation rate does not change. The latter implies that both curve $\hat{P}\hat{P}$ and line $\overline{P}\overline{P}$ remain in the same position. As the number of firms increases the optimal price is still smaller than the break-even entry price. This cannot be an equilibrium, hence the utilisation rate will change. Suppose instead that the utilisation rate of capital declines. This shifts the $\hat{P}\hat{P}$-curve down and the $\overline{PP}$-line up implying that in the new equilibrium the number of firms has fallen. Since the number of firms increases the rate of capital utilisation cannot fall. Hence the rate of capital utilisation rises if total demand increases. In a similar way, if demand falls the utilisation rate of capital falls, and if the drop in demand is large enough a number of firms will exit the market. So, suppose we are in a regime of capital and labour abundance, if demand does not increase it is likely that we stay in this regime. We can move to a regime in which one or both inputs are used completely only if demand increases.

Capital shortage and labour abundance

If the capital stock is fully utilised the optimal price firms charge is equal to the break-even entry price. If they charge a higher price new firms will enter the market as long as the actual price is higher than the break-even entry price. The new entrants reduce the production of existing firms and the equilibrium price. Hence the profits of the existing firms fall. It is therefore not optimal to charge a price that exceeds the break-even entry price. Charging a lower price does not affect production and employment, profits therefore decline. This again is not in accordance with profit maximisation. If firms charge the break-even entry price Inequality (11) becomes an equality and implies that the market value of the firm is equal to the replacement value of the firm. Since the latter is always positive the condition to exit the market, *i.e.* Equation (9), is never met.

If the capital stock is fully utilised and if there is an autonomous increase in demand the existing capital stock is insufficient to produce the additional demand. New firms enter the market until there is enough capacity to meet both the autonomous increase of demand and the extra demand brought about by the new investment. Existing firms cannot block the entrance of new firms by lowering their prices below the equilibrium break-even entry price. As long as capacity is insufficient potential entrants know that once they have entered the market they get their market share and receive the break-even entry price. If demand drops ultimately, *i.e.* if the drop in demand is large enough or is persistent, we may end-up in a regime in which both inputs are not fully utilised.

Capital abundance and labour shortage

If the workforce is fully employed the optimal price firms charge is equal to the break-even entry price. If firms charge a higher price new firms will enter the market as long as the actual price is higher than the break-even entry price. New entrants reduce the employment and therefore the production of existing firms and the equilibrium price. Hence profits of the existing firms fall if they charge prices higher than the break-even entry price. Charging a lower price does not alter employment and production and therefore reduces profits. This again is not in accordance with profit maximisation. So the optimal price firms charge is equal to the break-even entry price. As shown above this implies that the condition to exit the market is never met.

If the work force is fully employed and if there is an autonomous increase of demand the existing workforce is insufficient to produce the additional demand. Entry of new firms reduces the size of the firms but does not reduce excess demand. So, firms charge prices equal to the break-even entry price and the number of firms will stay put. The adjustment of the economy in response to a positive demand shock should come in another way. The excess demand for labour might result in an increase of labour supply and (or) an adjustment on any other market such that the autonomous increase of demand is (fully) offset. Again, if demand drops we ultimately, *i.e.* if the drop in demand is large enough or is persistent, may end-up in a regime in which both inputs are not fully utilised.

Capital and labour shortage

Using the same arguments as above one can show that the optimal price firms charge are equal to the break-even entry price. This implies again that the condition to exit the market is never met. In case of an autonomous increase of demand the capital shortage is absorbed by the entry of new firms the shortage of labour can be absorbed by an increase of labour supply and (or) an adjustment on any other market such that the autonomous increase of demand is (fully) offset. A decrease in demand may lead the economy ultimately into a situation of capital and/or labour abundance.

3. IDENTIFYING REGIMES IN THE DUTCH ECONOMY IN THE 19TH CENTURY

At the start of the 21st century the final estimates of the project *Reconstructing National Accounts* are published (Smits *et al.*, 2000). This project reconstructs national account data for the Netherlands for the period 1800-1913. The national accounts project does not provide information about the stock of capital and the utilisation rate of capital. We have constructed these variables. The stock of capital is calculated using a simple perpetual inventory method (lifetime of equipment is assumed to be 35 years). The calculation of the utilisation rate starts with assuming that productive capacity, approximated with a five-year moving average of actual output, is proportional to the stock of capital. Next, this ratio is re-scaled so that the utilisation rate of capital equals 0.85 on average which is generally accepted as a *normal* rate of utilisation, at least for the 20th century. Figure 3 shows some of the data used in this chapter. This figure shows that:

1. the utilisation rate increases until about 1850 and fluctuates around a more or less constant trend in the second half of the 19th century,
2. the unemployment rate reaches it peak of 6.5% in the early 1850s and drops to about 3% in the early 1900s,
3. the share of labour in income is rather low until about 1880, increases steadily in the next decade and falls back at the end of the 19th century, and
4. net investment is very low until 1860 and then picks up sharply, except for a short period towards the end of the 19th century.

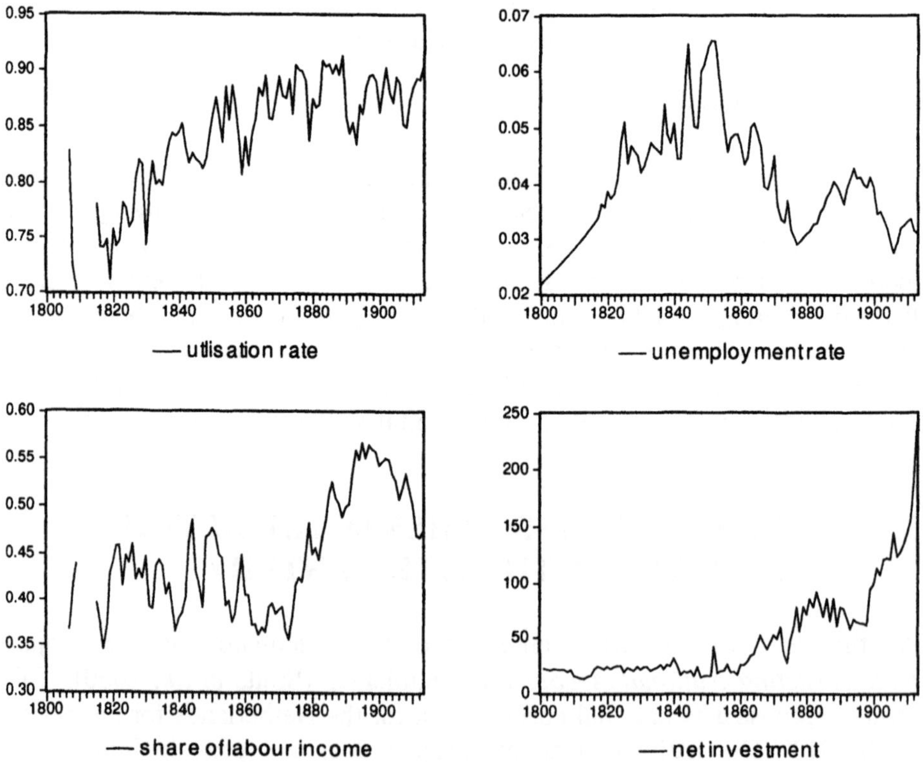

Figure 3. Data for the Netherlands in the 19th century. Source: Smits *et al.* (2000).

In the microeconomic model of entry and exit developed in Section 2, the level of output, the nominal wage rate, the weighted average cost of capital and the labour supply are assumed to be given. In a macroeconomic model these variables should be modelled consistently. For example, with labour fully employed, a positive demand shock should in some way be absorbed, *e.g.* by an increase in labour supply and/or a reduction of the interest or wealth related components of demand. We believe that a realistic macroeconomic model is not simply an aggregation of microeconomic quantities over all consumers and producers. This would imply that if all but one man is employed, labour is considered to be abundant and there is no need for the adjustment mechanisms just introduced. In real world adjustments take place gradually. Therefore we will not derive a full-fledged macroeconomic model which incorporates the microeconomics of Section 2. For the identification of the regimes we use the traditional criteria, the utilisation rate and the unemployment rate, and a model-based criterion derived from the microeconomic model presented in the previous section. This criterion is the share of labour income in total income. The time series of these variables and that of net investment are also shown in Figure 3.

We first turn to a classification based on the traditional criteria. We do not base our classification on the time series of the unemployment rate and the utilisation rate *per se*. If we look at graphs of these series more carefully we suspect that over time there are changes in trends. So, we classify the data using de-trended series. This choice also mitigates the effect of the way the time series of the stock of capital and the utilisation rate are constructed on our results. The trend is determined using the Hodrick-Prescott filter with a smoothing parameter of 100. This is the usual value for annual observations. Using a higher value of the smoothing parameter, say 1600, results in flatter trended series. However, the correlation coefficient between both sets of the de-trended series of the unemployment rate and the utilisation rate, *i.e.* with a smoothing parameter of 100 and 1600, are all above 0.90. This means that our classification will not be very sensitive to the smoothing parameter in the Hodrick-Prescott filter. We call capital scarce if the de-trended value of the utilisation rate is one standard deviation above its trend value. Similarly, labour is called scarce if the de-trended value of unemployment is more than one standard deviation below its trend value. The results of this classification are presented in Table 1.

We identify 24 years out of 99 in which there is a shortage of capital and/or labour. It should be noted that the one standard deviation cut-off point, which is *ad hoc*, implies that 50% of the data qualifies for possible shortage or scarcity. With two independent criteria (labour and capital) 25% of the data qualify for shortage of capital and/or labour.

Table 1. Years with capital and/or labour shortages

	Labour shortage	Labour abundance
Capital shortage	1841, 1856	1815, 1827, 1828, 1829, 1851, 1854, 1864, 1866, 1875, 1883, 1889, 1902
Capital abundance	1830, 1842, 1846, 1847, 1855, 1857, 1861, 1891, 1905, 1906	All other years between 1815 and 1913

We now turn to our model-based classification criteria. These criteria are supposed *ex ante* behaviour, *i.e.* they hint at future developments. In Section 2, the entry and exit decision of firms was discussed. Since capital goods are identified by the number of firms, changes in the stock of capital, that is net investment, are proportional to changes in the number of firms. If in the regime of capital and labour abundance demand falls sufficiently, a number of firms exits the market. Net investment is therefore negative. If in the same regime the (absolute) change in demand is small, net investment is zero. Similarly, in the regime of labour shortage and capital abundance there is no exit and no entry of firms and net investment is zero. In all other cases the number of firms increases or remains constant. Net investment is zero or positive. In all these other cases the investment function is of an accelerator type, and can using the macroeconomic counterparts of Equations (3) and (5) be written as:

$$\frac{I}{K_{-1}} = \delta + \left(\dot{Q} - \dot{\alpha}_K - \dot{v}\right), \tag{16}$$

where the dotted variables refer to the growth rates of these variables. In the period considered net investment is never negative or close to zero (see Figure 3). Using our model of Section 2 would imply that periods of labour shortages and periods economy-wide slumps are absent. Comparing instead the de-trended series of net investment with the trended series, that is assuming that firms take account of growth prospects in their entry and exit decisions, reverses this conclusion. However, using the deviations of net investment from its trend, it is still not possible to distinguish between periods of labour shortages and periods of economy-wide slumps. In addition, high net investments might be expected in periods of capital shortage as well as in periods of capital and labour abundance. This implies that the information contained in the net investment series is not suitable for the identification of periods of capital and/or labour shortages.

If firms expect that there will be a shortage of capital and/or labour they set there price equal to the break-even entry price. In all other cases they set a price lower or equal to that break-even entry price. This price can be rewritten in terms of the share of labour income in total income:

$$\frac{WL}{PQ} = 1 - \frac{r+\delta}{v\alpha_K}. \tag{17}$$

Therefore, if the share of labour income in total income is low, capital and/or labour is expected to be scarce. We call the share of labour income in total income as low as the de-trended value of the share of labour income in total income is more than 0.79 standard deviation below its trend value. This particular value of 0.79 is chosen in such a way that the resulting number of years in which any shortage is expected, that is in 24 years, is equal to the number of years in which any shortage is observed. The combined results of our identification criteria are presented in Table 2.

Table 2. Years in which shortages are expected and observed

	Shortage(s) expected	Shortage(s) not expected
Shortages realised	1841, 1846, 1847, 1854, 1855, 1856, 1857, 1864, 1889, 1891, 1906	1815, 1827, 1828, 1829, 1830, 1842, 1851, 1861, 1866, 1875, 1883, 1902, 1905
Shortages not realised	1817, 1818, 1823, 1831, 1832, 1839, 1840, 1872, 1873, 1874, 1882, 1890, 1911	All other years between 1815 and 1913

In roughly one-third of the years in which shortages are either expected or realised the expected shortages became reality. Roughly 50% of the shortages were expected and roughly 50% of the expected shortage were not realised. However this latter figure might be biased since firms set their prices equal to the break-even entry price — even if they expect that capital and labour are both abundant — if demand is expected to grow enough to invite new firms to enter the market.

4. CONCLUSIONS

Using a unique set of data for the Netherlands for the 19th century we classify this century in different regimes of capital and/or labour shortage and abundance. First, we use obvious measures of the unemployment rate and the utilisation rate of capital to determine these regimes. The years 1841 and 1856 are classified as years of both capital and labour shortage. A total of 24 years where classified either as years of shortage or abundance.

Second, we introduce an adjustment mechanism in a typical Post Keynesian model to come up with an expected, or *ex ante*, classification of regimes. It is argued that entrepreneurs invest in a situation of capital shortage based on the assumption that the existence of monopoly profits induces new firms to enter the market. The share of labour in income is found to be the crucial variable that captures information on future profitability of investment.

Third, this *ex ante* classification is confronted with the *ex post* classification based on the unemployment rate and the utilisation rate of capital. In roughly one-third of the years in which shortages are either expected or realised the expected shortages became reality. Roughly 50% of the shortages were expected.

REFERENCES

Abel, A.B. (1990), "Consumption and Investment," in F. Hahn and B.M. Friedman (eds.), *Handbook of Monetary Economics*, Amsterdam: North-Holland, pp. 725-778.

Brakman, S., H. Garretsen and L. Hoogduin (2001), "Overconfidence in Monetary Theory and Monetary Policy," in G.H. Kuper, E. Sterken and E. Wester (eds.), *Coordination and Growth: Essays in Honour of Simon K. Kuipers*, Boston: Kluwer Academic Publishers, pp. 163-180.

Campbell, J.R. (1998), "Entry, Exit, Embodied Technology, and Business Cycles," *Review of Economic Dynamics* 1, pp. 371-408.

Kuipers, S.K. and G.H. Kuper (2001), "Het contraire verloop van de productiviteitsgroei in de jaren 1919-1949 en 1973-1996," in H. Klok, T. van Schaik and S. Smulders (eds.), *Economologues, Liber Amicorum voor Theo van de Klundert*, pp. 253-270, Tilburg University, Tilburg.

Smits, J.-P., E. Horlings and J.L. van Zanden (2000), *Dutch GNP and Its Components, 1800-1913*, Groningen Growth and Development Centre, Monograph Series, No. 5, Groningen.

Solow, R.M. (1999), "Neoclassical Growth Theory," in J.B. Taylor and M. Woodford (eds.), *Handbook of Macroeconomics* 1A, Amsterdam: North-Holland, pp. 637-667.

Publications of Simon K. Kuipers

1960-1969

Kuipers, S.K. (1968), "Nogmaals structuur en conjunctuur," *Economisch Statistische Berichten* 63(26129), pp. 86-89.
Kuipers, S.K. (1969), "De inconsistentie in Professor Heertjes aanbodvariant van het model van Harrod en Domar," *De Economist* 117, pp. 695-698.
Haan, H. de and S.K. Kuipers (1969), "Een onderzoek naar de invloed van monetaire factoren op het reële groeiproces in enkele traditionele theorieën van economische groei (I)," *De Economist* 117(2), pp. 139-160.
Haan. H. de and S.K. Kuipers (1969), "Een onderzoek naar de invloed van monetaire factoren op het reële groeiproces in enkele traditionele theorieën van economische groei (II)," *De Economist* 117(4), pp. 381-401.
Haan, H. de and S.K. Kuipers (1969), "Een onderzoek naar de invloed van monetaire factoren op het reële groeiproces in enkele traditionele theorieën van economische groei (III)," *De Economist* 117(5), pp. 493-510.

1970-1979

Kuipers, S.K. (1970), "De betekenis van vraag- en aanbodfactoren in groeimodellen met één sector (The Significance of Demand and Supply Factors in One-Sector Growth Models. With English summary)," PhD-Thesis, Groningen.
Kuipers, S.K. (1970), "Gedragsmodellen van de economische groei (Behavioural Models of Economic Growth. With English summary)," *De Economist* 118(5), pp. 491-505.
Kuipers, S.K. (1970), "De existentie en de stabiliteit van het evenwicht van de goederenmarkt in geval van een proportionele spaarvergelijking en een flexibele-acceleratorvergelijking (The Existence and the Stability of the Equilibrium of the Goods Market in Case of a Proportional Saving Equation and a Flexible-Accelerator Investment Equation. With English summary)," *De Economist* 118(6), pp. 661-670.

Haan, H. de and S.K. Kuipers (1970), "De produktiestructuur van Nederland in de periode 1950-1966 (The Structure of Production in the Netherlands, 1950-1966. With English summary)," *De Economist* 118(4), pp. 370-394.

Kuipers, S.K. (With J.K.T. Postma) (1971), "Structurele begrotingspolitiek en economische groei," *Maandschrift Economie* 35, pp. 200-214.

Haan, H. and S.K. Kuipers (1972), "De neo-Keynesiaanse aanval op de neo-klassieke produktie- en verdelingstheorie," in H. de Haan, S.K. Kuipers and J.K.T. Postma (eds.), *Mens en keuze: opstellen aangeboden aan Prof. drs. S. Korteweg ter gelegenheid van de voltooiing van zijn zeventigste levensjaar*, Amsterdam: Noord-Hollandsche, pp. 139-154.

Haan, H. de, S.K. Kuipers and J.K.T. Postma (eds.) (1972), *Mens en keuze: opstellen aangeboden aan Prof. drs. S. Korteweg ter gelegenheid van de voltooiing van zijn zeventigste levensjaar*, Amsterdam: Noord-Hollandsche.

Kuipers, S.K. (1973), "Personele inkomensverdeling en produktiestructuur," in *Inkomensnivellering: verkenning van feiten, wenselijkheden, mogelijkheden en gevolgen, Preadviezen van de Vereniging voor de Staathuishoudkunde,* 's-Gravenhage: Martinus Nijhoff, pp. 63-94.

Kuipers, S.K. (1973), "A Demand and Supply Model of Economic Growth," *De Economist* 121(4), pp. 553-608.

Kuipers, S.K. and B.S. Wilpstra (1973), "Over Holtrops monetaire theorie," *Maandschrift Economie* 37(11), pp. 489-511.

Kuipers, S.K. and A. Nentjes (1973), "Pollution in a Neo-Classical World: The Classics Rehabilitated?," *De Economist* 121(1), pp. 52-67.

Kuipers, S.K. (1973), "The Positive Relation Between Average Labour Productivity and Labour Intensity," *Zeitschrift für Nationalökonomie,* 33(1/2), pp. 115-126.

Haan, H. de, S. Korteweg, S.K. Kuipers and J.K.T.Postma (1974/76), *Het moderne geldwezen* (13th revised edition), Stenfert Kroese, Leiden [Original Title: S. Korteweg and F.A.G. Keesing (1945), *Het moderne geldwezen,* Amsterdam: Noord-Hollandsche].

Kuipers, S.K. (With J. Muysken) (1974), "Bounded Substitutability and Utilization of Capital (Les proportions et intensités de facteurs), *Analyse sectorielle et intersectorielle*, Paris, pp. 115-160.

Kuipers, S.K. (With J.K.T. Postma and A.K. de Haan) (1975), "Regionale rendementsverschillen en de selectieve investeringsregeling," *Economisch Statistische Berichten* 60, pp. 200-205.

Kuipers, S.K. (1975), "A Vintage Model of Growth, Employment and Inflation," *De Economist* 123(4), pp. 531-558.

Kuipers, S.K. (1976), "Personal Income Distribution and Production Structure," *Economie Appliquée* 29(1), pp, 5-31.

Kuipers, S.K. (1976), "Imperfect Malleability of Capital and Economic Growth: An Attempt at Synthesis between Keynesian and Neoclassical Growth Models," *Maandschrift Economie* 40, pp. 530-542.

Kuipers, S.K. and H.F. Bosch (1976), "An Alternative Estimation Procedure of a Clay-Clay Type of Vintage Model: The Case of the Netherlands, 1959-1973," *De Economist* 124(1/2), pp. 56-82.

Groenveld, K. and S.K. Kuipers (1976), "Some Further Evidence on the Substitution Possibilities between Graduate and Other Labour," *Kyklos* 29(3), pp. 531-539.

Kastelein, T.J., S.K. Kuipers, W.A. Nijenhuis and G.R. Wagenaar (eds.) (1976), *25 Years of Economic Theory, Retrospect and Prospect*, Leiden.

Kuipers, S.K. (1976), "On the Estimation of Short Run and Long Run Production Equations," in F.L. Altmann, O. Kyn and H.-J. Wagener (eds.), *On the Measurement of Factor Productivities, Theoretical Problems and Empirical Results*, Göttingen, pp. 182-210.

Kuipers, S.K. (1977), *Over structurele en conjuncturele ontwikkelingen binnen de Nederlandse economie sinds de Eerste Wereldoorlog*, Inaugural Lecture, Amsterdam: Noord-Hollandsche.

Kuipers, S.K. and F.H. Buddenberg (1978), "Unemployment on Account of Market Imperfection in the Netherlands since the Second World War," *De Economist* 126(3), pp. 390-412.

Kuipers, S.K., J. Muysken and J. van Sinderen (1978), "De werkgelegenheidsontwikkeling in Nederland sinds 1970: een nadere analyse," *Economisch Statistische Berichten* 63(3160), pp. 648-652.

Kuipers, S.K. and B.S. Wilpstra (1978), "On the Estimation and Stability of Demand for Money Functions for the Netherlands, 1952-1976," *Economies-et-Sociétés* 12(10/12), pp. 1917-1942.

Haan, H. de, S. Korteweg, S.K. Kuipers and J.K.T.Postma (1978/81), *Het moderne geldwezen* (14th revised edition), Leiden: Stenfert Kroese [Original Title: S. Korteweg and F.A.G. Keesing (1945), *Het moderne geldwezen,* Amsterdam: Noord-Hollandsche], *Deel I, Macro-economische uitgangspunten* (1978), *Deel IIA, De techniek van het betalingsverkeer van een open volkshuishouding* (1979), *Deel IIB, De techniek van het internationale betalingsverkeer* (1979), *Deel III, De geldtheorie* (1979), *Deel IV, De geldpolitiek* (1981).

Kuipers, S.K. (With K. Groenveld) (1978), "The Influence of Substitution and Technical Progress on Income Differences between Graduate and Other Labour," in W. Krelle and A.F. Shorrocks (eds.), *Personal Income Distribution*, Amsterdam, pp. 399-414.

Kuipers, S.K. (With J. Muysken and J. van Sinderen) (1978), "Modernizacja Holenderskich Zdolnosci Produkcyjnych W Okresie Powojennym (The Modernization of the Dutch Productive Capacity in the Post-War Period: A Vintage Approach*), Wplyw modernizacji srodków pracy na wzrost gospodarczy*, Lódz, pp. 243-256 (Polish).

Kuipers, S.K. (1978), "Miljoenennota 1979: een uiterst somber macro-economisch perspectief," *Economisch Statistische Berichten* 63, pp. 1000-1004.

Kuipers, S.K. (1979), "Het verslag van De Nederlandsche Bank over het jaar 1978," *Economisch Statistische Berichten* 64(3204), pp. 476-482.

Kuipers, S.K., J. Muysken and J. van Sinderen (1979), "The Vintage Approach to Output and Employment Growth in the Netherlands, 1921-1976," *Welwirtschaftliches Archiv* 115, pp. 485-507.

Kuipers, S.K. (With Chr.L. Baljé, M.F.A. van Diessen and K. Groenveld) (1979), "Een liberale visie op de verdeling van inkomen en vermogen," *Geschrift van de Prof. Mr. B.M. Teldersstichting*, 34, 's-Gravenhage, pp. 221-224.

1980-1989

Kuipers, S.K. (1980), "Miljoenennota 1981: een keer ten goede," *Economisch Statistische Berichten* 65, pp. 1000-1004.

Kuipers, S.K. (1980), *Vooruitzichten voor de Nederlandse economie*, Leiden: Stenfert Kroese.

Kuipers, S.K. and G.J. Lanjouw (eds.) (1980), *Prospects of Economic Growth*, Amsterdam: North-Holland.

Kuipers, S.K. (1980), "Prospects of Employment Growth in the Netherlands: A Critical Survey of Prevailing Views," in S.K. Kuipers and G.J. Lanjouw (eds.), *Prospects of Economic Growth*, Amsterdam: North-Holland, pp. 117-130.

Kuipers, S.K., J. Muysken, D. J. van den Berg and A.H. van Zon (1980), *Sectorstructuur en economische groei: een eenvoudig groeimodel met zes sectoren van de Nederlandse*

economie in de periode na de Tweede Wereldoorlog. Voorstudies en achtergronden V14, Wetenschappelijk Raad voor het Regeringsbeleid, 's-Gravenhage: SDU.
Kuipers, S.K. (1981), "Keynesian and Neoclassical Growth Models: A Sequential Analytical Approach," *De Economist* 129(1), pp. 58-104.
Kuipers, S.K. (1981), "Disequilibrium, Power and Economic Systems: A Review Article of Schouten's New Book "Power and Disorder, a Comparison of Economic Systems"," *De Economist* 129(4), pp. 546-557.
Eijgelshoven, P.J. and S.K. Kuipers (1981), "A Note on Pasinetti's "Ricardian System" [A Mathematical Formulation of the Ricardian System]," *Review of Economic Studies* 48(1), pp. 185-186.
Kuipers, S.K. (1981), "Neoklassieke en Keynesiaanse verdelingstheorieën: een eclectische benadering," in P.J. Eijgelshoven and L.J. van Gemerden (eds.), *Inkomensverdeling en openbare financiën*, Utrecht and Antwerp, pp. 196-230.
Brakman, S., C.J. Jepma and S.K. Kuipers (1982), "The Deterioriation of the Netherlands' Export Performance during the Late 1970's: A Matter of Competitiveness or Export Structure?," *De Economist* 130(3), pp. 360-380.
Kuipers, S.K. and A.H. van Zon (1982), "Output and Employment Growth in the Netherlands in the Postwar Period: A Putty-Clay Approach," *De Economist* 130(1), pp. 38-70.
Kuipers, S.K. (1982), "Economisch herstel en de werking van de markteconomie," *Economisch Statistische Berichten* 67(337), 20 October, pp. 1122-1130.
Kuipers, S.K. (1982), "Stability in Keynesian and Neoclassical Growth Models: Reply," *De Economist* 130(1), pp. 123-130.
Kuipers, S.K. (With A.H. van Zon) (1983), "Substitution and Technical Progress: A Putty-Clay Model for the Netherlands," in D. Biehl, K.W. Roskamp and W.F. Stolper (eds.), *Public Finance and Economic Growth*, Detroit: Wayne State University Press, pp. 181-206.
Kuipers, S.K. (1983), "Interestvoet, spaartekort en liquiditeitskrapte," in J.A.H. Maks and E. Wester (eds.*), Met het oog op de werkelijkheid,* Leiden, 1983, pp. 69-93.
Kuipers, S.K. (1983), "Growth and Stagnation of the Dutch Economy: An Analysis of the Sixties and the Seventies," in A. Maddison and B.S. Wilpstra (eds.), *Unemployment: The Dutch Perspective*, The Hague, pp. 9-56.
Kuipers, S.K. (1983), "Macro-economische modelbouw in discussie (V): econometrische modellen een onmisbaar hulpmiddel," *Economisch Statistische Berichten* 68(3434), pp. 1140-1143.
Kuipers, S.K. (1983), "Internationale en nationale stagnatie: enkele beschouwingen naar aanleiding van het jaarverslag van De Nederlandsche Bank," *Economisch Statistische Berichten* 68(3408), pp. 500-506.
Kuipers, S.K. and B.S. Wilpstra (1983*), Conjunctuur- en groeitheorie: visies op de werking van een markteconomie*, Leiden: Stenfert Kroese.
Kuipers, S.K. (1984), "De ontwikkeling van de Nederlandse economie op middellange termijn in het licht van het gevoerde matigings- en bezuinigingsbeleid," *Maandschrift Economie* 48(6), pp. 437-453.
Brakman, S., C.J. Jepma and S.K. Kuipers (1984), "On Export Performance and Export Elasticities: A Reply," *De Economist* 132(2), pp. 232-233.
Kuipers, S.K. and G.H. Kuper (1985), "Een bouwjaaranalyse van de groeivertraging in Nederland sedert het begin van de jaren zeventig," in A. van der Zwan (ed.), *Nederland in zaken: investeren, winst en werkgelegenheid,* Utrecht-Antwerpen: Veen.
Kuipers, S.K, C.M. Andriesen, J.P.A.M. Jacobs and G.H. Kuper (1985), "A Putty-Clay Vintage Model for Sectors of Industry in the Netherlands," *De Economist* 133(2), pp. 151-175.

Kuipers, S.K. (1985), "Interest Rate, Savings Shortage and Liquidity Shortage: Theoretical Considerations in the Light of the Discussions about the High Rate of Interest during the Depression of the Early 1980's," *De Economist* 133(3), pp. 306-326.

Kuipers, S.K. (1985/86), *Het moderne geldwezen* (15th revised edition), Leiden: Stenfert Kroese [Original Title: S. Korteweg and F.A.G. Keesing (1945), *Het moderne geldwezen,* Noord-Hollandsche, Amsterdam], *Deel I, Macro-economische uitgangspunten* (1986), *Deel III, De geldtheorie* (1985).

Kuipers, S.K. (With C.G.M. Sterks) (1986), "De financieel-economische deugdelijkheid van CDA-en PvdA-programma's," *Openbare uitgaven* 18, pp. 25-40.

Kuipers, S.K. (1986), "De Nederlandse economie op middellange termijn," *Economisch Statistische Berichten* 71, pp. 444-450.

Kuipers, S.K. (1987), "Over het macro-economische beleid in de jaren tachtig," in A. Knoester (ed.), *Lessen uit het verleden: 125 jaar Vereniging voor de Staathuishoudkunde,* Leiden/Antwerpen: Stenfert Kroese, pp. 461-483.

Kuipers, S.K. (1988), "The Trade Cycle under Capital Shortage and Labour Shortage. On Witteveen's Synthesis of the Overinvestment and Underinvestment Theory of the Trade Cycle," in W. Eizenga, E.F. Limburg and J.J. Polak (eds.), *The Quest for National and Global Economic Stability,* Dordrecht, London.

Kuipers, S.K., B.W.A. Jongbloed, G.H. Kuper and E. Sterken (1988), *CESAM: het CCSO jaarmodel van de Nederlandse economie,* Groningen: Wolters-Noordhoff.

Kuipers, S.K. and B. Boertje (1988), "On the Causes of the Rise in the Liquidity Ratio in the Netherlands during the Early Eighties," *De Economist* 136(1), pp. 50-90.

Kuipers, S.K. (1989), "Het budgettaire beleid in de jaren negentig," *Economisch Statistische Berichten* 74, pp. 1016-1019.

1990-1999

Jongbloed, B.W.A., S.K. Kuipers, G.H. Kuper and E. Sterken (1990), "CESAM-voorspellingen voor 1990-1994," *Economisch Statistische Berichten* 75(3752), pp. 320-323.

Kuipers, S.K. (1990), "Special Issue on the Stability of Western Economies: Introduction," *De Economist* 138(4), pp. 395-396.

Kuipers, S.K. (1990), "Stabilization Policy: A Non-market Clearing View," in K. Groenveld, J.A.H. Maks and J. Muysken (eds.), *Economic Policy and the Market Process: Austrian and Mainstream Economics,* Amsterdam.

Kuipers, S.K., B.W.A. Jongbloed, G.H. Kuper and E. Sterken (1990), "CESAM: The CCSO Annual Model of the Dutch Economy," *Economic Modelling* 7(3), pp. 202-250.

Kuipers, S.K. and E. Sterken (1990), "Het Nederlandse monetaire beleid in de jaren '80: een portefeuillebenadering," in A.H.E.M. Wellink, A. Lamfalussy and S.K. Kuipers (eds.), *De mogelijkheden voor het monetaire beleid na de liberalisatie,* NIBE, Amsterdam, pp. 77-109.

Kuipers, S.K. and G.H. Kuper (1990), "De ontwikkeling van de Nederlandse economie in de eerste helft van de jaren negentig," *Maandschrift Economie* 54(6), pp. 425-438.

Wellink, A.H.E.M., A. Lamfalussy and S.K. Kuipers (1990), *De mogelijkheden voor het monetaire beleid na de liberalisatie,* NIBE, Amsterdam.

Kuipers, S.K. and H. van Ees (1990), "Macro-economische theorie en economisch politiek," *Economisch Statistische Berichten* 75, pp. 32-43.

Kuipers, S.K. and H. van Ees (1990), "Macro-economische theorie en economische politiek," in L. van der Geest (ed.), *Economische theorie: de stand van zaken*, Schoonhoven, pp. 11-46.

Kuipers, S.K. (1991), "Marktwerking en werkloosheid in Nederland in de jaren dertig en tachtig," *Mededelingen van de Afdeling Letterkunde*, Koninklijke Nederlandse Akademie van Wetenschappen, nieuwe reeks, dl. 54, no. 3

Kuipers, S.K. and G.H. Kuper (1991), "On the Persistence of Unemployment in the Netherlands: A Simple Theory and Some Evidence," in C. de Neubourg (ed.), *The Art of Full Employment: Unemployment Policy in Open Economies*, Amsterdam: North-Holland, pp. 105-127.

Bouma, J.L., Th. Junius, S.K. Kuipers and L. Schoonbeek (eds.) (1991), *Samenspel: opstellen aangeboden aan Prof. dr. G.F.W.M. Pikkemaat*, Groningen.

Kuipers, S.K. (1991), "Over geld, voorraden en buffers," in J.L. Bouma, Th. Junius, S.K. Kuipers and L. Schoonbeek (eds.), *Samenspel: opstellen aangeboden aan Prof. dr. G.F.W.M. Pikkemaat*, Groningen, pp. 127-154.

Kuipers, S.K. (1992), "Economische en Monetaire Unie," *Liberaal Reveil* 33(4) pp. 125-126.

Kuipers, S.K. (1992), "Imbalances in Public Sector Deficits: The Dutch Experience," in D.E. Fair and C. de Boissieu (eds.), *Fiscal Policy, Taxation and the Financial System in an Increasingly Integrated Europe,* Dordrecht: Kluwer Academic Publishers, pp. 165-184.

Brakman, S., H. Garretsen and S.K. Kuipers (eds.) (1993), *Met Jan Pen in debat (In Debate with Jan Pen)*, Amsterdam: Amsterdam University Press.

Brakman, S., H. Garretsen and S.K. Kuipers (1993), "Inleiding (Introduction)," in S. Brakman, H. Garretsen and S.K. Kuipers (eds.), *Met Jan Pen in debat (In Debate with Jan Pen)*, Amsterdam: Amsterdam University Press, pp. 1-5.

Kuipers, S.K. (1993), "Onder baggeraars," in S. Brakman, H. Garretsen and S.K. Kuipers (eds.), *Met Jan Pen in debat (In Debate with Jan Pen)*, Amsterdam: Amsterdam University Press, pp. 157-158.

Kuipers, S.K., H. van Ees, H. Garretsen, G.H. Kuper, E. Sterken and E. Wester (1994), *Evenwicht, conjunctuur en groei,* Utrecht: Lemma.

Kuipers, S.K. (1995), "Wanneer de veilingmeester faalt," *Economisch Statistische Berichten* 80(4028) pp. 900-903.

Kuipers, S.K. and E. Sterken (1995), "On the Scope for Dutch Monetary Policy," *Banca Nazionale del Lavoro Quarterly Review* 48(193), pp. 173-187.

Schoonbeek, L., E. Sterken and S.K. Kuipers (eds.) (1995), *Methods and Applications of Economic Dynamics,* Amsterdam: North-Holland.

Sterken, E., J.P.A.M. Jacobs, G.H. Kuper and S.K. Kuipers (1995), "Lagere overheidsschuld, minder economische activiteit?," *Economisch Statistische Berichten* 80(4034), pp. 1048-1051.

Kuipers, S.K. and G.H. Kuper (1996), "Wage Formation, Investment and Growth in the Netherlands in the Postwar Period: A Cross-section Analysis," *De Economist* 144(3), pp. 487-495.

Kuipers, S.K., J. Muysken and J. van Sinderen (1996), "The Vintage Approach to Output and Employment Growth in the Netherlands, 1921-1976," in J. Luiten van Zanden (ed.), *The Economic Development of the Netherlands since 1870,* Cheltenham: Elgar [Previously published: 1979], pp. 235-256.

Kuper, G.H. and S.K. Kuipers (1996), "Minder regulering, meer prestaties?," *Economisch Statistische Berichten* 81(4084), pp. 992-993.

Kuipers, S.K. (1996), "Coördinatie, concurrentie en doelmatigheid," in A. Nentjes (ed.), *Marktwerking versus coördinatie: preadviezen van de Koninklijke Vereniging voor de Staathuishoudkunde*, Utrecht: Lemma, pp. 37-51.

Kuipers, S.K. (1996), "De Economische en Monetaire Unie," in P.G.C. van Schie (ed.), *De Europese Unie: een perpetuum mobile?*, Prof. Mr. B.M. Teldersstichting, 's-Gravenhage, pp. 25-30.

Kuipers, S.K., H.van Ees and S.G. van der Lecq (1997), "Money and Stability: Some Preliminary Thoughts on the Functioning of a Monetary Economy," in H. Klenner (ed.), *Repraesentatio Mundi, Festschrift zum 70. Geburtstage von Hans Heinz Holz*, Köln: Dinter Verlag, pp. 369-378

Kuipers, S.K. (1997), "Het begrotingsbeleid in de komende kabinetsperiode: naar begrotingsevenwicht," in *Openbare Uitgaven, 1997* 29, pp. 207-215

Brakman, S., H. van Ees and S.K. Kuipers (eds.) (1998), *Market Behaviour and Macroeconomic Modelling*, London: Macmillan.

Brakman, S., H. van Ees and S.K. Kuipers (1998), "Introduction," in S. Brakman, H. van Ees, and S.K. Kuipers (eds.), *Market Behaviour and Macroeconomic Modelling*, London: Macmillan.

Kuipers, S.K. and V.C. Hoogenveen (1999), "Monetaire politiek, inflatie en natuurlijke werkloosheid," in D.W. Feenstra, G.J. van Helden and F.M. Tempelaar (eds.), *Over economie en bedrijf: Liber Amicorum voor Prof. dr. J.L. Bouma*, 's-Gravenhage: Delwel, pp. 77-95.

Kuipers, S.K. and G.H. Kuper (1999), "Coordination, Technical Progress and Economic Growth," in M.M.G. Fase, W. Kanning and D. Walker (eds.), *Economics, Welfare Policy and the History of Economic Thought: Essays in Honour of Arnold Heertje*, London: Edward Elgar.

Kuipers, S.K. (1999), "The Natural Rate of Unemployment: An Alternative Perspective," *CPB Report: Quarterly Review of CPB Netherlands Bureau for Economic Policy Analysis* 4, pp. 59-61.

2000-...

Ark, B. van, S.K. Kuipers and G.H. Kuper (eds.) (2000), *Productivity, Technology and Economic Growth*, Boston: Kluwer Academic Publishers.

Ark, B. van, S.K. Kuipers and G.H. Kuper (2000), "Introduction," in B. van Ark, S.K. Kuipers and G.H. Kuper (eds), *Productivity, Technology and Economic Growth*, Boston: Kluwer Academic Publishers.

Kuipers, S.K., G.A.W. van Dalen, K. Groenveld and R.H. Koning (2000), *Groei, inkomensverdeling en economische orde*, Prof. mr. B.M. Teldersstichting, 's-Gravenhage.

Hoogenveen, V.C. and S.K. Kuipers (2000), "The Long-Run Effects of Low Inflation Rates," *Banca Nazionale del Lavoro Quarterly Review* 53(214), pp. 267-85.

Kuipers, S.K. and G.H. Kuper (2001), "Het contraire verloop van de productiviteitsgroei in de jaren 1919-1949 en 1973-1996," in H. Klok, T. van Schaik and S. Smulders (eds.), *Economologue: Liber Amicorum voor Theo van de Klundert*, Tilburg: Tilburg University.

Kuipers, S.K. and G.H. Kuper (2001), "On U.S. Capital Productivity Growth Between 1919 and 1949," in D.A. Albregtse, L. Bovenberg and L.G.M. Stevens (eds.), *Er zal geheven worden!*, Boston: Kluwer Academic Publishers.

PhDs supervised by Simon K. Kuipers

09-02-1978	T.J. Broersma *De lange golf in het economische leven: Empirische en theoretische onderzoekingen*
05-04-1979	J. Muysken *Aggregation of putty-clay production functions*
17-06-1982	P.J. Eijgelshoven *De kritiek op de neo-klassieke allocatie- en verdelingstheorie*
22-06-1982	P.K. Keizer *Inflatie, een institutionele benadering*
30-09-1982	K. Groenveld *Onevenwichtige markten*
20-06-1985	J. Snippe *Macro economic adjustment processes: A sequential analytical approach*
16-01-1986	A.H. van Zon *A simple multi-sector model of the Dutch economy for the period 1950-1968*
22-05-1986	J. van Dijk *Migratie en arbeidsmarkt*
25-01-1990	E. Sterken *DUFIS: An econometric model of the Dutch financial system*
28-06-1990	H. van Ees *Macroeconomic fluctuations and individual behaviour: The implications of real and nominal inertia*

13-09-1990	A. van Witteloostuijn *Rationality, competition and evolution: Entry (deterrence) in dynamic barrier market theory*
06-12-1990	J.W. Drukker *Waarom de crisis hier langer duurde: Over de Nederlandse economische ontwikkeling in de jaren dertig*
21-02-1991	L.H. Hoogduin *Some aspects of uncertainty and the theory of a monetary economy*
15-10-1991	H. Garretsen *Beyond the invisible hand: How to extend Keynes' analysis of the coordination problem*
28-10-1993	B.B. Bakker *Saving in the Netherlands: Sources, trends and mobility*
15-12-1994	N. Brunia *Jugatio: A macroeconometric model of the six largest OECD countries*
05-01-1995	G.H. Kuper *Investment behaviour and vintage modelling*
29-06-1995	H.J. Nieuwenhuis *Continuous-time macroeconometric modelling: With an application to the Dutch economy*
15-01-1998	J.P.A.M. Jacobs *Econometric business cycle research: With an application to the Netherlands*
10-09-1998	S.G. van der Lecq *Money, coordination and prices*
03-06-1999	J.I. Kakes *Monetary transmission: The credit view*
18-06-1999	K.F. Wallis Honorary Doctorate
in preparation	M. Rensman *Productivity differentials and technology diffusion: An international comparison* (working title)
in preparation	V.C. Hoogenveen *The relationship between inflation and growth* (working title)

MIX
Papier aus verantwortungsvollen Quellen
Paper from responsible sources
FSC® C105338

If you have any concerns about our products,
you can contact us on
ProductSafety@springernature.com

In case Publisher is established outside the EU,
the EU authorized representative is:
Springer Nature Customer Service Center GmbH
Europaplatz 3, 69115 Heidelberg, Germany

Printed by Libri Plureos GmbH
in Hamburg, Germany